The Case for
Intercultural
Education
in a
MULTICULTURAL
WORLD

Library and Archives Canada Cataloguing in Publication

Gundara, Jagdish S. (Jagdish Singh), author
    The case for intercultural education in a multicultural
world / Jagdish Gundara.

Issued in print and electronic formats.
ISBN 978-0-88962-936-3 (pbk.).-- ISBN 978-1-77161-013-1 (html).--
ISBN 978-1-77161-014-8 (pdf)

    1. Multicultural education. I. Title.

LC1099.G85 2014   370.117   C2014-900632-2
                                              C2014-900633-0

Pubished by Mosaic Press, Oakville, Ontario, Canada, 2015.
Distributed in the United States by Bookmasters (www.bookmasters.com).
Distributed in the U.K. by Gazelle Book Services (www.gazellebookservices.co.uk).

MOSAIC PRESS, Publishers
Copyright © 2015, Jagdish Gundara
Printed and Bound in Canada.
Cover design and book layout by Eric Normann

ISBN: Paperback 978-0-88962-936-3 ePub 978-1-77161-013-1 ePDF 978-1-77161-014-8

We acknowledge the financial support of the Government of Canada through the Canada Book Fund (CBF) for this project.

Nous reconnaissons l'aide financière du gouvernement du Canada par l'entremise du Fonds du livre du Canada (FLC) pour ce projet.

 Canadian Patrimoine
Heritage canadien

Canada

Mosaic Press gratefully acknowledges the assistance of the OMDC (Ontario Media Development Corporation) in support of our publishing program.

Mosaic Press
1252 Speers Road, Units 1 & 2
Oakville, Ontario L6L 5N9
phone: (905) 825-2130

info@mosaic-press.com

www.mosaic-press.com

The Case for
Intercultural
Education

in a

MULTICULTURAL
WORLD

Essays by
Jagdish Gundara

mosaicPRESS

Contents

Brief Biographical Note

Jagdish S. Gundara is Emeritus Professor of Education at the Institute of Education at the University of London. He holds the UNESCO Chair in International Studies and Teacher Education at the School of Culture and Lifelong Learning. In this capacity he has been appointed as the Director of the reestablished International Centre for Intercultural Studies at the Institute of Education in March 2012.

He received his school education in Kenya where he grew up and undertook an undergraduate degree at Bowdoin College, Maine, USA as Bowdoin Plan Scholar. He was awarded the Steinberg Fellowship and received M. Beatty Bursary to study for his post-graduate degree and received his M.A. from McGill University, Montreal, Canada and a doctorate from Edinburgh University, Scotland, U.K. He subsequently taught in schools and adult and further education institutions in London till the summer of 1979.

He was appointed as the first Head of the pioneering institute wide multidisciplinaryInternational Centre for Intercultural Education in the autumn term of 1979 and retained this position until his retirement in 2006. He was a Visiting Scholar at the Harvard University Graduate School of Education 1987–8.

He is the founding member and the current President of the International Association of Intercultural Education which is based in The Hague, Netherlands. He was the Chairman of the Board of Trustees of the Scarman Trust, based in London and following the death of the first President of the Trust Lord Leslie Scarman, he was elected as the second President of the Trust. Professor Gundara is a founding member of the International Broadcasting Trust (IBT), and Vice-Chairman of the Board of IBT and was a Commissioner of the Commission for Racial Equality until its closure in August 2007. He was an Assessor for Combined Arts Projects and Judge of the Raymond Williams Publishing Prize from 1995–1999 at the Arts Council of Britain. He was the President of Jury of Evens Foundation Intercultural Education Jury, Antwerp, Belgium from 1997 to 2009.

He was one of the Founding members of the Friends of UNESCO Committee and after the U.K. rejoined UNESCO was a member of the Education Committee of the UK UNESCO Commission from 2004–2011. Under the auspicious of the Korean UNESCO Commission he conducted a Feasibility Study which led the establishment of the Asia-Pacific Centre for Education for International Understanding based in Seoul, Korea.

He has been a Fellow of the Centre for African Studies, and the Institute of Commonwealth Studies, University of London,; the Canberra Centre for Research on Indian and Pacific Region Studies, Canberra, Australia and the New Ethnicities Unit at the University of East London. In June 2013 he was elected as the Senior Research Fellow of the Institute of Commonwealth Studies at the University of London. He has been an examiner for Diploma, Masters and Doctoral level dissertations at a number of British universities which include Cambridge, Glasgow, London and Anglia Ruskin University

From 1990–1996 he was Member of the Council of St. Georges House, Windsor Castle, Windsor (Chair: HRH the Duke of Edinburgh; and Chairperson the South Asian Literature Society from 1994–2000).

His research interests include curriculum studies; sustainable development; comparative education; citizenship education; human rights education; multilingualism and asylum and refugee issues. He has been an examiner for a number of higher education institutions in Britain and overseas.

Professor Gundara has organised major international conferences and seminars, has, been a keynote speaker, chaired sessions and organised workshops for institutions like the European Union, the Council of Europe, UNICEF, UNESCO, the Commonwealth Ministers of Education and major universities and professional associations.

He is the author of *Interculturalism, Education and Inclusion* (Paul Chapman, 2000) and coeditor of *Intercultural Social Policy in Europe* (Ashgate, 2000) and has published extensively in the fields of human rights and education in multicultural studies. He is on the Editorial Boards of the journals *Intercultural Education* and *Multicultural Education Review.*

Professor Gundara has received various awards for numerous contributions for his work. These include the Asian Jewel Award, United Kingdom (2003) for excellence in contributions to education and the community; the Indian Council of World Affairs Award (2004) for contributions to intercultural and international understanding; His Highness the Dalai Lama presented him with the Bhai Vir Singh International Award for contributions to education in socially diverse societies and the Scarman Trust Award (2006) for exceptional contributions to CAN DO democratic citizenship in local communities.

He was elected a Fellow of the Royal Society of Arts (1990).

Notes on the Chapters

Global and Civilisational Knowledge: Eurocentrism, Intercultural Education and Civic Engagements was presented at the Education in the Global World conference, University of Verona, April 15 – 18, 2103.

Interculturalism, Dialogue and Cooperation in Higher Education Institutions was presented at the Eurasian Inter-University Dialogues on Cooperation for Higher Education Development, University of Bucharest, May 27 – 28, 2011.

Educational Issues for Young and Vulnerable Groups During Periods of Intercultural Conflict and War was presented at IAIE Zagreb Conference, September 17 – 21, 2013.

Inclusive Education Policies for Vulnerable Groups in Multicultural Societies was presented at Education and Social Integration of Vulnerable Groups conference at the University of Macedonia, Thessalonki, June 24 – 26, 2011.

Intercultural Education Policies for a Multicultural and Democratic Europe was prepared for the Centre for Migration Studies and Intercultural Coexistence, Nº 13 Education and Interculturality.

Intercultural and International Understandings Non-Centric Knowledge and Curriculum in Asia was presented as the keynote address at the Kame International Conference, Hanyang University, May 10, 2013.

Critical Intercultural Education: Challanges for the Nation State Systems was presented at the Intercultural Versus Critical Education – Contrast or Concordance? conference, Sodertorn University, April 14 – 16, 2011.

The Third World Project: Imperialism, Interculturality in the Post World War II Period was presented at Joint AESA/IAIE Conference, Toronto, October 29 – November 2, 2014

Issues of Religious and Cultural Diversity in Modern States was presented at the Cottbus Conference on World Heritage and Cultural Diversity: Challenges for University Education, Brandenburg University of Technology, October 23 – 26, 2006.

Inequality, Diversity and Life-long Learning: Intercultural Perspectives was presented as "Inequality and Diversity Across the Life Course: Intercultural Perspectives" at the Galway University UNESCO Centre Conference, May 18, 2011.

Civilisational Knowledge:

Civic Engagement, Intercultural and Citizenship Education

There is currently a fair amount of discussion about issues of citizenship and the curriculum within educational institutions. A fair amount of discussion about these issues takes place in the context of globalisation but even the most enlightened initiatives which take account of universal principles still revolve around the nation. In Britain the issues are generally about the 'National Curriculum' and issues of citizenship which have received a fair amount of attention tend to assert the national British context and apart from gestures towards the 'global' there are very few substantive changes to take cognisance of the more broadly based and universal basis of knowledge. Recently, the Qualifications and Curriculum Authority has announced that the history curriculum will be changed to include aspects of Black history, the US Civil Rights Movement and Mughal India within the history curriculum at the secondary school. (The Indepenent, London. 26-8-2008) The article will adapt a different set of lenses on these issues in relation to the curriculum and education for citizenship.

Intercultural and Citizenship Education: Historical Legacies of Difference

Intercultural and citizenship education and civic engagement raise a complex set of issues at the present time. In Bosnia, attempts to develop intercultural understandings and common citizenship entail bringing Bosnian, Croatian, and Serbian children into the same school. There is, however, no agreement on a locally developed curriculum or common set of textbooks because the memories of the three groups are very different and they use curricula and textbooks developed by an external agency called the Atlantic College. Work undertaken in Kosovo by Jack Peffers and me from the University of London for UNICEF demonstrated similar problems in agreeing on a common curriculum between all the groups in Kosovo, including the Albanian and Serb communities.

1

The contention of this article is that the biologically derived versions of the nation of 'blood and soil' only tell a narrow and singular version of the story of nation states. The substantive historical and contemporary realities necessitate the telling of much broader stories which are inclusive of good citizenship values derived from diverse sources in complex multicultural societies. In order to achieve this it is necessary to negate the powerful legacies of the dominant groups who have used brutal power to provide long term legitimacy of their control based on notion of 'civilising the natives'.

The Spanish thinker Sepulveda justified the right to intervene in Amerindian societies because of their barbarity. Las Casa's on the other hand purported that evil existed everywhere and that therefore there was no theological justification for interference. This sixteenth century debate has continued for five centuries and as a consequence has barbarised both the brutalisers and the brutalised and led massive intercultural conflicts. (I. Wallerstein: 2006: 16–21)

The early years of the twenty first century are an opportune moment to take stock of these negative legacies and develop new and different intellectual and academic discourses. In the absence of this happening the very grave inequalities as a consequence of deep racism and sexism will continue to corrode the progressive developments which are universal humanistic and nurture 'seige mentalities' which will in turn lead to the entrenchment of multiply divided 'seige communities.' There is as such, no evidence from within the humanities, the social sciences or pure scientific research including the genome studies that there is a concept of 'race'. Concepts of 'race' are social constructs and have no basis in the domain of education or within societal contexts. Therefore, these issues have no basis whatsoever in the in teaching and learning about citizenship, especially if they relate to notions of belonging on the grounds of 'blood and soil.'

In England, citizenship education was introduced in secondary schools in 2002 and, according to a recent OFSTED[1] Inspectorate Report, only a minority of schools have embraced it with any enthusiasm and the quality of the lessons is considered inadequate (The Guardian, 9-28-06). The Inspectorate may, however, have only a partial understanding of why intercultural and citizenship education in the country is inadequate: another aspect could simply be the learners' lack of interest. Their underlying concerns may range from being disengaged from the fissiparous tribes of electronically engaged members of the body politic and not being susceptible to the modern politics defined by 'control freakery'. They also might have inflated career expectations and at the same time confront the grim realities that large numbers of young people face.

1 OFSTED stands for the Office for Standards in Education, Children's Services and Skills. It is the non-ministerial government department of Her Majesty's Chief Inspector of Schools in England.

In Japan, Shinzo Abe, former the Liberal Democratic Party Prime Minister intended to follow a more nationalistic course and to revise the US-imposed pacifist constitution and the Fundamental Law of Education which was enacted in 1947 as a basis for post-war schooling in order to emphasize moral values, patriotism, and tradition (*The Guardian*, 9-27-06). He has however, subsequently had to resign on charges of corruption and these measures are currently in abeyance.

These examples—taken from the Balkans, England and Japan—raise some difficult issues in three different countries. These include questions about the nature of intercultural education, citizenship, and civic engagement in comparative contexts. Is a nationally based understanding of local and central government and human rights sufficient? If one moves to the next level of regions, are the Eurocentric (Bernal 1987), Indo-centric (Chaudhuri 1990), and Sino-centric (Hamashita 1988) memories, histories, and understandings of the past a sufficient basis for citizenship education? Would such narrow national, regional learning about citizenship not in turn raise the spectre of Afro-centrism (Asante 1987), Islamo-centrism (John Voll 1994), or other 'centrisms' at the continental and global levels because of the diasporas of African, Muslim, and 'other' peoples? The attempt therefore, is not to replace one type of centrism with another, which reinforces centric intellectual tunnel visions, but to develop a more holistic formulation of issues about the substance of intercultural and citizenship education.

At one level, the rise of 'siege mentalities' and singularized identities of communities based on religious, ethnic, tribal or linguistic loyalties, as well as the negations of nation-state and social class identities, may partly be a result of the discontinuities, binary/oppositional memories and mentalities that may have been informed by past experiences of servitude or slavery, and colonial and imperial legacies that have become extenuated with the rise of economic globalization. However, histories and societal development are not necessarily one-dimensional or negative: issues of intercultural understandings and citizenship are based on struggles that can embody positive aspects of struggles and memories. However, at this level, too, one is again confronted with complex issues of how to accord legitimacy to the multiple identities and the discourses based on the progressive struggles of the subaltern groups.

Normally in most nation states citizenship values are based on the dominant and largely nationalistic stories of citizenship. These are largely exclusive of groups which have been subdued or conquered and therefore are not inclusive of all the good values of all groups which constitute a polity. Samir Amin (1997) suggests the process of delinking from the dominant and exploitative global forces. It is being argued here that such a delinking must also be accompanied by a process of linking or bridging (Puttnam 2000) with the progressive forces that form part of the current agendas for constitutionally based citizenship and human rights.

A significant part of the content of these agendas is a result of struggles by serfs, peasants, slaves, indentured labour, agricultural and industrial workers, and universally oppressed women against subjugation. While the exceptional nature of each oppression or genocide is recognized, the educational challenge is to determine how the divides and differences can be used to develop shared understandings and common struggles. In the absence of these shared understandings, Freud's concerns about the 'narcissism of small differences' come into play, deepening the divides between groups.

During the UNICEF project conducted in Kosovo, referred to earlier, the issue of singular group identities was raised with different communities, and some members claimed that narrow 'ethnic' or 'racial' identifications exist because they were part of 'human nature'. This is too complex an issue to discuss here but it needs to be stressed at the outset (as stated earlier in this article) that there is no scientific basis or evidence concerning the notion of 'human nature'. If such a thing did exist, then any ideas about intercultural and citizenship education in the context of contemporary schooling stand no chance of succeeding. Hence, a focus on immutable human nature negates the possibilities of unravelling either the historical legacies or current realities of inequalities, and detracts from the positive dimensions of human history and progressive struggles for equality, citizenship, and human rights.

The challenge for intercultural and citizenship education is how to recognize 'bonding' within a group and use this as a basis for bridging or linking with other groups on a sustained basis (Putnam and Feldsten 2003: 280–1). This is important at the present time because most diverse societies have become increasingly fragmented and individuals 'bowl alone' whereas, it is necessary to reconnect isolated individuals, groups and communities through active citizenship engagements so that people can 'bowl together' in safe democratically organised communities.

Furthermore, these issues are not only a prerogative of Eurocentric notions of the 'modern world system' (1974) as articulated earlier by Wallerstein. He has recently recognised the limitations of Eurocentric universalis and reviews three aspects of the structure of knowledge in the modern world: the modern university system, the epistemological divide between the so-called two cultures, and the special role of the social sciences. He states:' all three were essentially nineteenth-century constructions. And all three are in turmoil today as a consequence of the structural crises of the modern world systems.' (I. Wallerstein: (2006) p. 59) These changes are part of a universal repertoire and do not pertain only to the 'West', which is perceived as constituting the 'centre' and at a distance from the 'peripheries'. The content of these issues and their implications of how citizenship and human rights can be taught and learned, and the resulting knowledge can help create a clearer understanding of the newer, changing but substantive realities within a community or a society. Herein, there is also a major role for public and social policies, including those concerning education (not schooling) and the need to recognize the issue of differences, diversities, and commonalities at the global level.

Developing Inclusive Globalism

Many national communities embody notions of particularism as well as those of universalism. Educators and others have an important role in examining these complex notions, both real and imaginary, to analyse the myths, feelings, understandings, and concepts that underlie these differences, and to develop rational ways of dealing with the resultant dilemmas. Can educators, for instance, pool civilizational knowledge in ways that do not polarize peoples but help to develop more syncretism, which can then inform the educational process and citizenship education differently?

From the Cultural Revolutions Founding the Tributary Era to Interfaith Dialogue

The first universalist phase in civilisational development based on the development of ideologies of major religions can be described as the millennium that extended from the fifth century BC to seventh century AD, when the great religions of Zoroastrianism, Buddhism, Christianity, and Islam were founded, and the great Confucian and Hellenistic philosophies were formulated. It is also important to note that these River Valley Cultures were places where the 'tools' of science were also fashioned. These included the handling of 'natural materials and a degree of abstraction which resulted in writing and symbolism.' (H.J.J. Winter: Eastern Science. John Murray. 1952) Hence, in both religious and scientific ways these systems affirmed the common dimension and destiny of all human beings, if only in the life beyond. As Samir Amin writes:

> This declaration of a universalist vocation did not establish a real unification of humanity. The conditions of tributary society did not permit it, and humanity reformed itself into major tributary areas held together by their own particular universalist religion-philosophy (Christendom, Dar el Islam, the Hindu world, the Confucian world). It is still the case, however, that the tributary revolution, like all the great revolutionary moments in history, projected itself forwards and produced concepts ahead of its time (Amin 1997: 80).

While it can be accepted that these earlier movements form an important part of a set of universalistic norms and values, they also continue to present unresolved dilemmas during the contemporary period. Here one need to consider what is necessary from the perspective of the religiously diverse nation-states and regions to develop some inclusive norms that might allow these religions and philosophies to become part of progressive struggles that can lead to interfaith understandings. Hans Küng writes about the need for peace among nations being derived from dialogue between religions and nations. The dialogue between religions requires knowledge about their theological foundations and necessitates, according to Küng that three basic propositions be in place:

> Hans Küng speaking after the events of 9/11 stated that: 'attacking Iraq is likely to worsen the terrorist threat'
> *Catholic New Times*, December 15, 2002

He summarized his view in four propositions: no peace among the nations without peace among the religions; no peace among the religions without dialogue among the religions; no dialogue among the religions without common ethical standards; and finally, no peace without a common global ethic.

Hans Küng's suggestion raises the whole issue of dialogue. First, such dialogues are nothing new. The Umayyad Caliphate which functioned in the eleventh-century Andalusia is an example of intercultural dialogue and cooperation between the southern Mediterranean rim and the North African region with the northern European part of the Mediterranean Sea. It represents the nature of an inter-cultural dialogue between Christians, Jews, and Muslims. Scholars like Al Kundi, Averroes, and Avicenna represent those who translated Aristotelian philosophy into Arabic; these texts were subsequently used for translations into Latin. The common sense understandings are the developments during the Renaissance were based direct translations from Greek texts into Latin. Yet, the work of these philosophers, scientists, and thinkers was undermined by Islamic literalists and fundamentalists like Al Ghazzali, who was part of the Almohad dynasty and resonates with the Christian and Islamic literalists at the present time who are negating ideas of evolutionary science and substituting it with 'essentialists' Christian and Isamic versions of 'science'.

Second, from an educational perspective, a dialogue among religions is insufficient: from the point of view of intercultural and citizenship education there is a need for a more substantive educational engagement. Educational initiatives and interfaith education are among the ways to engage with religions and their relationship to society. The challenge is how, in socially diverse societies, to build intellectually rigorous interfaith education, one that recognizes difference and diversity but also allows for the nurturing and the development of points of mutuality and similarity between faiths.

Many of the current religious strife's are based on memories of wars, terror and persecution derived from religious particularisms and the specificities of their belief systems. Montaigne decries then fact that religious pluralism in France did not bring peaceful coexistence because bitter disputation between the Catholics and Huguenots and led to rhetoric's of hate and was accompanied by vicious circle of violence. Monatigne states 'All are alike in using religion for their violent and ambitious schemes and observes that 'Christians excel at hating enemies.' Other religions however, may not only equal the Christians but even surpass them in their capacities for hatred, viciousness and terror.

What kind of teacher education and support for teachers and schools can help to deal with these historically based politico-religious legacies? For a start it is a very difficult task for educators to give different versions of these stories because religious stories and imaginations are deeply engraved into the psyches of believers and therefore are not amenable to rational discussion or argument. Furthermore, interfaith initiatives that enhance mutual understandings also need to deal with issues of relations between believers of different faiths and those who are non-believers in today's complex and diverse school populations.

One fruitful way inter-faith education initiatives maybe used by schools is the way in which some religions do not comprehend the divine. These religions and the doubts at the heart of Eastern Christianity, Orthodox Judaism, Buddhism, Hinduism and Sufi traditions in Islam constitute an important basis for dialogue and education.

While issues concerning religious instruction and ways of life may be considered as part of a community's private and communal life, knowledge about faiths that circulates within the larger public domain and public institutions may also have an important role to play. Religious identities also are but one aspect of peoples multiple identities and the education systems cannot only deal with them at the exclusion of other, and perhaps more important aspects of different identities of students. Many rational and sensible believers have turned their backs on their faiths because of the limitations and hatreds perpetrated by religions which are not matched by their capacities to constructively and substantively enhance inter-faith and inter-cultural understandings.

These complicated legacies of the hegemony of theological knowledge necessitate fresh thinking by different faiths. This is necessary because it can lead separate as well as collective religious renaissance. Faith communities cannot allow legacies of difference based on hierarchies and in egalitarian values especially against women to continue. Values of secular humanism are deeply ingrained in the consciousnesses of oppressed peoples who have struggled over centuries to acquire greater levels of equalities. Rejuvenated and religious renaissance of religions at the present time can help peoples who have uplifted themselves through popular political struggles as well as educators and schools to heal ancient wounds and negative legacies of the past which continue to be divisive during the contemporary period.

The Enlightenment and the Modern Period

The second phase of the history of societies that can be used to inform citizenship education is that period following the Renaissance, to which the Mediterranean civilizations contributed. It was also the time of the conquest of the Americas by the Atlantic-facing European countries. One of the legacies of the conquests of the Americas is that after 1500 the Europeanization of the globe and the definition of the world from a Eurocentric perspective increased. Did the voyages of Columbus and Vasco da Gama divide the world or were they also a way of connecting the small European peninsula with the rest of the globe? If they are connective then how can the inequalities and unequal relations between and amongst the different regions are ironed out so that the connections establish greater levels of mutualities and solidarities across the regions.

During the Western Enlightenment, one of the important legacies that occurred in the wake of the Renaissance was a shift which from the purely religious to the secular domain and one of whose results was the idea of 'nation'. Enlightenment philosophy's social vision of society, and following the French Revolution, was based not on the ideas of some biological myth of ancestors but on the notions of a social contract—'a nation of free men [sic]'. This nation-state included Alsatians and Occitanians, who did not speak French, as well as Jews. With the abolition of slavery in Santo Domingo, black African peoples were also considered to be 'citizens'.

Compared to the concept of secularism, religion occupied a very different dimension since it was seen as part of the tyranny of an *ancien regime*. As Amin states:

> In forging the concept of 'secularism', it goes beyond religious toleration; it claims to rid the new nation of references to the past and sees Christianity as no more than a personal philosophical opinion like any other, not an ideological structure of society (S. Amin (1997): 81).

Here, the nation is not an affirmation of the particular but an affirmation and an expression of the universal. While the securing of human rights was one of the core objectives of the French Revolution, those rights were applied selectively, with women being denied full citizenship rights. The assimilation of 'other' peoples and the abandoning of local languages in favour of the French language were additional indicators that the nation-state was to take priority. The role of building the modern French nation around this new cultural and linguistic unity was assumed by the school system under the Republic.

The legacy of officially nullifying and overriding differences has had manifestations in the twenty-first century. In 2005 and 2006, French cities were rocked by riots of young, poor, and disenfranchised French citizens, largely from minority and North African backgrounds. The challenge for educators is how to use this complex legacy of the universal and the particular; the local and the national which provides the substantive basis for intercultural understandings and accords equality of citizenship, within the currently unequal nation-state.

In the economically unequal societies the basis of difference is a barrier to developing the notions of similarity, so under those circumstances, what can be done to bring about greater levels of equality? In many contexts these inequalities have become inter-generational and have thwarted possibilities for improving socio-economic conditions through knowledge and skills provided by the school and the educational system.

The English bourgeois revolution of the seventeenth century was earlier than the French Revolution and was less radical. The domination by the English of the different peoples within the islands of Britain and Ireland also led to the loss of local languages and cultures. The role of the monarchy, aristocracy, and Protestant Reformation was based on compromises and a less assertive break with the past. In England, France, and Holland— where bourgeois revolutions had taken place—the changes in terms of the biological basis of the nation-state were different from those that continued to nurture the myths of 'the nations of the mists', i.e., of the remote past, which was sociologically referred to as 'Gemeinschaft'. Given that there are many differences between England, France, and Holland the right to be different is muted by notions of the right to be similar. The modern forms of Enlightenment thought had been developed by cosmopolitans in the salons of Paris, London, Edinburgh, and Berlin.

Immigration Societies

The French and American Revolutions have a lot in common since both were informed by similar ideas during this period of history. Both societies embody features of equality and inequality on various indices, including racial ones.

In immigration societies such as the United States, assimilation allowed subsequent groups to be incorporated into the cultural identity and imposed a fragment of Anglo-Saxon Protestant norms and these have become construed as the public political values of the American national culture. Hence, the American public and national story is not inclusive of the broader range of stories and diversities which are represented historically and contemporaneously within American society. Scholars (like Samuel Huntington) and commentators who cite the American national story as an example for other nation states have in fact misunderstood the narrow American story as being an inclusive broader story of the American polity and society.

The United States also accepted the right to be different, which further perpetuated the differences for the African-American and indigenous American peoples, who, being racially different, had been hierarchically positioned in an unequal society. This conceals the notions of the right to be similar based on principles of equity.

Samuel Huntington's notion of the 'clash of civilizations' at the global level was based on the dominant Anglo-Saxon values juxtaposed to those of the subordinated groups in the American polity. In educational terms this can be illustrated by the 1954 Supreme Court opinion written by Chief Justice Warren that 'separate is not equal'. The year 2008 marks the fifty-fourth anniversary of that Supreme Court decision, and yet the right to be similar and to be equal continues to be denied to African American students as well as to the Native American populations and the more recent Hispanic immigrants. Hence, the right to equality under the United States Constitution is not a reality for large numbers of American citizens, and exclusion due to racism manifests itself throughout American institutions and society. This does not bode well for either equality or the possibilities of better intercultural understandings amongst very diverse and unequal groups in American society.

Socialism

The socialists in the nineteenth century had to operate within the framework of the reactionary ideas of the past, the rise of nationalism within Europe, and, subsequently, within the larger colonial context. They attempted to strengthen the consciousness of solidarity within the subordinated social classes across the lines of nationalist ideologies and tried to optimize the equalities of rights and entitlements. In many cases it was the Eurocentric and messianic versions of socialism that informed struggles outside Europe.

From the period of the Enlightenment to the present time there have also been misplaced notions of progress with the development of pseudo-science and eugenics, with the most appalling consequences, been used against national minorities and 'other' groups in society. In other words the actualisations of socialist societies necessitated the 'purification' of the human stock and eradicate the mental and physical disabilities by shedding the weaker sections of society. In educational terms the concept of 'defectology' used in many socialist and communist states which stressed the genetic basis of intelligence of minority groups and use the majority or dominant nationality as a norm. Hence, groups like the Jews, Roma and other nationalities continue to face disastrous consequences in these states. There are therefore, ways of being circumspect of 'secular Western science' as it was vulgarised by the Nazis, as one needs to be wary of vulgarised fundamentalist religions at the universal level.

One of the problems resulting from the dissolution of the Soviet Union and the Yugoslav Republic was the acceptance of the right to be different which was carried to great lengths. Marxism went through a series of gradual developments under the Second and then the Third International broke from the ethno-centric perspective and placed anti-imperialism at the heart of strategies for struggle. However, the acceptance of the right to be different, common to the Third International, did not allow these states to deepen the notions of inclusive citizenship based on shared values.

National Liberation Movements and Bandung

The colonial world was not directly exposed to the democratic values of the Enlightenment by the European colonial elite, including those of democratic political rights and secularism. Hence, it was the national liberation movements that had to confront the challenge of the values of universalism. This was reinforced by the fact that socialists in Europe were not able to shift their thinking beyond its Eurocentric origins.

The national liberation movements opted for the unity of peoples in the struggle against imperialism and for the constructions of the nation-state beyond ethnic or religious horizons. Those who were on the right invoked the nations shrouded in the 'mists of time', and these myths flew in the face of ethnic, religious, or linguistic diversity, harking back to the tributary systems of Hinduism, Islam, or the ideas of the biological and racial rather than the modern constitutional bases of for instance, the Arab nation. They were in this sense not very different from European nations, which also believed in mythic beginnings. The Janus-faced nature of the nation with 'blood and soil' on the one hand and the modern civic nation based on democratic constitutions on the other have continued as problems in the present.

There are also differences and divides within the national liberation struggles between the right and left, the centralists and the federalists, those who opted for multi-party political systems, and those who espoused unitary political party systems. Those nationalist leaders who subscribed to the progressive ideas were of the leftist tradition within the national liberation, and drew their inspiration from the philosophy of the Enlightenment.

These ideas and perspectives were not something that European elites and colonialists shared with progressive nationalists. For instance, the speech by Jawaharlal Nehru on the 14th August 1947 when India become independent included the following sentence: "And so we have to labour and to work, and work hard, to give reality to our dreams. Those dreams are India, but they are also for the world, for all the nations and peoples are too closely knit together today for anyone of them to imagine that it can live apart." (The Guardian, London 2007; Great Speeches of the 20th century No. 11 in series of 14) Nehru derives his ideas from Western, Indian and other sources from the colonised world and this syncretism of ideas do not have a purely European pedigree but result of struggles for freedom in different societies.

In addition to the recognition of diversity and difference at local and regional levels or in religious or linguistic terms, they have also stressed the notion of unity across these particularistic divides. The Non-Aligned Movement (NAM was founded in 1961) which grew out of the Bandung Conference in Indonesia, in 1955, and made an important contribution towards the democratisation of the United Nations and to develop it into an instrument of justice and to develop it as an instrument for justice. NAM brought together the progressive and democratically oriented nation-states and lasted till about 1975. The Bandung proposals for 'economic cooperation' and for an international system to diversify their economic base led despite resistance of the Western powers to the formation of the UN Conference on Trade and Development (UNCTAD. The most powerful agreement at Bandung came over 'cultural cooperation' and condemned the cultural chauvinism of the imperialists and there was greater unity on this than on issues of political economy. The UNESCO based studies by Claude Levi-Strauss and Marie Jahoda on the biological fiction of race led to twenty nine new states to condemn 'racialism as a means of cultural suppression' (V.Prasad: 2007. p. 45) and laid the foundations of what ultimately became the basis for intercultural exchange and cooperation and educational initiatives including the arts, culture, science and technology.

The movement was reactivated in Havana in the summer of 2006 and it remains to be seen if it will gather strength and become a force in progressive struggles of peoples around the world or if it will be suppressed by the major imperialist powers.

If societies within the rubric of this system are analysed in horizontal terms, they reflect vast reverses experienced by the national liberation movements, peoples, and the negation of citizenship rights across many countries of eastern, central, and southern Europe and the Southern Hemisphere, which present a major challenge for reinstating the intercultural understandings, citizenship and human rights of the masses. For hundreds of millions of peoples in war-torn, corrupt, and collapsed states across the globe, this is a distant dream.

The challenge for inclusive polities, deeper levels of intercultural and citizenship education is not only to engage with the retreats of the ideologies and religions of the tributary epochs, because these need to be deepened with the philosophy of the Enlightenment as well as the socialist movement and the progressive ideas of national liberation, as exemplified by the Bandung Movement.

The democratic practices organized around the notions of respect for difference need to be informed by the right to be similar. These ought to bring about an erosion of the many injustices within and between societies and establish commonalities between and with struggles for equality and human rights globally. In order to help construct a new notion of 'us' and of shared belonging in European societies, progressive ideas from the Third World ought to become part of the ideas of inclusive citizenship in the body politic of Europe in the same way that Western ideas and ways of life have penetrated the Third World.

These issues present cumulative challenges to political systems and especially the education systems on how to socialise and educate young people who can live in diverse and unequal communities with a semblance of stability and intercultural amity.

Contemporary Struggles and Solidarities

Do the past and common struggles for equality, human and citizenship rights provide any basis for progressive struggles to work together and learn from each other? William Katz has uncovered the hidden history of the shared and common struggles of the African and Amer-Indian peoples from New England to Brazil. This history of relationship and collaboration between the reds and blacks remains largely unwritten. (See W. L. Katz: Black Indians: A Hidden Heritage (New York: Simon Pulse: 2005) More recently, the Civil Rights Movement in the United States in the 1960s inspired the feminist movement in its struggle to obtain greater degrees of gender equality. While in the bourgeois national and global contexts this has helped certain classes of women, there are many millions more who are still at the margins of society. In the next stage, can these contemporary struggles lead to some sharing of learning from the past?

The year 2008 commemorates the bicentenary of the abolition of the slave trade, especially the trading in peoples of African origin, who were transported by force to the Americas in large numbers and to the Arabian Peninsula in smaller numbers. One of the challenges posed at the present time is how these events can mark issues of better intercultural relations and equality of citizenship, not only for the descendents of slaves but for the many millions more who are currently denied citizenship and human rights.

How can educators functioning in modern state systems establish commonalities and mutualities with those who have experienced other kinds of oppressions? As an example, the liberation of slaves led to the recruitment of indentured labour, largely from India to work in the plantation economies in the Indian Ocean and Pacific Ocean and the Caribbean region. Are there possibilities of connecting the struggles of these two peoples to attain equality, not only in the Americas, Australasia and Europe, but also feeding into the struggles of the first peoples in the countries where they were transported? Amerindian and Aboriginal peoples also suffered oppression and continue to wage isolated struggles without making connections with others who have fought similar battles.

There is also the massive movement of women who eke out a living in the globalized capitalist economies in the world. For every female executive there are multitudes of poorer women who migrate for work in factories and farms or as cleaners, caregivers, maids and sex workers. This feminization of poverty represents a fundamental denial of citizenship and human rights. How can these millions upon millions of people be accorded their rights, and what can be learned from previous oppressions and struggles out of which new solidarities, similarities, and mutualities of interest can be established?

Concluding Section

This contribution has pointed out the dichotomies which exist in most societies at the present time and the need to deal with inequalities into greater levels of equality; to turn the negative aspects of unities and diversities into more productive and creative aspects of these disconnected and polarised aspects of difference which are construed as deficits and unities which are interpreted as being assimilation. Hence, the notions of unities ought to include basic and fundamental rights of peoples and citizens and which vest them with rights and responsibilities.

This article has raised challenges for intercultural education and for being active citizens in cohesive democratic contexts where people continue to struggle against hierarchies, inequalities and disenfranchisement. It also raises the issues of divides amongst peoples along gender, faith, social class and racial divides which the dominant groups and political institutions have failed to tackle in practical terms from the local, national to the global levels.

At the core of all these issues are ways in which the academe needs to universalise knowledge and shift away from dominant and 'centric' knowledge systems which have continued to provide singular and dominant versions of humanity and its histories. During this period of global transitions these separate realities and developments need to acquire multiple as well as universal legitimacies so that cohesive futures are based on more inclusive and realistic understandings of humanity.

Discussions about the intercultural curriculum within many countries including Britain cannot ignore these broader underpinnings of knowledge at the universal level. As mentioned earlier there a some attempts to make the history curriculum more inclusive of the knowlsge of minority communities as well as the impact of slavery and colonialism.The issues raised in this article have substantive implications for citizenship education but they do not appear to be currently taken on board by the national educational policy makers and educational institutions.

Bibliography

Amin, S. *Capitalism in the Age of Globalisation*. London: Zed Press, 1997.

Asante, M.K. *The Afrocentric Idea*. *Philadelphia*. Temple University Press, 1987.

Bernal, M. *Black Athena*. London: Free Association Press, 1987.

Chaudhuri, K.N. *Asia before Europe*. *Economy and Civilisation of the Indian Ocean from the Rise of Islam to 1750*. Cambridge: Cambridge University Press, 1990.

Hamashita, T. "The Tribute Trade System and Modern Asia." *The Toyo Bunko*, no. 46; 7–24. Tokyo: *Memoirs of the Research Department of Toyo Bunko*, 1988

Huntington, Samuel. *The Clash of Civilizations and Remaking the World Order*. New York: Simon and Schuster, 1996.

Küng, Hans. *Global Responsibility: In Search of A New Global Ethic*. London: SCM Press, 1991.

Prashad, Vijay. *A People's History of the Third World: The Darker Nations*, New York: The New Press, 2007.

Putnam, R. *Bowling Alone*. New York: Simon Shuster, 2000.

Putnam, R. D., Feldstein, L. M. and Cohen, D. (2003) *Better Together: Restoring the American Community*, New York.

Voll, J. I. "Islam as a Special World-System." (1994) *Journal of World System History*, 5, 2: 213–26.

Wallerstein, Immanuel (1974): *The Modern World-System, vol. I: Capitalist Agriculture and the Origins of the European World-Economy in the Sixteenth Century*. New York/London.

Wallerstain, Immanual (2006) *European Universalism: The Rhetoric of Power*. New York: The New Press, p. 59

Global and Civilisational Knowledge:

Eurocentrism, Intercultural Education and Civic Engagements

Dedication

This paper is dedicated to my very good friend and colleague P.L.B (Bev) Woodroffe

There is currently a fair amount of discussion about issues of civic engagement and the curriculum in an increasingly globalised world. A fair amount of discussion about these issues takes place in the context of globalisation but even the most enlightened initiatives which take account of universal principles still revolve around the nation. In Britain the issues are generally about the 'National Curriculum' and issues of citizenship which have received a fair amount of attention tend to assert the national British context and apart from gestures towards the 'global' there are very few substantive changes to take cognisance of the more broadly based and universal basis of knowledge. Recently, the Minister of Education, Michael Gove has announced that the history curriculum will be changed to reflect a more narrowly English history. It will replace the previous curriculum which included aspects of Black history, the US Civil Rights Movement and Mughal India within the history curriculum at the secondary school. (The Independent, London. 26-8-2008) Cannadine, Sheldon and Keating (2011) suggest young people need to acquire a historical perspective within a broad framework so that they have an understanding of the wider world.

Intercultural and Civic Education: Historical Legacies of Difference

Intercultural and civic engagement raise a complex set of issues at the present time. In Bosnia, attempts to develop intercultural understandings and common citizenship entail bringing Bosnian, Croatian, and Serbian children into the same school.

There is, however, no agreement on a locally developed curriculum or common set of textbooks because the memories of the three groups are very different and they use curricula and textbooks developed by an external agency called the Atlantic College. Work undertaken in Kosovo by Jack Peffers and me from the University of London for UNICEF demonstrated similar problems in agreeing on a common curriculum between all the groups in Kosovo, including the Albanian and Serb communities.

The contention of this paper is that the biologically derived versions of the nation of 'blood and soil' only tell a narrow and singular version of the story of nation states. The substantive historical and contemporary realities necessitate the telling of much broader stories which are inclusive of good citizenship values derived from diverse sources in complex multicultural societies. In order to achieve this it is necessary to negate the powerful legacies of the dominant groups who have used brutal power to provide long term legitimacy of their control based on notion of 'civilising the natives'.

The Spanish thinker Sepulveda justified the right to intervene in Amerindian societies because of their barbarity. Las Casa's on the other hand purported that evil existed everywhere and that therefore there was no theological justification for interference. This sixteenth century debate has continued for five centuries and as a consequence has barbarised both the brutalisers and the brutalised and led massive intercultural conflicts. (I. Wallerstein: 2006: 16–21)

The second decade of the twenty first century is an opportune moment to take stock of these negative legacies and develop new and different intellectual and academic discourses. In the absence of this happening the very grave inequalities as a consequence of deep racism and sexism will continue to corrode the progressive developments which are universal humanistic and nurture 'siege mentalities' which will in turn lead to the entrenchment of multiply divided 'siege communities.' There is as such, no evidence from within the humanities, the social sciences or pure scientific research including the genome studies that there is a concept of 'race'. Concepts of 'race' are social constructs and have no basis in the domain of education or within societal contexts. Therefore, these issues have no basis whatsoever in the in teaching and learning about civic engagement, especially if they relate to notions of belonging on the grounds of 'blood and soil.'

In England, citizenship education was introduced in secondary schools in 2002 and, according to an OFSTED[1] Inspectorate Report, only a minority of schools have embraced it with any enthusiasm and the quality of the lessons is considered inadequate (*The Guardian*, 9-28-06). The Inspectorate may,

1 OFSTED stands for the Office for Standards in Education, Children's Services and Skills. It is the non-ministerial government department of Her Majesty's Chief Inspector of Schools in England.

however, have only a partial understanding of why intercultural and citizenship education in the country is inadequate: another aspect could simply be the learners' lack of interest. Their underlying concerns may range from being disengaged from the fissiparous tribes of electronically engaged members of the body politic and not being susceptible to the modern politics defined by 'control freakery'. They also might have inflated career expectations and at the same time confront the grim realities that large numbers of young people face.

In Japan, a series of pronouncements by the previous prime minister Kaizumi in 2005 promised 'never to take the path of war' but Shinzo Abe the Liberal Democratic Party Prime Minister intended to follow a more nationalistic course and to revise the US-imposed pacifist constitution and the Fundamental Law of Education which was enacted in 1947 as a basis for post-war schooling in order to emphasize moral values, patriotism, and tradition (*The Guardian*, 9-27-06). After facing changes for corruption he is back in office.

These examples—taken from the Balkans, England and Japan—raise some difficult issues in three different countries. These include questions about the nature of intercultural education civic engagement in comparative contexts. Is a nationally based understanding of local and central government and human rights sufficient? If one moves to the next level of regions, are the Eurocentric (Bernal 1987), Indo-centric (Chaudhuri 1990), and Sino-centric (Hamashita 1988) memories, histories, and understandings of the past a sufficient basis for civic education and engagement? Would such narrow national, regional learning about citizenship not in turn raise the spectre of Afro-centrism (Asante 1987), Islamo-centrism (John Voll 1994), or other 'centrisms' at the continental and global levels because of the diasporas of African, Muslim, and 'other' peoples? The attempt therefore, is not to replace one type of centrism with another, which reinforces centric intellectual tunnel visions, but to develop a more holistic and non-centric formulation of issues about the substance of intercultural and civic education.

At one level, the rise of 'siege mentalities' and singularized identities of communities based on religious, ethnic, tribal or linguistic loyalties, as well as the negations of nation-state and social class identities, may partly be a result of the discontinuities, binary/oppositional memories and mentalities that may have been informed by past experiences of servitude or slavery, and colonial and imperial legacies that have become extenuated with the rise of economic globalization. However, histories and societal development are not necessarily one-dimensional or negative: issues of intercultural understandings and civic engagements and are based on struggles that can embody positive aspects of struggles and memories. However, at this level, too, one is again confronted with complex issues of how to accord legitimacy to the multiple identities and the discourses based on the progressive struggles of the subaltern groups.

Normally in most nation states civic values are based on the dominant and largely nationalistic stories of belonging to the polity. These are largely exclusive of groups which have been subdued or conquered and therefore are not inclusive of all the good values of all groups which constitute a polity. Samir Amin (1997) suggests the process of delinking from the dominant and exploitative global negative forces of neoliberal economics. It is being argued here that such a delinking must also be accompanied by a process of linking or bridging (Puttnam 2000) with the progressive forces and struggles that form part of the current agendas for constitutionally based civic and human rights.

A significant part of the content of these agendas is a result of struggles by serfs, peasants, slaves, indentured labour, agricultural and industrial workers, and universally oppressed women against subjugation. While the exceptional nature of each oppression or genocide is recognized, the educational challenge is to determine how the divides and differences can be used to develop shared understandings and common struggles. In the absence of these shared understandings, Freud's concerns about the 'narcissism of small differences' come into play, deepening the divides between groups.

During the UNICEF project conducted in Kosovo, referred to earlier, the issue of singular group identities was raised with different communities, and some members claimed that narrow 'ethnic' or 'racial' identifications exist because they were part of 'human nature'. This is too complex an issue to discuss here but it needs to be stressed at the outset (as stated earlier in this paper) that there is no scientific basis or evidence concerning the notion of 'human nature'. If such a thing did exist, then any ideas about intercultural and citizenship education in the context of contemporary schooling stand no chance of succeeding. Hence, a focus on immutable human nature negates the possibilities of unravelling either the historical legacies or current realities of inequalities, and detracts from the positive dimensions of human history and progressive struggles for equality, civic and human rights.

The challenge for intercultural and civic education and engagements is how to recognize 'bonding' within a group and use this as a basis for bridging or linking with other groups on a sustained basis (Putnam and Feldsten 2003: 280–1). This is important at the present time because most diverse societies have become increasingly fragmented and individuals 'bowl alone' whereas, it is necessary to reconnect isolated individuals, groups and localities through active citizenship engagements so that people can 'bowl together' in safe democratically organised communities.

Furthermore, these issues are not only a prerogative of Eurocentric notions of the 'modern world system' (1974) as articulated earlier by Wallerstein. He has subsequently recognised the limitations of Eurocentric universalist and reviews three aspects of the structure of knowledge in the modern world: the modern university system, the epistemological divide between the so-called two cultures, and the special role of the social sciences. He states:' all three were essentially nineteenth-century constructions. And all three are in turmoil today as a consequence of the structural crises of the modern world systems.' .(I. Wallerstein: (2006) p. 59) These changes are part of a universal repertoire and do not pertain only to the 'West', which is perceived as constituting the 'centre' and at a distance from the 'peripheries'. The content of these issues and their implications of how civic and human rights can be taught and learned, and the resulting knowledge can help create a clearer understanding of the newer, changing but substantive realities within a community or a society. They can also enable young people to be actively involved in civic activities within local communities and the larger polity. Herein, there is also a major role for public and social policies, including those concerning education (not schooling) and the need to recognize the issue of differences, diversities, and commonalities at the global level.

Developing Inclusive Globalism

Many national communities embody notions of particularism as well as those of universalism. Educators and others have an important role in examining these complex notions, both real and imaginary, to analyse the myths, feelings, understandings, and concepts that underlie these differences, and to develop rational ways of dealing with the resultant dilemmas. Can educators, for instance, pool civilizational knowledge in ways that do not polarize peoples but help to develop more syncretism, which can then inform the educational process and civic education differently?

From the Cultural Revolutions
Founding the Tributary Era to Interfaith Dialogue

The first Universalist phase in civilisational development based on the development of ideologies of major religions can be described as the millennium that extended from the fifth century BC to seventh century AD, when the great religions of Zoroastrianism, Buddhism, Christianity, and Islam were founded, and the great Confucian and Hellenistic philosophies were formulated. It is also important to note that these River

Valley Cultures were places where the 'tools' of science were also fashioned. These included the handling of 'natural materials and a degree of abstraction which resulted in writing and symbolism.' (H.J.J. Winter: Eastern Science. John Murray. 1952) Hence, in both religious and scientific ways these systems affirmed the common dimension and destiny of all human beings, if only in the life beyond. As Samir Amin writes:

> This declaration of a universalist vocation did not establish a real unification of humanity. The conditions of tributary society did not permit it, and humanity reformed itself into major tributary areas held together by their own particular universalist religion-philosophy (Christendom, Dar el Islam, the Hindu world, the Confucian world). It is still the case, however, that the tributary revolution, like all the great revolutionary moments in history, projected itself forwards and produced concepts ahead of its time (Amin 1997: 80).

While it can be accepted that these earlier movements form an important part of a set of universalistic norms and values, they also continue to present unresolved dilemmas during subsequent periods of history and especially during the contemporary period at a global level. Here one need to consider what is necessary from the perspective of the religiously diverse nation-states and regions to develop some inclusive norms that might allow these religions and philosophies to become part of progressive struggles that can lead to interfaith understandings. Hans Küng writes about the need for peace among nations being derived from dialogue between religions and nations. The dialogue between religions requires knowledge about their theological foundations and necessitates, according to Küng that three basic propositions be in place:

Hans Küng speaking after the events of 9/11 stated that: 'attacking Iraq is likely to worsen the terrorist threat'

Catholic New Times, December 15, 2002

> He summarized his view in four propositions: no peace among the nations without peace among the religions; no peace among the religions without dialogue among the religions; no dialogue among the religions without common ethical standards; and finally, no peace without a common global ethic.

Hans Küng's suggestion raises the whole issue of interfaith dialogue and these same issues are stressed by the Dalai Lama and more recently with the rise of missonising at the global level by Christianity and Islam a critical analysis by Nobel Prize winner Wole Soyinka of the way in which traditional African cultures and spiritual systems like the Orisa are being destroyed. (W. Soyinka: 2012)

The Renaissance and Intercultural Scholarship.

The second phase of cultural development is the Renaissance, which has largely been perceived as a Christian and European phase of cultural development. This understanding of the Renaissance ignores the contributions which were made by various cultural traditions around the Mediterranean region. The Umayyad Caliphate which functioned in the eleventh-century Andalusia is an example of intercultural dialogue and cooperation between the southern Mediterranean rim and the North African region with the northern European part of the Mediterranean Sea. It represents the nature of an inter-cultural dialogue between Christians, Jews, and Muslims. Scholars like Al Kundi, Averroes, and Avicenna represent those who translated Aristotelian philosophy into Arabic; these texts were subsequently used for translations into Latin. The common sense understandings are the developments during the Renaissance were based direct translations from Greek texts into Latin. Yet, the work of these philosophers, scientists, and thinkers was undermined by Islamic literalists and fundamentalists like Al Ghazzali, who was part of the Almohad dynasty and resonates with the Christian and Islamic literalists at the present time who are negating ideas of evolutionary science and substituting it with 'essentialists' Christian and Islamic versions of 'science'.

Second, from an educational perspective, a dialogue among religions is insufficient: from the point of view of intercultural and civic education there is a need for a more substantive educational engagement. Educational initiatives and interfaith education are among the ways to engage with religions and their relationship to society. The challenge is how, in socially diverse societies, to build intellectually rigorous interfaith education, one that recognizes difference and diversity but also allows for the nurturing and the development of points of mutuality and similarity between faiths.

Many of the current religious strife's are based on memories of wars, terror and persecution derived from religious particularisms and the specificities of their belief systems. Montaigne decries then fact that religious pluralism in France did not bring peaceful coexistence because bitter disputation between the Catholics and Huguenots and led to rhetoric's of hate and was accompanied by vicious circle of violence. Monatigne states 'All are alike in using religion for their violent and ambitious schemes and observes that 'Christians excel at hating enemies.' Other religions however, may not only equal the Christians but even surpass them in their capacities for hatred, viciousness and terror.

What kind of teacher education and support for teachers and schools can help to deal with these historically based politico-religious legacies? For a start it is a very difficult task for educators to give different versions of these stories because religious stories and imaginations are deeply engraved into the psyches of believers and therefore are not amenable to rational discussion or argument. Furthermore, interfaith initiatives that enhance mutual understandings also need to deal with issues of relations between believers of different faiths and those who are non-believers in today's complex and diverse school populations.

One fruitful way inter-faith education initiatives maybe used by schools is the way in which some religions do not comprehend the divine. These religions and the doubts at the heart of Eastern Christianity, Orthodox Judaism, Buddhism, Hinduism and Sufi traditions in Islam constitute an important basis for dialogue and education.

While issues concerning religious instruction and ways of life may be considered as part of a community's private and communal life, knowledge about faiths that circulates within the larger public domain and public institutions may also have an important role to play. Religious identities also are but one aspect of peoples multiple identities and the education systems cannot only deal with them at the exclusion of other, and perhaps more important aspects of different identities of students. Many rational and sensible believers have turned their backs on their faiths because of the limitations and hatreds perpetrated by religions which are not matched by their capacities to constructively and substantively enhance inter-faith and inter-cultural understandings.

These complicated legacies of the hegemony of theological knowledge necessitate fresh thinking by different faiths. This is necessary because it can lead separate as well as collective religious renaissance. Faith communities cannot allow legacies of difference based on hierarchies and in egalitarian values especially against women to continue. Values of secular humanism are deeply ingrained in the consciousnesses of oppressed peoples who have struggled over centuries to acquire greater levels of equalities. Rejuvenation and religious renaissance rather than the fundamentalism as a result of essentialising of the faith systems at the global level at the present time can help peoples who have uplifted themselves through popular political struggles as well as educators and schools to heal ancient wounds and negative legacies of the past which continue to be divisive during the contemporary period.

The Enlightenment and the Modern Period

The third phase of the history of societies that can be used to inform civic and citizen education is that period following the Renaissance, to which the Mediterranean civilizations contributed. It was also the time of the conquest of the Americas by the Atlantic-facing European countries. One of the legacies of the conquests of the Americas is that after 1500 the Europeanization of the globe and the definition of the world from a Eurocentric perspective increased. Did the voyages of Columbus and Vasco da Gama divide the world or were they also a way of connecting the small European peninsula with the rest of the globe? If they are connective then how can the inequalities and unequal relations between and amongst the different regions are ironed out so that the connections establish greater levels of mutualities and solidarities across the regions.

During the Western Enlightenment, one of the important legacies that occurred in the wake of the Renaissance was a shift which from the purely religious to the secular domain and one of whose results was the idea of 'nation'. Enlightenment philosophy's social vision of society, and following the French Revolution, was based not on the ideas of some biological myth of ancestors but on the notions of a social contract—'a nation of free men [sic]'. This nation-state included Alsatians and Occitanians, who did not speak French, as well as Jews. With the abolition of slavery in Santo Domingo, black African peoples were also considered to be 'citizens'.

Compared to the concept of secularism, religion occupied a very different dimension since it was seen as part of the tyranny of an *ancien regime*. As Amin states:

> In forging the concept of 'secularism', it goes beyond religious toleration; it claims to rid the new nation of references to the past and sees Christianity as no more than a personal philosophical opinion like any other, not an ideological structure of society (S. Amin (1997): 81).

Here, the nation is not an affirmation of the particular but an affirmation and an expression of the universal. While the securing of human rights was one of the core objectives of the French Revolution, those rights were applied selectively, with women being denied full citizenship rights. The assimilation of 'other' peoples and the abandoning of local languages in favour of the French language were additional indicators that the nation-state was to take priority. The role of building the modern French nation around this new cultural and linguistic unity was assumed by the school system under the Republic.

The legacy of officially nullifying and overriding differences has had manifestations in the twenty-first century. In 2005 and 2006, French cities and in 2011 English cities were rocked by riots of young, poor, and disenfranchised young people who experienced institutionalised racism backgrounds. The challenge for educators is how to use this complex legacy of the universal and the particular; the local and the national; the regional and the global which provides the substantive basis for intercultural understandings and accords equality of citizens, within the currently unequal nation-state systems.

In the economically unequal societies the basis of difference is a barrier to developing the notions of similarity, so under those circumstances, what can be done to bring about greater levels of equality? In many contexts these inequalities have become inter-generational and have thwarted possibilities for improving socio-economic conditions through knowledge and skills provided by the school and the educational system.

The English bourgeois revolution of the seventeenth century was earlier than the French Revolution and was less radical. The domination by the English of the different peoples within the islands of Britain and Ireland also led to the loss of local languages and cultures. The role of the monarchy, aristocracy, and Protestant Reformation was based on compromises and a less assertive break with the past. In England, France, and Holland—where bourgeois revolutions had taken place—the changes in terms of the biological basis of the nation-state were different from those that continued to nurture the myths of 'the nations of the mists', i.e., of the remote past, which was sociologically referred to as 'Gemeinschaft'. Given that there are many differences between England, France, and Holland the right to be different is muted by notions of the right to be similar. The modern forms of Enlightenment thought had been developed by cosmopolitans in the salons of Paris, London, Edinburgh, and Berlin.

Immigration Societies

The French and American Revolutions have a lot in common since both were informed by similar ideas during this period of the Enlightenment. Both societies embody features of equality and inequality on various indices, including racial ones.

In immigration societies such as the United States, assimilation allowed subsequent groups to be incorporated into the cultural identity and imposed a fragment of Anglo-Saxon Protestant norms and these have become construed as the public political values of the American national culture. Hence, the American public and national story is not inclusive of the broader range of stories and diversities which are represented historically and contemporaneously within American society. Scholars (like Samuel Huntington) and commentators who cite the American national story as an example for other nation states have in fact misunderstood the narrow American story as being an inclusive broader story of the American polity and society.

At the more international level the United Nations University has launched a Research Centre under the rubric of Alliance of Civilisations in June 2011 and at the global level and for intercultural understandings is an important initiative to counteract the arguments of people like Huntington on the Clash of Civilisations.

The United States also accepted the right to be different, which further perpetuated the differences for the African-American and indigenous American peoples, who, being racially different, had been hierarchically positioned in an unequal society. This conceals the notions of the right to be similar based on principles of equity.

Samuel Huntington's notion of the 'clash of civilizations' at the global level was based on the dominant Anglo-Saxon values juxtaposed to those of the subordinated groups in the American polity. In educational terms this can be illustrated by the 1954 Supreme Court opinion written by Chief Justice Warren that 'separate is not equal'. The year 2008 marks the fifty-nineth anniversary of that Supreme Court decision, and yet the right to be similar and to be equal continues to be denied to African American students as well as to the Native American populations and the more recent Hispanic immigrants. Hence, the right to equality under the United States Constitution is not a reality for large numbers of American citizens, and exclusion due to racism manifests itself throughout American institutions and society. This does not bode well for either equality or the possibilities of better intercultural understandings amongst very diverse and unequal groups in American society.

Socialism

The fourth development at the universal level has been the way in which ideas of socialism took roots across the world. Socialists in the nineteenth century had to operate within the framework of the reactionary ideas of the past, the rise of nationalism within Europe, and, subsequently, within the larger colonial context. They attempted to strengthen the consciousness of solidarity within the subordinated social classes across the lines of nationalist ideologies and tried to optimize the equalities of rights and entitlements. In many cases it was the Eurocentric and messianic versions of socialism that informed struggles outside Europe.

From the period of the Enlightenment to the present time there have also been misplaced notions of progress with the development of pseudo-science and eugenics, with the most appalling consequences, been used against national minorities and 'other' groups in society. In other words the actualisations of socialist societies necessitated the 'purification' of the human stock and eradicate the mental and physical disabilities by shedding the weaker sections of society. In educational terms the concept of 'defectology' used in many socialist and communist states which stressed the genetic basis of intelligence of minority groups and use the majority or dominant nationality as a norm. Hence, groups like the Jews, Roma and other nationalities continue to face disastrous consequences in these states.

There are therefore, ways of being circumspect of 'secular Western science' as it was vulgarised by the Nazis, as one needs to be wary of vulgarised fundamentalist religions at the universal level.

One of the problems resulting from the dissolution of the Soviet Union and the Yugoslav Republic was the acceptance of the right to be different which was carried to great lengths. Marxism went through a series of gradual developments under the Second and then the Third International broke from the ethnocentric perspective and placed anti-imperialism at the heart of strategies for struggle. However, the acceptance of the right to be different, common to the Third International, did not allow these states to deepen the notions of inclusive citizenship based on shared values.

National Liberation Movements and Bandung

The colonisation of the world by Europe after 1492 began to be reversed in the middle of the twentieth century and provides the fifth phase of civilizational development through national liberation movements. The colonial world was not directly exposed to the democratic values of the Enlightenment by the European colonial elite, including those of democratic political rights and secularism. Hence, it was the national liberation movements that had to confront the challenge of the values of universalism. This was reinforced by the fact that socialists in Europe were not able to shift their thinking beyond its Eurocentric origins.

The national liberation movements opted for the unity of peoples in the struggle against imperialism and for the constructions of the nation-state beyond ethnic or religious horizons. Those who were on the right invoked the nations shrouded in the 'mists of time', and these myths flew in the face of ethnic, religious, or linguistic diversity, harking back to the tributary systems of Hinduism, Islam, or the ideas of the biological and racial rather than the modern constitutional bases of for instance, the Arab nation. They were in this sense not very different from European nations, which also believed in mythic beginnings. The Janus-faced nature of the nation with 'blood and soil' on the one hand and the modern civic nation based on democratic constitutions on the other have continued as problems in the present.

There are also differences and divides within the national liberation struggles between the right and left, the centralists and the federalists, those who opted for multi-party political systems, and those who espoused unitary political party systems. Those nationalist leaders who subscribed to the progressive ideas were of the leftist tradition within the national liberation, and drew their inspiration from the philosophy of the Enlightenment.

These ideas and perspectives were not something that European elites and colonialists shared with progressive nationalists. For instance, the speech by Jawaharlal Nehru on the 14th August 1947 when India become independent included the following sentence: "And so we have to labour and to work, and work hard, to give reality to our dreams. Those dreams are India, but they are also for the world, for all the nations and peoples are too closely knit together today for anyone of them to imagine that it can live apart." (The Guardian, London 2007; Great Speeches of the 20th century No. 11 in series of 14) Nehru derives his ideas from Western, Indian and other sources from the colonised world and this syncretism of ideas do not have a purely European pedigree but result of struggles for freedom in different societies.

In addition to the recognition of diversity and difference at local and regional levels or in religious or linguistic terms, they have also stressed the notion of unity across these particularistic divides. The Non-Aligned Movement (NAM was founded in 1961) which grew out of the Bandung Conference in Indonesia, in 1955, and made an important contribution towards the democratisation of the United Nations and to develop it into an instrument of justice. NAM brought together the progressive and democratically oriented nation-states and lasted till about 1975. The Bandung proposals for 'economic cooperation' and for an international system to diversify their economic base led despite resistance of the Western powers to the formation of the UN Conference on Trade and Development (UNCTAD). The most powerful agreement at Bandung came over 'cultural cooperation' and condemned the cultural chauvinism of the imperialists and there was greater unity on this than on issues of political economy. The UNESCO based studies by Claude Levi-Strauss and Marie Jahoda on the biological fiction of race led to twenty nine new states to condemn 'racialism as a means of cultural suppression' (V.Prasad: 2007. p. 45) and laid the foundations of what ultimately became the basis for intercultural exchange and cooperation and educational initiatives including the arts, culture, science and technology.

The movement was reactivated in Havana in the summer of 2006 and it is hoped that after Hugo Chavez's recent death, where the cry was 'We are all Chavez' (The Guardian, London, 9-March 2913) that the movement will gather strength and become a force in progressive struggles of peoples around the world or if it will be suppressed by the major imperialist powers.

If societies within the rubric of this system are analysed in horizontal terms, they reflect vast reverses experienced by the national liberation movements, peoples, and the negation of citizenship rights across many countries of eastern, central, and southern Europe and the Southern Hemisphere, which present a major challenge for reinstating the intercultural understandings, citizenship and human rights of the masses. For hundreds of millions of peoples in war-torn, corrupt, and collapsed states across the globe, this is a distant dream.

The challenge for inclusive polities, deeper levels of intercultural and civic education is not only to engage with the retreats of the ideologies and religions of the tributary epochs, because these need to be deepened with the philosophy of the Enlightenment as well as the socialist movement and the progressive ideas of national liberation, as exemplified by the Bandung Movement.

The democratic practices organized around the notions of respect for difference need to be informed by the right to be similar. This is important to establish greater levels of mutualities and resemblances. These ought to bring about an erosion of the many injustices within and between societies and establish commonalities between and with struggles for equality and human rights globally. In order to help construct a new notion of 'us' and of shared belonging in European societies, progressive ideas from the Third World ought to become part of the ideas of inclusive citizenship in the body politic of Europe in the same way that Western ideas and ways of life have penetrated the Third World.

These issues present cumulative challenges to political systems and especially the education systems on how to socialise and educate young people who can live in diverse and unequal communities with a semblance of stability and intercultural amity. In this respect Mwalimu Nyerere, the former President of Tanzania practised statecraft which held the diverse Tanzanian polity together. He was therefore known as Mwalimu, a Teacher. (M. Mamdani: 2012)

Contemporary Struggles and Solidarities

Do the past and common struggles for equality, human and citizenship rights provide any basis for progressive struggles to work together and learn from each other? William Katz has uncovered the hidden history of the shared and common struggles of the African and Amer-Indian peoples from New England to Brazil. This history of relationship and collaboration between the reds and blacks remains largely unwritten. (See W. L. Katz: Black Indians: A Hidden Heritage (New York: Simon Pulse: 2005)

Subsequently, the Civil Rights Movement in the United States in the 1960s inspired the feminist movement in its struggle to obtain greater degrees of gender equality. While in the bourgeois national and global contexts this has helped certain classes of women, there are many millions more who are still at the margins of society. In the next stage, can these contemporary struggles lead to some sharing of learning from the past?

The year 2008 commemorated the bicentenary of the abolition of the slave trade, especially the trading in peoples of African origin, who were transported by force to the Americas in large numbers and to the Arabian Peninsula in smaller numbers. One of the challenges posed at the present time is how these events can mark issues of better intercultural relations and equality of citizenship, not only for the descendents of slaves but for the many millions more who are currently denied citizenship and human rights.

How can educators functioning in modern state systems establish commonalities and mutualities with those who have experienced other kinds of oppressions? As an example, the liberation of slaves led to the recruitment of indentured labour, largely from India to work in the plantation economies in the Indian Ocean and Pacific Ocean and the Caribbean region. Are there possibilities of connecting the struggles of these two peoples to attain equality, not only in the Americas, Australasia and Europe, but also feeding into the struggles of the first peoples in the countries where they were transported? Amerindian and Aboriginal peoples also suffered oppression and continue to wage isolated struggles without making connections with others who have fought similar battles. At the global level these struggles and solidarities are important forces to enhance intercultural understandings and unities.

There is also the massive movement of women who eke out a living in the globalized capitalist economies in the world. For every female executive there are multitudes of poorer women who migrate for work in factories and farms or as cleaners, caregivers, maids and sex workers. This feminization of poverty represents a fundamental denial of citizenship and human rights. How are these millions upon millions of people to be accorded their rights, and what can be learned from previous oppressions and struggles out of which new solidarities, similarities, and mutualities of interest can be established?

Concluding Section

This contribution has pointed out the dichotomies which exist in most societies at the present time and the need to deal with inequalities into greater levels of equality; to turn the negative aspects of unities and diversities into more productive and creative aspects of these disconnected and polarised aspects of difference which are construed as deficits and unities which are interpreted as being assimilation. Hence, the notions of unities ought to include basic and fundamental rights of peoples and citizens and which vest them with rights and responsibilities.

This paper has raised challenges for intercultural education and for being active citizens in cohesive democratic contexts where people continue to struggle against hierarchies, inequalities and disenfranchisement. It also raises the issues of divides amongst peoples along gender, faith, social class and racial divides which the dominant groups and political institutions have failed to tackle in practical terms from the local, national to the global levels.

At the core of all these issues are ways in which the academe needs to universalise knowledge and shift away from dominant and 'centric' knowledge systems which have continued to provide singular and dominant versions of humanity and its histories. During this period of global transitions these separate realities and developments need to acquire multiple as well as universal legitimacies so that cohesive futures are based on more inclusive and realistic understandings of humanity.

Discussions about the intercultural curriculum within many countries including Britain cannot ignore these broader underpinnings of knowledge at the universal level. As mentioned earlier there are some attempts to make the history curriculum more inclusive of the knowledge of minority communities as well as the impact of slavery and colonialism. The issues raised in this paper have substantive implications for citizenship education but they do not appear to be currently taken on board by the national educational policy makers and educational institutions.

Bibliography

Amin, S. *Capitalism in the Age of Globalisation*. London: Zed Press, 1997.

Asante, M.K. *The Afrocentric Idea. Philadelphia*. Temple University Press, 1987.

Bernal, M. *Black Athena*. London: Free Association Press, 1987.

Chaudhuri, K.N. *Asia before Europe. Economy and Civilisation of the Indian Ocean from the Rise of Islam to 1750*. Cambridge: Cambridge University Press, 1990.

Hamashita, T. "The Tribute Trade System and Modern Asia." *The Toyo Bunko*, no. 46; 7–24. Tokyo: Memoirs of the Research Department of Toyo Bunko, 1988

Huntington, Samuel. *The Clash of Civilizations and Remaking the World Order*. New York: Simon and Schuster, 1996.

Katz, William, *Black Indians: A Hidden Heritage*. New York: Simon Pulse: 2005

Küng, Hans. *Global Responsibility: In Search of A New Global Ethic*. London: SCM Press, 1991.

Mamdani, Mahmood Mamdani, *Define and Rule: Native as a Political Identity*. Cambridge: Harvard University Press: 2012

Prashad, Vijay. *A People's History of the Third World: The Darker Nations*, New York: The New Press, 2007.

Putnam, R. *Bowling Alone*. New York: Simon Shuster, 2000.

Putnam, R. D., Feldstein, L. M. and Cohen, D. (2003) *Better Together: Restoring the American Community*, New York.

Soyinka,Wole (2012) *Of Africa*. New Haven and London, Yale University Press.

Voll, J. I. "Islam as a Special World-System." (1994) *Journal of World System History*, 5, 2: 213–26.

Wallerstein, Immanuel (1974): *The Modern World-System, vol. I: Capitalist Agriculture and the Origins of the European World-Economy in the Sixteenth Century*. New York/London.

Wallerstain, Immanual (2006) *European Universalism: The Rhetoric of Power*. New York: The New Press, p. 59

Citizenship Education

in a Multicultural Britain and Europe

Introduction

This article will examine the pressures on contemporary democratic societies during a period of contradictory changes. There are pressures for localisation on the one hand as well as those of centralisation at national and regional levels. In contemporary terms the rise of religiosity in many contexts is also perceived to present particular problems. The development of multicultural policies, in many European countries (including Britain, Netherlands and Sweden) are criticised by many as privileging issues of particular group identities and ignoring the larger question of inequality in societies. The article deals with these complex issues by focussing on educational dimensions in relation to citizenship education. Firstly, it addresses the question of multiculturalism and intercultural education and points the way forward in educational terms. Secondly, it addresses the challenges for developing 'communities of development and hope', through active citizenship at grass roots and local levels. Thirdly, it deals with the institutional challenges at the public level for developing features of transparency and good governance through joined up intercultural agendas which lead to greater levels of equalities through social and public policy measures. This article argues that intercultural public and social policies are a step in the direction of actualising a cosmopolitan and social democratic polity. Education of citizens at formal and informal levels and greater levels of educational equality of outcomes within a state are important to enhance peace and stability in modern polities.

The following discussion on education and democracy takes as its premise that issues of multiculturalism pertain not only to the contemporary aspects of diversity based on linguistic, religious, nationality and social class grounds but also to the historical diversities in society. There are however, changing topographies of contemporary and historical aspects of differences and diversity and they raise in their wake various complex issues for many societies across the world.

In the political domain the German Chancellor Angela Merkel has stated that multiculturalism in Germany has failed. More recently the British Prime Minister David Cameron has also attacked Britain's multicultural policies and raised issues of national security as being endangered by these policies.

Multiculturalism

Social diversities which are evident in the European context are also evident in most other societies. In some of the ex-colonial European countries the experience of decline of the imperial power and external colonialism and the distance from it, allows the members of the polity (ies) an opportunity to reflect on the dominant nature of historical 'internal colonialism'. This reflexive distance can provide an opportunity to 'see themselves from the perspective of the defeated in the questionable role of victors who were called to account for the violence of an imposed and disruptive process of modernisation.' (Habermas 2007)

In this article the term 'multiculturalism' is used as a descriptive term and refers to aspects of social and cultural differences in institutions, communities and societies. However, in many English speaking countries the term 'multicultural' is used as a policy term and has led to interminable debates about 'political correctness'. In many European countries and other societies these multicultural policies are also perceived to have consequences for 'Western' and 'Enlightenment values', which are perceived by these critics as being undermined by 'the others' and especially Muslims in Europe. These tensions between the religious and the secular have been highlighted by Ian Buruma and other contemporary writers. (Buruma 2010) Another writer Gilles Kepel argues that multiculturalism used by British and Dutch has echoes of the old colonial practices of indirect rule through organised religious and ethnic communities and that this 'communal' approach, prevents successful integration of Muslims and other immigrants in Europe. (Kepel 1997). These issues of immigration, integration and the role of Islam are also raised by other authors as, are the dilemmas which have resulted from them for the policy makers in most European societies. (Caldwell 2009); Anderson 2009)

Another fairly strong critique of the use of multiculturalism as a policy term is that this tends to obfuscate the much bigger questions of inequalities in society. It tends to legitimise economic inequality and diverts attention away from the deeper issue of class politics in societies like the United States. (Michaels 2007). Worse still is the way in which conservatives in many societies try to underplay the importance of equalities for all groups in society. Richard Wilkinson and Kate Pickett's research and book on 'evidence based politics' received praise from British Conservatives but soon after assuming power, they have used their right-wing think tanks to rubbish the evidence used by the authors. (Wilkinson and Pickett 2009); and *The Guardian*, London 14-8-2010: 3.) However, Wilkinson and Pickett, claim that where inequality exists in socially diverse communities 'ethnic divisions may increase social exclusion and discrimination, but ill health and social problems become more common the greater the relative deprivation people experience—whatever their ethnicity'. (Wilkinson and Pickett: 178) Where there are class differences, people nearer the bottom of society almost always face downward discrimination and prejudice. Where there is also racial discrimination there is a greater social division and greater levels of discrimination which may impede the processes of intercultural understandings through educational and other social and public policy measures.

There is also another argument about the need to break from the national container of history and to develop a 'transnational memory'. This would enable societies to reflexively modernise by institutionalising a cosmopolitan civil society having learnt lessons from the Holocaust, imperialism and colonial history. This normative cosmopolitanism would need to correct the democratic deficit of the public institutions and create levels of institutional equality and inter-dependence. These measures would lead to cosmopolitan integration both internally and externally, by reinterpreting the creative tension between unity and diversity. Beck and Grande state that this is 'a paradigm shift resting on the principle that diversity is not a problem but a solution'. (Beck and Grande 2007: 242). They however, recognise that living together can be explosive and therefore necessitates enhanced capacities for intercultural interaction. (Beck and Grande: 249). The school curriculum and the learning process have an important role to play in giving substance to enhancing intercultural understandings.

This difficulty of living together is most pronounced for groups who are viewed as being very different by those who are settled and consider the norm as being the national sovereign territories which have boundaries. They view those groups which are nomadic as not having the same rights and there are huge tensions between settled and nomadic communities, like the Roma and Traveller communities in Europe. The French government has recently deported 1,000 members of this community to Romania and Bulgaria and has been forced into a defensive stance by the European Union's Justice Commissioner, Viviane Reding, who cited this as a violation and a denial of fundamental right of the freedom of movement. The Sarkozy government may land in the European Court in Luxemburg for this violation. (*The Guardian*, London, 15-9-2010: 17) The constitutional, human and social rights of these groups are ignored and the education of their children is generally of a very low standard. This issue presents one of the greatest challenges for intercultural education in democratic societies and schools within them.

Within the British context, the devolution of Scotland, Wales and Northern Ireland is an indication of the political acknowledgement of the historical multinational nature of British society. This historical legacy presents ongoing challenges. Wales has a functioning Assembly but in Northern Ireland the Assembly has functioned sporadically; while Scotland has a Parliament which has greater powers than an Assembly.

The complex processes of devolution, centralisation and integration are simultaneously taking place within many socially diverse societies. It is important to reflect on the features of democracy, citizenship and public and social policy issues within most societies generally. There is also a need to educate young people about the multicultural nature of societies and the importance of democratic features and cosmopolitan citizenship issues within such complex societies and region. The multicultural contexts in historical and contemporary terms are dynamic and not static. (Bakhtin) There are also transcultural crossings, shifts and leaps which can result in dissensus since the dominant group may attempt to undermine consensus to remain dominant. There is an ethical imperative to engage in a dialogue with issues of difference in society. While the need for grounding by many groups can be understood, it can be temporary and changing, and based on critical reflection. Grounding and uncertainty can go together and open possibilities which are not necessarily relativist in nature. It can open up in pedagogical terms where dissensus and consensus can be seen to be contingent on changing circumstances. In Raymond Williams terms this would require the unlearning of the 'inherent dominative mode.' (Williams 1958: 376). This sort of perspective can form the basis for intercultural dialogue and intercultural education.

The liberal market economies have deepened the divides between winners and losers, but the elites continue to use the political rhetoric and conventions of compromise. They try not to allow the basis of discontent and opposition to 'respond energetically or imaginatively to new challenges.' (Judt 2010: 157). While democratic societies provide constitutional protection for dissent, there is a general swing towards conformity and the minority dissenters may find themselves as outcasts. Neither at the level of citizens or of contemporary intellectuals are there informed discussions about public policy issues, which are undertaken by policy specialists and 'think tanks.' In the U.S. the mantra of holding taxes to the minimum and 'keeping the government out of our affairs' is further strengthened by the demagogy of keeping 'socialism' out of government. In Switzerland a referendum banned the building of minarets by Muslims; in Britain citizens have accepted high levels of closed circuit television and intrusive policing and in most European countries citizens find it difficult to challenge economic policies. The education systems bear part of the responsibility for not educating young people to be well informed critical citizens, and allow them to remain apolitical. Young people are more likely to join single issue interest groups but do not engage in 'the management of public affairs,' and the development of strategies to dissent within the law. This can happen if young people develop a new language of politics which recasts public conversation. (Judt: 156–173). This is partly the result of young people not being taught history properly and the absence of understanding of who 'we' are and who the 'others' are. A critical reading and understanding of the past can help young people to refine their analytical skills to understand the complexity of contemporary societies. At the underlying level the absence of the study of history may add to the failure of citizenship education to deal with issues of dissensus.

A consideration of such a pedagogic practice is necessary because most states face similar issues which have led to pressures on the political, economic and social systems. At this level contrasting valuations can be placed on politics and the market and reinforce 'confidence in the civilising power of a state that they expect to compensate for "market failures.' (Habermas: 47) There are pathological consequences of capitalist modernisation which requires an ongoing political evaluation to promote citizen's 'awareness of the paradoxes of progress'. (Habermas: 47) This can possibly form the basis for the bringing together of differentiated regions in most continents to develop cosmopolitan strategies beyond the national boundaries.

Education has a powerful role to play in the strengthening of democracies and to make them more inclusive. It can also enable young people to understand their rights, obligations and responsibilities as active citizens, within most complex democratic societies. This presents educational institutions with a challenge of bridging divides by providing access to diverse groups to social goods in society. They can also assist in nurturing conversations which can lead to the creation of shared values within the public domain and public institutions. However, educational processes should not only be considered to be taking place in the formal school system but they should include the use of visual media and a critical reading of media messages.

There are also some elements of diversity which can be counterproductive if they conflict with citizenship and liberal democratic principles. Given that there are deep divisions caused by historically derived 'hidden hatreds' and uneven development, what can be done to develop new friendships and creative imaginations? There is already a legacy of exclusive and negative imaginations of racism, xenophobia, chauvinism and sexism. These issues pose complex challenges to teachers of citizenship to try to bridge these divides which cannot easily be dealt through rational discussions. While at the classroom level these issues present pedagogical challenges they also present institutional challenges. In democratic educational institutions, intercultural and anti-racist policies which disallow negative behaviours. These policies can also be used to provide greater levels of access to knowledge, skills and shared values through institutional initiatives. Hence, while there have been genocides and Holocausts of particular groups and peoples the role that educators along with other public and social policy makers have to undertake is how to build solidarities and commonalities between and within these different groups at transnational levels. The issue at this level is: without losing sight of the particularities of a loss of different groups: what can be done to bridge the divides between different groups?

To ensure that young people do not accept binary divides but adhere to their rights, obligations and responsibilities, the political culture has to have a broad basis. It cannot be based on the narrow national, dominant group or on the acceptance of simplistic ethnic divides. Young people need to develop notions of inclusivity which symbolically and substantively are based on inclusive good values from all groups and which capture the imagination and enchant the disenchanted young people, especially those from subordinated and marginalised communities. The cosmopolitan constitutional and human rights principles and other progressive and democratic struggles can also form part of this teaching and learning process.

Amongst many young people the notion of being part of, and belonging to complex localities is important. Hence, the acceptance of territorial belongingness which is not exclusive but shared is worth exploring within schools and youth clubs. There is a need to develop non-exclusivist neighbourhoods which are not no-go areas for others but are as Bookchin has called them "confederal communities". It entails turning the biological affinities into social affinities. (Bookchin: 1992). Such communities would be based on shared resemblances which are neither racist nor patriarchal. This necessitates the revamping of the old Greek concept of "paidea" or the German notion of "bildung" to develop their interactive and intercultural aspects within complex and socially diverse schools and communities. These purposes of education ought to ensure that they are enablers of citizens in contributing to the life of the communities and societal institutions. These confederal values ought perhaps to give a new meaning to an intercultural paidea or an intercultural bildung. Chinese and Indian civilizations also embody similar notions which can lend strength to developing intercultural shared value systems which strengthen the social affinities within multicultural polities in Europe.

Communities of Development and Hope

Processes of devolution, national or regional integration and mass migration place complex pressures on national educational systems to engage in teaching democratically at local levels while recognising the centralisation of power at national or supra-national levels. (Baumann: 2008) Democratic schools and socially diverse class-rooms can organise teaching and learning which enables young people to understand complexity of societies and develop shared understandings. Provision for life long learning and informal education can also form the basis of inclusive learning communities which have collective voices and cut across communal divides. Education systems need to create public spaces so that whole democratic communities at the local level can influence educational and public policies in general. This type of learning within modern cities and rural areas have to be connective since both these contexts are at the intersection of the local, national, regional and global; and also since there are intersections of perceived, conceived and lived space. As David Harvey states in (1989) the compression of learning is needed because of space time compression and learning is not restricted to formal or informal but also in the contexts of the family, community and the workplace. Hence, both rural and urban communities become 'learning communities' through active learning strategies which are sustainable.

Such developments can contribute to the rebuilding of communities and establishing of a connection with what Judith Green calls "communities of development and hope" (Green 1998: 431). Individuals and groups need a sense of agency as the citizens of a democratic society which moves beyond the merely institutional basis and engages with issues of exclusion within diverse communities. It allows for what Green refers to as deeper democratic features of diverse and complex modern societies. These features include a critical understanding of intercultural issues highlighted by indigenous or immigrant minorities. In some contexts such groups are defined as "the others" and demonised. However, these diverse communities also present the possibilities of complex interactions at individual and community levels to form a basis of resemblances and fraternities across group divides.

Hence, deep democracy has dynamic and imaginative features which draw upon and connect one's own stories and those of the community. One's personal knowledge confers the confidence to deal with issues and to contribute to public life and public institutions with greater competence. It also has the potential of initiating and helping to shape public and social policy from a local context. Such a development of a collective critical consciousness would contribute to rebuilding the "public square", as discussed by Cornel West (West: 1994). The public square includes public institutions and the need to engage with issues of deep divisions, democratic and intercultural relations and to turn exclusions into inclusions. Schools and other civic institutions which have greater levels of autonomy need to be supported, as Green writes:

> For their effectiveness in facilitating public discussions, coalition development and multinational community building ... fostering deeply democratic attitudes and by offering opportunities to

develop skills and capacities that active democratic citizenship requires (Green 1998: 437).

Small beginnings at grassroots and community levels are one way of initiating involvement with deep democracies. They use experience as a basis of active citizenship, which can form the beginning of developing broader analysis and conceptualisation of citizenship engagement, not necessarily based on established political parties or machines. An impressive recent British pioneer in this field, the Novas Scarman Trust, sponsors small self-help projects in run-down communities. These projects are not just temples of democratic talk but are of the "Can-Do" mentality which leads to practical action at local community level, using the community's own capacities and initiatives. They have included turning a derelict rubbish dump into a small park, reopening and running a closed-down village shop on which the community depended, and enabling a group of jobless youngsters to acquire the house they were squatting in—renovate it as a hostel, and then go on to renovate other derelict properties. It also includes the provision of practical skills, training for jobs and generating local economies through microeconomic projects. (Scarman Trust: 1999). The way into the instrumentalist initiatives mentioned above includes the generation of interest in the creative faculties of those who are marginalised in society and to engage them by using their imaginations and imaginative faculties. In short, they are a way of using community assets to reduce inequalities and bridge group divides.

Transparency and Good Governance

There are numerous hurdles in developing community involvement and transformative institutions in the present context because:

> Persistent fundamentalism and differentiation in religious, ethnic and national identities are juxtaposed with increasingly interpenetrated cultures. It is a context of global economic competition along with global consciousness of disparities of wealth and well being (March & Olsen 1995: 7).

What makes divisions based on above issues particularly threatening to the prospects of deep democracy is the success of appeals to ethnic, gender, religion, racial and ethnic identities which undermine confidence in reason and the Enlightenment and, coupled with the pessimism engendered by the uncertainties and introspection during the early years of the New Millennium, which may have led to a decline in confidence not only in democracy but in good governance. At this level it is particularly important that governments in democratic polities are transparent. The pressures of an economic urban and rural underclass, rising population pressures and depleting resources are a major challenge which most states at the international level need to confront. These pressures can lead to greater divides through pressures of economic globalisation.

Institutions in society have an educative role so that they can foster sacrifices not selfishness, and self-discipline through cooperation. (March & Olsen 1995: 49). Invoking the consciousness of the civic and the collective develops notions of the common good, and requires the shaping of a sense of inclusive solidarity based on a sense of security and belonging. Specific personal identities need to be shaped to that of being a citizen, so that the private self is confirmed in the public domain through critical conversations and evaluations. This requires the state to provide a framework within which the social and cultural pluralism of multiethnic and multicultural societies can establish a sense of inclusive and collective solidarity.

March and Olsen write:

> Part of the craft of democratic governance is developing institutions that simultaneously accommodate the ideals of pluralism and diversity, institutions that are capable of maintaining trust and mutual affection within a polity while simultaneously accommodating enduringly in constituent subgroups demands based on family ties, religion, ethnicity, language or personal affinity. That craft involves strengthening identities based on broad and long term conceptions of a community of citizens and a concern for others in that community, including future citizens and unborn generations, and developing institutions that encourage both solidarity and civility (March & Olsen 1995: 55).

The state-craft entailed in cultivating this community of citizens who are defined by a bundle of rights, duties and responsibilities should be an essential aspect of diverse polities where the ethos of civic virtue is absent. Nevertheless introducing a civic education which critically informs young and adult learners in diverse polities of their roles in society is a complex task. It entails an involvement in critical public debate based on insights which acknowledge the legitimacy of multiculturalism and can accept both conflict and opposition as an aspect of the knowledge required to deal with the complexities of life not only in a national society but within the larger and developing cosmopolitan polity.

Such a political life assumes that the young citizens have a set of identities rather than one dominant or singular identity. It also assumes that good governance will empower the positive experiences of the key political identities. It entails the management of conflicts as well as inconsistencies. Deep democracies however also need to deal with seeds of deep conflict, also the simpler ones of self interest and public interest which are in continual tension. Education for democratic citizenship entails the learning of rules needed to negotiate reasonably in situations of such complex conflicts and to become active citizens in complex communities.

Establishing processes which are acceptable to learners requires teachers and learners to understand the difficulties of teaching and learning in diverse polities, and of the resolution of conflicts through deep conversations and mediation of differences. In many cases there can also be an agreement about what constitutes 'the common good.' In a democratic context, teaching and learning demands accepting a commitment to the democratic processes, even when differences and contradictions remain unresolved. The powerful rules governing democratic negotiation and civility are not only difficult to teach but to learn. Nevertheless knowledge, skills and competencies can be acquired and sharpened through education and democratic learning experiences in democratically organised schools and institutions.

Democratic engagements are more complex in societies which have higher levels of inequalities and social differentiation. Hence greater levels of equity between rights, resources, competencies, knowledge and organisational capacities would help the chances of democratic accommodations and solutions being worked out.

> The objective may include not only education into the obligations and rights of the key identities of the policy, but also the establishment of widespread agreement on the main substantive purposes and ends of the policy, a sense of common good and common destiny. A key objective is to produce a political community within which citizens can discuss political issues in an atmosphere of mutual trust, tolerance and sympathy (March & Olsen 1995: 244).

The absence of these measures and the inability to strengthen cohesive democratic cultures may lead to the fragmentation of such polities or to alternative models of authoritarian government (Dahl 1998: 145–65).

Most contemporary societies embody complexities, paradoxes, contradictions and a deepening of differences, as a result of high levels of socio-economic inequalities. These contradictions need to be addressed in forthright ways in all areas of public, social and private lives to enable aspects of deep democracy to be forged. At a community level, there needs to be more of the interaction between enablers and can-doers who are active citizens in many countries around the world. Some of the community activists in England have managed to develop micro-economies using assets within the community. In the absence of these engagements the linguistic, cultural, religious and nationality divides can become deeper and create exclusive imaginations of difference. Hence, it is critical that educational measures are instituted to ensure that separatised groups do not 'bowl alone' but 'bowl together.' (Putnam:2000; Putnam and Feldstein: 2003)

Schools, Universities and Civil Society

Schools, universities and institutions of life long learning have an important role to uncover the hidden and ignored pasts of most European societies to build a more inclusive notion of the polities. Such a critical understanding of the complexity of societies can be acquired through work within individual academic disciplines as well as, inter-disciplinary studies by teachers and learners.

Schools and universities can also assist education systems in devising the intellectual basis of inclusive policies which can assist in making contemporary societies more socially just. These include the asymmetries resulting from social-economic inequalities. In the absence of integrative or inclusive policies which the governments need to develop and implement, progressive forces can become galvanised and reinforce singular identity politics and strengthen singular identity-based organisations and activities. In the new millennium the schools and higher education system also confront the more complex task of having to use the very specific concerns expressed by identity based organisations, as well as the intensification of the issues of race, ethnic and gender specific politics, which challenge the possibilities of reconstructing a more inclusive and shared basis of knowledge which is part of the mainstream educational curriculum.

Yet, as Peter Kwong writes:

> The objective of defining identity should not be an abstract theoretical exercise. In fact, the original mission of ethnic studies and Asian American studies was to end racism in the spirit of the larger struggle for equality and social justice (South End Press Collective 1998: 65–6).

Deepening democracy means strengthening the institutions of civil society, especially the so-called non-governmental sector. However, this raises another problem, because the civil society sector is stronger in the more democratic societies, and weaker in the less democratic polities and where the 'narcissism of small differences' as Freud states can fragment communities and societies.

Identity-based movements or single issue politics need not necessarily lead to balkanisation. Forging overlapping interests can allow the development of a movement with a broader base of popular support and political power which can help to establish frameworks and influence the state institutions to become more just, inclusive and democratic. Here the issue of human rights is particularly important in the demands for greater justice for socially excluded groups. Those who have worked around these issues are also able to see the connections between them and develop agendas on a broader front, based on these interconnections. However, this joined up globalisation is not yet a reality, partly because of the democratic deficit in national, regional and international institutions. However, unfortunately neither the Council of Europe, the African Union or the UN system have developed coherent policies and action oriented approach to deal with these complex set of issues. It is possible that the national education systems can develop effective strategies to deal with some of these broader issues and the education systems can act as enabling agencies in this process. Organisation like UNESCO have developed agendas for Education for All, the Convention for Cultural Rights and for providing Universal Primary Education, yet the issues of equalities do not feature very prominently within them or their schools.

Over the years the Council of Europe, which started as a political institution based on levels of mutualities, has developed increasingly as a norm-based organisation which has involved itself not only in conflict resolution but also asserting issues of human rights within democratic contexts to develop values of democracy, diversity and human rights among young people. Yet, as its membership increased after the fall of Communism these progressive initiatives have been undermined by the new member states on very narrow nationalistic grounds.

Many of the European and post-colonial ideals of democratic states which were formulated in the post-World War II period to avoid the catastrophes of inter-state violence have been negated. There is also growing evidence of these becoming more institutionalised in an effective manner not between but within many countries. In Europe, the devastation and ethnic cleansing in South East Europe has occurred fifty years after these abominable ideas were defeated in the WWII. Moreover the multicultural and multilingual Europe is a powerful counterweight to other regional organisations which do not embody the vast elements of social diversities. The same is the case for countries in other continents where ethnic cleansing has taken place. These differences when channelled through appropriate educational initiatives can on the other hand, lend strength to developing greater levels of fraternity and unity.

Citizenship and Difference

The challenge for citizenship is the moulding of the one out of the many and to construct appropriate educational responses to difference and diversity within the numerous modern societies. Education policy initiatives of anti-racism or multiculturalism which are merely directed at immigrants or indigenous minorities and do not include the dominant groups or majority populations may not be useful. The essentialist rhetoric of some of these policies in some contexts has led to "the othering" of groups and created binary oppositions (e.g. majority/minority; belongers/non-belongers; black/white). Given these divides and the varying level of inequalities the state also tries as, Marshall states through citizenship to initiate a "tendency towards equality" (Marshall 1977) by creating basic conditions leading towards social equality. It is also a dynamic and an active not a passive concept. Hence, social equalities can be achieved by removing hindrances like "institutional racism", exclusionary practices including 'glass ceilings', whereby women or minorities never reach the top of institutions or organisations.

Education systems also confront the challenge of helping to build inclusive polities along with other social and public institutions by accommodating notions of difference and also creating conditions of belongingness of diverse groups. In educational institutions such initiatives can be a 'creative moment' since notions of citizenship can be utilised to develop integrative mentalities by reducing inequalities and differences between groups.

EQUALITY AND DEMOCRATIC ENGAGEMENT

How can there be the framework for universal norms which can encompass the particularistic demands and establish solidarities? Citizenship as a modern concept is realisable only in the context of a democratic and constitutional state. Modern citizens have rights which have been acquired after long struggles which cannot be easily ignored or denied. One of these rights is the access to institutions within a society and is particularly relevant for girls, women or vulnerable groups. In some cases it is not the state but the patriarchal or particular community which may deny women their rights to education or employment

The conferring of citizenship rights entails opposing such particularistic practice which would deny girls the equality in education or employment. At this level the public institutions need to distinguish which values of different communities are acceptable and do not violate the universality of the rights of girls, women or vulnerable groups. At this level there are fairly serious issues about the public and private domains amongst groups with few shared political identities and fears that their legitimate religious, traditional and familial rights would be infringed and lead to the homogenisation of the minority communities and their cultures. There can be three important ways of ensuring that this does not happen: (i) that the modern constitutional principles used by the state are universalistic and cosmopolitan and not purely those of the dominant nation of the shared descent and culture; (ii) that the secular notions are reviewed to ensure that that are not oppositional to the faith and religion, but have an interpretation which ensures the protections to all groups to believe or not to believe and to protect the legitimate private rights; (iii) the asymmetries in socio-economic terms are reduced between majorities and minorities and issues of fairness, equalities, mutualities, reciprocities and social justice are seriously dealt with. Hence, there are institutional and structural basis of exclusivities to be removed.

If citizens are excluded or marginalised within the education system then does the state stay neutral or does it intervene? In other words is the state fair or is it impartial? Rawls, using the difference principles would argue that the better off should not do better than the "worst off". (Rawls 1971: 60, 124, 132, 199). So, to accord equity the state is "fair" but not impartial. In a democratic context a citizen is entitled to access to education and knowledge to equalise their life chances. Hence, the state has a role in creating level playing fields and in educational terms, it can do this by intervening. This is especially true where marginalised or excluded minorities are subordinated by dominant or majority groups.

Contemporary societies also currently face a dilemma because old solidarities and mutualities have been destroyed, especially as the younger generation are divided into those who are winners and losers. The notion of a citizenship education during the period of economic globalisation the losers owe nothing to the winners is a difficult but critical issue. Habermas writes:

> 'Today, as the nation-state finds itself challenged from within by the explosive potential of multiculturalism and from without by the pressure of globalisation, the question arises of whether there exists a functional equivalent for the fusion of the nation of citizens with the ethnic nation". (Habermas 1998:117).

Constitutional principles, human rights declaration, progressive and democratic struggles can also form part of this teaching and learning process.

Deep Citizenship

Within most contexts internationally the narrow nationalistic and destructive power a government can unleash need to be restrained. As Habermas writes about Europe: 'A culture that has over the centuries been torn apart more than any other by conflicts between city and country, ecclesiastical and secular power, the competition between religion and science, and the struggles between political authorities and antagonistic classes, had to learn the painful lessons of how differences can be communicated, oppositions institutionalised, and tensions stabilised. The recognition of differences, the mutual recognition of others in their otherness, can become a distinguishing mark of a shared identity.' (Habermas: pp.44–5)

Notions of how to develop deep democracy based on deep social participation and citizenship requires urgent attention because the private market has no public obligations and the role of mixed economies becomes more important. The role of social capital amongst citizens is now also recognised by the World Bank.

Deep democracy demands deep citizenship. The activation of civic values in public and private domains puts into place a new non-traditional understanding of citizenship. Here deep democracy can be assisted by eliminating the previous private/public divide:

> The fundamental change in the way in which the particular and the universal are related to the public and the private is to admit the civic virtues to wide areas of life: most generally wherever one can act towards the universal, therein lie the civic virtues and therein lies deep citizenship (Clarke 1996: 118).

SOME FUTURE DIRECTIONS IN EDUCATION

European education systems need to seriously reexamine the earlier history of the Mediterranean region. This involved interactions between Greeks, Egyptians and Phoenicians, amongst other people in that complex region. These interactions have left a legacy of complex knowledge which has been largely ignored by the north European historiography of 18th and 19th century. Greece has been viewed as the pure childhood of Europe and thus set a basis for Eurocentrism in construction of knowledge about this continent. This issue needs to be revisited to form a much more inclusive basis of knowledge within the European education systems. For instance, during the 11th and 12th centuries Muslim, Jewish and Catholic scholars formed an intercultural basis of constructing knowledge inherited from ancient Greece which laid the foundation for knowledge leading to the Renaissance.

These earlier historical aspects of intercultural intellectual collaboration in European history can form the basis for a non-Eurocentric and trans-national curriculum for the school in the twenty first century. For instance, a trans-national history curriculum can lead to friendships across national boundaries by delimiting triumphalism and militarism.

Measures to reduce educational inequalities are needed to enchant the disenchanted young people with the reinstatement of the power of education and not to merely 'school' young people which replicates the existing socio-economic roles and divides. The exciting task of educating young people to improve their life chances requires interculturally educated teachers who are not merely 'trained' but also 'educated'. These teachers need to understand theory and practice of learning and teaching as well as the rich, diverse and complex underpinnings of the society and communities reflected within the curriculum and functioning of the school.

The divides within many communities within European cities can be bridged within common state school systems which are provided by accountable and democratically elected local authorities. Good comprehensive educational measures to ensure that the common and shared curriculum which draws on both the broader intercultural pool of knowledge as a basis for the official school curriculum. This ought to build on the subjectivities of knowledge which young people bring to the school. This would lay the basis of developing common and shared public democratic values.

In many European countries concepts of the 'secular' and the 'religious' are perceived as being oppositional. The reality in most polities is that the secular constitutional democracies protect the private rights of groups to believe or not to believe; to attend or not attend the church, mosque or the temple. The patriarchal dimensions of faith may restrict citizenship and human rights of girls and women and in the public domain and institutions rights should remain inviolable, Private institutions may 'instruct' believers about the faith. The role of educational institutions is not to instruct but to inculcate the critical faculties amongst the learners and to educate young people across particularistic group divides based on singularised identities. The school cannot also afford to ignore the multiple, hybrid and mestizo identitities of many young people. In this respect the educational institutions may choose to educate learners about secular societal values and inter and multi-faith issues.

A number of countries follow the neoliberal economic model in judging school performances by publishing by school league tables and setting narrow performance targets. This process entails an inspection system where there is no space for intercultural and anti-discriminatory policies and practices which regulate behaviours. Perhaps the European schools can follow the system in Finland which allows schools to self-evaluate themselves. This ought to contain an important dimension of the absence of racist and xenophobic behaviours and measure the state of intercultural understandings within the school.

A democratic school practices which provide a lived reality of basis of democratic engagement can contribute to the learning of citizenship and human rights values which are then translated by young learners into active citizenship values and engagement within their communities and society generally. This in turn can form the basis of create safe and stable inclusive communities of 'development and hope.' It also provides a basis for the protecting rights of the new as well as the old minority groups like the Roma and the Samish people in Europe.

Conclusion

This article is being submitted for publication to initiate a more informed and rational political and policy dialogue which can lead to evidence based research; intercultural public and social policies. It is anticipated that these can help to tackle meaningfully some of the underlying challenges which are laced with social and class divides. The current tokenistic and rhetorically oriented multicultural policies only help to strengthen superficial, simplistic identity based politics and feed to sustain siege communities and mentalities. The secular state has the duty to protect the autonomous and private religious and traditional identities of groups. However, state support and funding of schools and other institutions is an intrusion into the private domain. It also helps to entrench particularistic group identities diminishes the broader integrative powers of the state. The state therefore, has an even greater obligation to strengthen inclusive public institutions, protect constitutional and human rights of all citizens. This necessitates the enhancement of public spaces for across group conversations. These are necessary to build reciprocities and trust across divides in multicultural communities also divided on class basis.

The narrowly based policies of the state also obviate the development of politically creative and imaginative capacities of citizens to help in the process of revitalising statutory and civic institution and cultures. These initiatives of citizens can genuinely help the state in resolving some of the underlying causes which feed narrow nationalism, xenophobia and racism.

Conversely, the political cultures and many institutions in the European continent have the capacities to remove democratic inequalities and deficits. These capacities draw upon the past and contemporary struggles of the under classes, subordinated and oppressed groups to acquire democratic and citizenship rights. Seeds of these experiences are reflected in many communities, localities, regions and national states. To enhance cosmopolitan citizenship the European Union and the Council of Europe provide the constitutional and institutional basis to help build a stable, peaceable and diverse European continent.

Bibliography

Anderson. P: (2009) The New Old World (London: Verso)

Beck, U and Grande, E. (2007) Cosmopolitan Europe. (Cambridge: Polity Press)

Bauman, Z. (2007) Liquid Times: Living in an Age of Uncertainty. (Cambridge: Polity Press)

Bookchin, M. (1992) Urbanization without Cities: The Rise and Decline of Citizenship (Montreal: Black Rose Books).

Buruma. I (2010). Taming the Gods: Religion and God in Three Continents. (Princeton: Princeton University Press)

Kepel. G (1997) Allah in the West: Islamic Movements in America and Europe (Stanford: Stanford University Press)

Caldwell. C. (2009). Reflections on the Revolution in Europe. (London: Allen Lane)

Clarke, P.B. (1996) Deep Citizenship (London: Pluto Press).

Dahl, R.A. (1998) On Democracy (New Haven: Yale University Press)

Green, J. (1998), "Educational Multiculturalism: Critical Pluralism and Deep Democracy" in Willett, C. (Ed.) *Theorizing Multiculturalism: A Guide Current to Debate* (Oxford: Blackwell).

Habermas, J. (1998) The Inclusion of the Other: Studies in Political Theory (Cambridge, Mass: MIT Press).

Habermas, J. (2007). The Divided West. (Cambridge: Polity Press)

Kepel, G. (1997) Allah in the West: Islamic Movements in America and Europe. (Stanford: Stanford University Press)

Judt, T (2010) Ill Fares the Land. (London: Allen Lane)

March J.G. & Olsen, J.P. (1995). Democratic Governance (New York Press).

Marshall, T.H. (1977) Class, Citizenship and Social Development (Chicago: University of Chicago Press).

Michaels, W. B. (2007). The Trouble With Diversity: How We Learned To Love Identity And Ignore Inequality. (New York: Henry Holt and Company)

Putnam, R. D. (2000) Bowling Alone: The Collapse and Revival of American Community (New York: Simon and Schuster)

Putnam, R. And Feldstain, L. M. (2003): Better Together: Restoring the American Community. (New York: Simon and Schuster)

Rawls, J. (1971) Theory of Justice (Cambridge: The Belknap Press).

The Scarman Trust (1999) Getting Self-Propelled–They Can do Challenge (London: The Scarman Trust).

South End PRESS Ccollective (1998) In Talking about a Revolution (Cambridge, Mass: South End Press).

Wallerstein, I. (1991) Unthinking Social Science: The Limits of Nineteenth Century
Paradigms (Cambridge: Polity Press).

West, C. (1992) Race Matters (New York: Vintage).

Wilkinson R and Pickett, K (2009) The Spirit Level: Why Equality is Better for
Everyone (London: Penguin)

Williams, R. (1958). Culture and Society, 1780–1950. (London: Chatto and Windus)

Interculturalism, Dialogue and Cooperation:

In Higher Education Institutions

Introduction

This paper aims to explore a range of issues related to civilizational knowledge, cultural diversity and dialogue, academic learning and teaching, and interculturalism in generation of cooperation between higher education institutions. At the outset it is important to highlight that essence of the terms 'multicultural' and 'intercultural'. The essence of the 'multicultural' is that it is a descriptive term of a society inhabited by different socio-cultural groups. These include those based on linguistic, social class, religious, ethnic, territorial and non-territorial (Roma and Traveller groups.) Nicholas Hans the comparative educationalist stated that these were the historical basis of the national states. The term 'intercultural' is the basis of social interactions; developmental dialogues as well as policies and practices which enable interactions and can help reduce social inequalities. Hence, the term 'multicultural' is a descriptive term and 'intercultural' is about dynamic activities which include a broad vision of knowledge.

In our own time there is a necessity to consider at the widest political level the necessity of negating intercultural conflicts and to enhance intercultural understandings. Governments need to ensure that they create public, educational and social policies which enable the higher education systems to operate a autonomous and independent institutions where there is total academic freedom. All higher education institutions need to ensure that the humanities and the social sciences are taught at the undergraduate level with a great deal of intellectual rigour. The one very good example of this kind of teaching is represented by the American liberal arts colleges where students have access to learning across a very broad range of academic disciplines ranging from the sciences, humanities, arts and the social sciences. Hence, students require a critical understanding of knowledge at the broadest possible level and these can then be deepened at postgraduate levels with more specialist knowledge. Young people can also acquire an understanding of the nature of democratic societies as well as "some of the goals of critical thinking and world citizenship." (M. Nussbaum: 2010 p. 126) This paper suggests that issues of civilizational knowledge, social diversity are also highly relevant to issues of genuine dialogue, and provide higher education institutions with challenges which so far largely remain unaddressed. This paper argues that there are many and varied forms of knowledge around the world, and that these—and particularly those of subordinated or minority groups—need to be represented within higher education curriculum, especially in the historically and strategically very important Eurasian region where there is an enormous meeting, as well as subordination of cultures and civilisations and needs to be critically reappraised.

At the national level, one means of promoting such as holistic approach to education would be to take into account the different forms of knowledge that are represented by diverse languages, histories, and cultures in a society. But perhaps, an even greater challenge is for the universities to develop cooperative and collaborative work which has syncretism and a multiplier effect.

As will be argued in the next section, promoting this approach internationally would demand a more intercultural perspective. Given that many different forms of knowledge do exist, both nationally as well as internationally, the paper further argues that curricula within higher education institutions should be non-centric. In other words, curricula should not draw heavily from one source of knowledge while excluding or marginalising others. Higher education institutions in particular often have a great deal of access to intellectual knowledge and expertise, and so are in a position to make a significant contribution to both intercultural education and development of intercultural dialogue. However, the connections between intercultural dialogue and diversity are rapidly changing and necessitate a sustained social science analysis. The paper therefore considers the conceptual links between interculturalism, civilizations and cultural diversity, and discusses the implications for research and teaching in higher education.

It is also important that higher education institutions establish institutional mechanism of cooperating across different regions since these will have dividends as multipliers of new and shared knowledge across cultural and national divides.

Higher education institutions also educate numbers of people who work in the formal and informal continuing, adult and lifelong learning institutions. It is important to stress that visual, audio and print media play a critical role in informing, educating as well as miseducating people. It is therefore necessary to consider the role of not only using these media for teaching purposes but also of a critical reading and understanding of messages portrayed by these media.

In this respect the role of sports, the rules of the game which include fair play and include winning or losing are important. When the Armenian leader Serzh Sarkiisian shook the hand of his Turkish colleague after Turkey scored the first goal of the match is an important and 'rare good news' and symbol of rapprochement in the Caucasus. (De Waal: 2010) How and what can Higher Education Institutions do to strengthen the role of sports to nurture intercultural understandings across this whole region?

Interculturalism and Cultural Diversity in Education

A range of international initiatives have relevance for the role of higher education in both the promotion of intercultural dialogue and the protection of cultural diversity. UNESCO has been actively engaged in work related to the protection of cultural diversity, including through the creation of the Universal Declaration on Cultural Diversity (2001) and the more recent Convention on the Protection and Promotion of the Diversity of Cultural Expressions (2005). However, the work of these multiple international agencies is not joined up, and the various initiatives concerning intercultural dialogue and cultural diversity remain disconnected and disparate. (UNESCO: Intercultural Education: Paris: 2006)

The Eurasian region has been a bridge between the south-west, southern and eastern Asia which were separated by mountains and deserts. This was a route through which economic goods, trade, arts and religions travelled. Hence, the UNESCO History of Civilisation of Central Asia (Bosworth and Asimov: 2009) places this region as part of human history in its own right. It has been the meeting point and at the crossroads of making societies to the east and the west of it important. This history is undertaken by UNESCO in the 1980's which brought 180 scholars to work on this project. Perhaps it is now time that some of these and other scholars collaborate to map out how this region contributed to the development of civilisations in Asia and Europe.

National, Regional and International Contexts

The role of education within these legislative frameworks is also complex. Specifically, education is commonly seen as a route not only to enhance strategies to deal with intercultural conflicts, but also to develop proactive initiatives which enhance the knowledge, skills and competences which learners, activists and others need to work towards developing viable and sustainable intercultural futures.

This paper suggests, however, that many of the substantive challenges to establish intercultural cooperation are frequently perceived to relate only to the Eurasian or the eastern of the continent, and that institutions in the Western Europe and hemisphere tend to provide leadership rather than partnership to address—what are problems relevant to all academic institutions. This also requires that those groups who in the Eurasian region are considered subordinated are not constructed as being frozen in time and place, and with a fixed status, but as vibrant and dynamic cultures, especially in their struggles to build new futures on the margins of capitalist economic globalisation.

Such an intercultural perspective would necessitate an understanding of the legacies of resistance of oppressed peoples, their cultures and civilisations. In this respect it is important to consider Edward Said's notion that 'the production of knowledge best serves communal as opposed to sectarian ends; how knowledge that is non-coercive can be produced in a setting that is deeply inscribed with the politics, the considerations, the positions and strategies of power' (Said 1978). This perspective necessitates in the first instance the unlearning of what Raymond William describes as the 'inherent dominative mode' (William 1958: 376).

It is clear that educational institutions have a critical role to play in international relationships through maintaining critical and academic distance and opening up scientific spaces to generate and disseminate knowledge. Globalisation has contributed to the creation of networks of knowledge which span the whole globe and can enable educational institutions to participate in building a democratic and equitable world. However, agreements which seek to include higher education as one of a range of 'trades and services' included within the General Agreement on Trade and Services drafted by the World Trade Organisation also present danger in the form of the increased 'commodification of knowledge' based on market principles. This treatment of knowledge is inimical to idea of using knowledge for the common good.

It is necessary during this globalising period to enhance cooperation at the higher education level between the industrialised, Eurasian and emerging economies, however, these international agreements can also be used to close the rising knowledge gaps, and to reduce brain drain as well as social tensions through emigration of the qualified people. The reduction of the brain drain from research and teaching institutions in the Eurasian region is particularly important because it has diminished the capacity of those institutions to contribute to new knowledge in the fields of generating societal development, intercultural cooperation and understanding and conflict resolution. These initiatives may necessitate institutional support from international organisations to build research capacities within the Eurasian region.

Higher education at national levels, within the European Union and the Council of Europe, and among institutions in the Eurasian region needs to adopt a strategic approach to issues of intercultural education and institutional cooperation. Such an approach would ensure that the whole of the education sector would autonomously take a lead in the critical analysis of issues and the focus on the policies necessary in helping to implement positive measures in these fields.

'People without History': The civilised and the Barbarian

An anthropologist like Eric Wolf who was born in 1923 in the multicultural and socially diverse city of Vienna was a crossroads of people in Northern Bohemia. Wolf explained that it is important to explain a society in a historical context and in his book (Wolf: 1983) he challenged the notion of many anthropologists that many societies were static entities. He explained that in the course of global expansion of capitalism those who were considered as, peoples without history who were in fact part of the history of European expansion from 1400–1800 and the interconnectedness between isolated societies.

The initiatives to implement meaningful measures to create an Alliance of Civilizations need to deal with the issues those who argue for the Clash of Civilizations. (S. Huntington:) This is necessary because there is a very long history of the differences and distinctions made between those who are civilised, semi- or un-civilised and even barbaric. However, authors like the late S. Huntington tend to ignore that those who colonised and dominated the so-called less civilised peoples have in fact, had a brutalising effect both on the dominating groups as well as the colonisers and the colonised. The Spanish thinker Sepulveda justified the right justified the right to intervene in Amerindian societies because of their barbarity. Las Casas, on the other hand, purported that evil existed everywhere and that therefore there was no theological justification for interference. However, it was Sepulveda's argument which carried the day and people in many parts of the world were barbarised. The Caucasus is a jagged land with powerful neighbours like Iran to the south, Russia in the north and Turkey to the west, hemmed by the Black Sea on one side and the Caspian on the other.

Who have been considered as conquerors in this region? These include Genhgis Khan, Alexander the Great, Tamalane, a caravan of Persian Kings, Peter the Great,

Hitler, and Stalin—and all of them have claimed the conquest of the Caucasus region. In religious terms: there are Shiite Muslims to the south, Sunnis to the north; three schisms of Christianity push from separate fronts. (N. Griffin: 2001) Conflicts in this region erupted after the collapse of the Soviet Union and countries like Azerbaijan lying at the epicentre of the Russian-Turkish-Iranian geopolitical triangle and made its process of nation-building very difficult. (T. Swietochowski: 1995)

It would be presumptuous of an outsider like me to pretend to know the complexities of relationship and fractures for instance, in the South Caucasus region, because it is for the academics within the region to begin the long journey to begin to think of themselves as one because of the strong ties of culture between the different nations as well as shared histories of economic collaboration. In the globalised world of today the region needs bring the commonalities of culture and shared economic interests to deal in a positive way with the negative features of neoliberal global economies which can devastate fragmented national economies.

In the Central Eurasian Cultural Complex many people's have been designated as barbarians and have been subjugated by oppressive foreign regimes: these include the Tibetans of Tibet, the Uighurs of East Aturistan with both being labelled as 'minorities' by China and have suffered deep repression by China. Within the Russian ambit there are the Turkic Tuvins of Altai region and the Mongolic Kalmyks of the North Caucasus Steppe, the Evenkis of Siberia who remain under Russian rule.

The nomad-ruled empires created a powerful trade-oriented Central European economy combining the efforts and products of the pastoral nomadic peoples, the agricultural peoples and the urban peoples of central Asia. What drove the economic engine of the Silk Route was first of all the internal Central Eurasian trade, based on the internal demands not only of the products of their own people but for those of the neighbouring Central Eurasian states or products acquired through them. The connection of these by interregional trade produced a healthy international commerce. At the centre of the Silk Road system was the Central Eurasian aristocracy of native states in which most rulers were of the steppe nomadic origin. The destruction of the Silk Road is not a mystery because in the 17th century the Russian and the Manchu China partitioned Central Eurasia between themselves and domination by both these powers led to the collapse of the Silk Road economy which was the heartland of peoples of Central Eurasia and the civilisation of Central Asia and Tibet sank into poverty and backwardness. In this history lie seeds of shared and common cultural values and economic interests and mechanism which higher education institutions need to uncover.

The universities in this region need to readdress the historical basis of the reverses in these multiethnic and multicultural states in the region as well as their contemporary social science analysis since the modern nation-state systems are generally dominated by one ethno-linguistic group. (C. Beckwith: 2009). Hence, at one level the stereotypical interpretations of the Silk Road related around the peripheral states with China at one end and the Goths in Europe at the other, thus ignoring the 'barbaric nomads of Central Eurasia'. In short, the word 'barbarian' embodies a complex European cultural construct, a generic pejorative term for a 'powerful foreigner with uncouth, uncivilised, nonurban culture who is militarily skilled and somewhat heroic, but inclined to violence and cruelty.' The Russians however, had a great deal of difficulty conquering the mountain peoples of the Caucasus who spoke different languages and practised different religions and resisted Russian domination (D. Headrick: 2010) The legacy of this history is that it goes beyond the 'narrow nationalist container histories into a trans-national cosmopolitan past. It is currently buried but can be reactivated to develop inclusive thinking.

As an illustration in another region, namely the south-east Asian region, there are 100 million people who are referred to as minorities and occupy 2.5 million square kilometres stretching from western China to eastern India. These people at the present time are trying to escape from the oppressions of state making projects in this region and all the neighbouring countries consider them as barbarians. (J. C. Scott: 2009)

Curricular Issues

The central argument of this paper is that within socially diverse or multicultural communities, in order to obviate intercultural conflicts and to enhance intercultural understandings across cultural and civilisation divisions, there is a need for the development of a non-centric curriculum. Essentially, this means that in socially diverse learning contexts the subjectivities of knowledge are important so that learners have an access to the curriculum. In most institutions it is the knowledge of the dominant group or the majority populations which is reflected in the curriculum. It is therefore not surprising that the poorer students and those from minority communities do not do well in education.

In the south East Europe and in Central Asia the societies have been historically multicultural and to have sustainable futures these differences and diversities need to be nurtured. Recent conflicts in these regions have marred the possibilities of intercultural understandings. (UNICEF: Ferguson, Gundara and Peffers: 2006 and 2009).

The Silk Route leaves an important historical legacy of shared experiences, interstate economic exchanges and aspects of these can be used to develop non-centric and syncretic basis of knowledge in the higher education institutions in the region.

There is however even deeper and longer term legacy of the exclusions of knowledge in historical terms at the universal level. For instance, the divided and divisive notions of curricula centred on European, Asian, African or Islamic identities are inimical to developing intercultural understandings. Education institutions in most regions of the world need to instead consider inclusive and non-centric knowledge to be valid at the level of the community, locally, regionally and universally.

In the European context, non-centric curricula at the school and higher education level are essential to ensure that students also have non-Eurocentric knowledge and skills. Research done by Samir Amin (1989) and Martin Bernal (1987, 1991), for instance, has made important historiographic analyses of the reconstruction of European history in the 18th and 19th centuries. These have shown that with the rise of racism and of anti-Semitism, the learning and understanding that the ancient Greeks acquired from the Egyptians (perceived to be Africans) and Phoenicians (seen as forebears of the Jewish faith) was excluded from the canon of history.

Learning inherited from Greek civilisation thus became reconstructed as 'pure' European, with no links to other civilisations or their knowledge systems. This reconstruction of history is of critical importance because it highlights the subjectivities of knowledge which learners bring to teaching and learning contexts. Academic engagements which involve the 'love of learning and learning for the sake of learning', on the other hand, can provide a firm foundation for citizens' democratic engagement within modern polities.

Largely, however, the above is not the case. Education systems commonly exclude the linguistic and knowledge systems of groups which are considered to be less or uncivilised (Gundara 2000: 183–199). Apart from the languages, histories and knowledge of subordinated European nationalities, this construction also excludes the languages and knowledge of other groups who are present in Europe, such as the Roma peoples. One problem in the implementation of intercultural education is that the languages, histories and cultures of these subordinated groups are not seen as having equal value to those of dominant European nationalities. An entitlement to an intercultural and non-centric curriculum is perhaps one of the greatest challenges to bringing about the development of intercultural education.

The development of a non-centric curriculum in all education institutions therefore requires academics and teachers to work closely with historians, social scientists and other researchers in their respective fields. Sheila Aikman's (1997) work on iintercultural bilingual education (IBE), for instance, has been undertaken in many parts of the world and has explored fourth world peoples' languages and knowledge about societal differences. The importance of IBE is that it can help to improve the quality of education by enhancing student's access to the curriculum.

Nevertheless, the mainstream educational discourses continue to ignore languages and knowledge of groups who are referred to as uncivilised or barbaric.

The key issue worth exploring here is how to develop relevant curriculum from the local to the global levels which encompass shared aspects of knowledge and which can enable the development of confederal values and democratic engagements. In the Eurasian regions there are examples of both intercultural understandings as well of conflict. The Tbilisi Initiative was initiated by the Ministry of Education in Georgia in September 1997 to reform the teaching of history and was supported by Armenia, Azerbaijan and the Russian Federation. The favourable political climate at the time helped the launch of this Initiative, as a process, which would help strengthen the reconciliation process in the Caucasus through education to enhance intercultural dialogue as well as principles of equality, mutual respect and transparency. The multiperspectivity in the teaching of history would negate concepts of triumphalism and militarism and enhance creativity. The pedagogical materials have not been published and I do not know how this Initiative supported by the Council of Europe is doing at the present time.

Another example in South East Europe is the Mostar Bridge which was built in in the city of Mostar. Bosnia and Herzegovina and crosses the River Neretva and connect two parts of the city and was built by Sulaiman the Magnificient in 1557 and the builder Mimar Hayruddin a student of the famous Ottoman architect Sinan records its building. It had the widest man-made arch in the world. It has been a powerful symbol of uniting and not dividing groups but was destroyed on 9th November 1993 by artillery fire during the Croat-Bosniak War and it was rebuilt and opened again on 23rd July 2004. Since the bridge does not have strategic value it was destroyed as an example of deliberate cultural property destruction, or as Andras Riedlmayer states the destruction was an act of "killing memory." Higher education institutions need to consider how to negate the deep hatreds of this period and to use its value of shared cultural heritage and peaceful coexistence to develop common meanings to inform the development of common democratic values in the country at the present time.

A more complex example is the Battle of Kosovo still divides the Albanian and the Serb peoples and perhaps common and shared meaning needs to be developed for this 14th century battle for both the groups.

Students and Academic Work

Drawing attention to some of the issues concerning higher education specifically, a few examples are taken in this section: Roma and other socially diverse as well as, international students and female students. These groups, it is argued, largely have their forms of knowledge ignored by the institutions in which they study. This is despite the fact that women as well as students from other cultural backgrounds may not necessarily be a societal minority, because they may constitute a majority where they come from and also have a very different understanding of issues of identity.

In the Eurasian region many minorities and the Roma peoples were referred to be as 'defective' by the previous communist governments. This psychological labelling of these groups through 'defectology' has had long term negative implications on the groups. Since, all people have multiple intelligences as defined by Howard Gardener this labelling of groups in higher education institutions and schools needs an urgent reconsideration. These policies and practices need to be revered because they diminish life chances of those who are labelled as being 'defective'.

Diverse Student Bodies

One issue in many polities is that different communities have varying levels of access to school and higher education. In Britain, for instance, there has recently been an increase in chiefly middle-class, African and Asian minority students. An estimated 60% of these students are studying at the new (post-1992) universities, and many of them do very well. However, according to the 1996 policy of Higher Education Funding Council (HEFCE), the representation of Afro-Caribbean men and of Pakistani and Bangladeshi women in higher education remains low. There is also evidence of low representation of young people from white, working class communities. These divides do not bode well for sustainable societal futures, and have the potential to increase intercultural community conflicts.

Institutional customs, practices and procedures, may overtly and covertly discriminate against students from certain social classes or racially and culturally different backgrounds. At this level, formal policies are needed to ensure that institutional arrangements and practices do not discriminate against groups defined as being 'different'. Monitoring such policies ought to ensure that student admissions, staff appointments and promotions are transparent. This is essential both for the optimum functioning of higher education institutions and in ensuring quality control in relation to equity in school, professional and higher education. Importantly, however, what should be monitored is the effectiveness or otherwise of policies of equality, and not the 'ethnicity' of groups.

Of course, one of the very positive aspects of having a diverse student body in higher education is that students can contribute new and different ways of thinking, behaving and interacting with each other and their tutors. In certain cultures, for example, an appropriate behaviour towards those who are learned and academic is to demonstrate respect and to maintain what is seen as a proper distance (Jones 2010). However, the hierarchical character of academic institutions in some cultures can also prevent some cultural groups from treating members of faculty informally or from challenging statements made by academic staff, even if that is the norm both in Eurasian region and European countries.

Female Students

Female students have historically played key roles in intercultural education and sustainable development, and need to be further enabled and empowered to continue to contribute to both areas in the future. The involvement of women from minority communities can present a rather different set of potentials and problems, however. Such students may be even more motivated than some men from their communities, as well as more disciplined and committed. Their focus and concentration may partly arise from their involvement with carrying out chores in their personal capacities at home. In certain cases, they may, however, have a lower order of academic skills and knowledge than their male counterparts as a result of the educational inadequacies of the learning institutions they attended previously (Jones 2010).

Ideally, institutions taking on female students from diverse backgrounds should create an inclusive intellectual and academic structure to enable them to make intellectual contributions at tutorials, lectures and seminars. One particular challenge for female students from patriarchal societies may be that male dominance in general, but also from men within their communities, needs to be addressed both before entry and within institutions during seminar and classroom interactions. Female students can then, in turn, help to ensure a supportive context in which other students from similar backgrounds can make positive intellectual contributions.

Institutional Policies and Orientation Programmes

Where some of the academic and support staff of an institution are from non-majority backgrounds themselves, this may help to provide the contexts which enable students from diverse social and cultural backgrounds to more easily adjust to an academic milieu. An intellectually and materially supportive environment is a prerequisite to establishing collegiality. However, or enhance both academic understanding of and policy oriented studies within higher education, institutions also require long-term strategies and effective structures for addressing issues of interculturalism.

Strong institutional policies and sanctions should be in place to regulate the behaviour of all staff and students, whether in dealing with xenophobia, racism or sexism, in order to ensure that no student feels excluded or victimised. Named equal opportunity consultants in academic contexts, for instance, can prove highly supportive of tutors and students. These policies need to be devised and implemented in a systematic manner to ensure that they are not simply seen as attempts to be 'politically correct'. A preliminary orientation programme can help to ensure, for example, that male students from patriarchal communities can work positively with female tutors or fellow students. In the absence of such a collective ethos, both students and tutors are likely to confront awkward situations and misunderstandings. It is therefore important to work to ensure that exclusivist behaviours of any kind are not accepted within higher education institutions.

Such institutional policies are far more important than the recommendations of writers such as Phillips and Pugh (1994), who suggest that minority students should learn 'assertion techniques' to cope with exclusion or victimisation. This approach leaves the onus for institutional change on the students when, in fact, it is the institutions themselves which are responsible for promoting change and facilitating positive understandings of diversity among staff and students. The central task of higher education institutions is not to encourage 'assertiveness' among particular groups, but to promote conversation and dialogue across cultural divides so that students have open minds. These conversations ought to cut across academic, disciplinary, group, social class or nationality divisions and to encourage a critical approach to received wisdom and stereotyped identities.

Of course, students from different backgrounds have different strengths and weaknesses, and academic departments and tutors may need to acquire resources and expertise to deal with the complex levels of understanding and skills—as well as the lack of them—that diverse students bring to institutions. Tutors, in particular, require greater 'resources and capabilities so that the student, once accepted, does not fail for want of adequate tutorial support'. Teaching and supervisory functions should enable each individual student from a disparate background to shift from being a relatively 'ill-informed and undisciplined thinker to the author of a limited but definitive enquiry' (Eggleston and Delamont 1983: 62–63).

In an even broader sense, the relationships between institutions and communities have an particular significance for students from diverse backgrounds. In other words, if institutions have good relationships with the communities in which they are located, then students from minority backgrounds are likely to feel safer and freer to study and develop. If not, then they can be particularly vulnerable to xenophobia, exclusion and racism and therefore good relations between 'town and gown' are important.

Intercultural Education for Teachers and Professionals

Educational initiatives and changes referred to through this paper are contingent upon how well the higher education system is managed. The management of these institutions is an issue of highest priority and this becomes especially true when the institutions need to manage change. The changes which need to made in higher education level are dependent on the quality of research which is undertaken and centres of excellence need to be established to ensure that teaching, learning, knowledge and the curriculum are based on evidence based research.

Higher education institutions perform an enormous service to society not only by providing opportunities for academic study, but also by providing professional training. Many of these professionals—and particularly those working in areas related to teaching and social policy—may in turn be responsible for ensuring delivering equality, providing good education, and developing mechanisms for intercultural understandings in their societies. The key questions to be asked are, therefore: What is the status of academic work on issues of intercultural studies at disciplinary and inter-disciplinary levels? What types of intellectual and institutional measures need to be implemented to raise the profile of these fields within higher education?

Firstly, in order to develop the best educated and optimally qualified teaching and social policy professionals, their professional education should be undertaken at universities or institutions with comparable standards to those of high status professions such as, for example, law, medicine, and architecture. Furthermore, by joining an accredited professional education programme after completing an undergraduate degree, public, teaching and social policy personnel could potentially achieve a professional status and autonomy similar to those in other highly-regarded professions. As a part of this accreditation process, intercultural dimensions need to be formally built into courses.

An accredited professional competence, which is validated and includes an integral intercultural dimension, is needed to ensure that what is at heart an essential academic issue is not marginalised. Nor should intercultural education be seen as issue relevant only to culturally diverse urban institutions, but one that is important to all institutions, including suburban and rural ones. Likewise, issues of intercultural studies ought not to be perceived as only being relevant to the Eurasian region and therefore marginalised within higher education systems in Western Europe and the western hemisphere generally.

Furthermore, at present many students from minority backgrounds who do well at university tend to choose high status professions, rather then what are considered to be 'lower level' teaching profession. Yet, to make intercultural education more effective and part of the mainstream work of higher education, academic institutions need to have representation from diverse students and teachers at all academic and professional levels. Approaches to education for minority students therefore also need to be improved, and measures instituted to ensure that a number of them will ultimately work on intercultural issues or related areas.

Quality and Structure of Intercultural Teacher Education

The issues for academic and professional education in general, and for its intercultural dimensions, are twofold: What do educators and teachers need to know in terms of knowledge? What kinds of key skills do they need? Regardless of the specific answers to these complex questions for particular areas of work, we argue that the central role of educational institutions should be to ensure that professionals' understandings and skills are of a high order. The status and structure of the teaching and social policy professional institutions are therefore critical for the role and position of professional education itself. For example, if professional educators are seen largely as former teachers or practioners whose understanding of the field and academic knowledge of academic and intellectual issues and research may itself be quite limited, then the education they provide is unlikely to be perceived as adequately rigorous. There is, therefore, a need to enhance the expertise of those who educate professionals, giving them a sound and rigorous academic background and an ability to work together with others to develop sound cultural diversity and intercultural dimensions within programmes.

Professionals education at the postgraduate level also needs to provide both systematic academic study as well as opportunities for closely supervised and monitored 'field' experience. Higher education institutions should therefore work to establish good links with other local institutions, for example, in the way that many medical schools are linked with hospitals. This would help to create possibilities for the cross-fertilisation of ideas across knowledge systems and their practice, and would benefit and enhance both cultural development and the implementation of intercultural education.

One of the key critiques of intercultural education is that it 'waters down' the educational process and does not help to raise educational standards. While such critiques need to be seriously considered, they should also be tempered by recognition that these fields are based on a sound intellectual basis. As such, the focus on good intercultural education should be seen to raise the level of quality and of equality of education. For instance, equality of opportunity needs to lead to greater levels of equalities in educational outcomes. Hence quality and equality go hand in hand—a conclusion that is based on rigorous research, analysis and the effective implementation of work in the field. Similar critiques might also be directed towards issues of access, and will need to be similarly addressed by evidence from research and practice. This ought to give further depth to the issues discussed by the UNESCO-CEPES Forum on Higher Education in Bucharest from 21 to 24th May 2009 and widen access, quality and competitiveness. (UNESCO-CEPES: Bucharest: 2009)

However, such efforts should not be left to the initiative of a few academic members of staff who are interested in these fields, but there is a need to make structural arrangements are made to allow for a more integrated approach, they are likely to continue to be marginalised. Each disciplinary field or area has to acquire and develop its own expertise, and also work to of interdisciplinary and cross-institutional frameworks to implement change. These large-scale efforts therefore require the involvement not only of a few enthusiasts, but also of structural measures—resources, mechanisms and infrastructure—to ensure that any changes will be institutionalised.

Policies for intercultural academic or teacher education also cannot be effective unless they have the support of all staff, and changes are seen to be made in (a) student admissions, (b) staff recruitment, development and promotions, and (c) initiation of research and curriculum developments. Moreover, as has been stated before, such changes require an evaluation of their effectiveness, and cannot simply be tokenistic. Academic and teacher educators will need support through staff development to update their knowledge and skills in these areas. Higher education institutions ought therefore to ensure that the intellectual and professional development of academics and staff includes intercultural competencies as well as in the area of their professional expertise. This entails a complex evaluation of values, standards and methods across a range of their academic disciplines and other activities (Gundara 1997). It should be acknowledged therefore that academic and intellectual knowledge has conceptual, theoretical and practical dimensions, and it is likely that there will be tensions about the appropriate balance between these conflicting demands.

Conclusion

This paper has discussed a wide range of issues that need to be considered in engaging with intercultural dialogue and education through an intercultural perspective. It has outlined the need for inclusive and non-centric knowledge to be included in the curricula and socio-cultural development thinking and efforts, and also particularly emphasised the role that higher education institutions must play in this endeavour. For instance, curricula need to be genuinely inter- and multi-disciplinary, to include the languages and histories of whole communities including the subordinate groups, as well as the knowledge of women (particularly those from disadvantaged backgrounds). In many cases the issues may include international students who are studying across cultural divides. The paper has explored a range of issues that need our urgent attention, including working with student diversity to build inclusion within higher education institutions.

In summarising the relevance of linking intercultural education with socio-cultural development, the paper has highlighted the need for the intercultural at academic levels and the education of professionals; for interdisciplinary work, and for cross-institutional frameworks in the Eurasian region to implement these changes. One of the foremost challenges for developing teaching programmes of these kinds is that academics and educators in the first instance need to acquire intercultural knowledge and understandings themselves, so that that intercultural dialogue can be deepened. These competences in turn need to be related to public, educational and social policies and practices especially in complex secular and religious ethical issues which are found in diverse societies and polities within this region (cf. Kung 1990). This research and developmental work would enable lecturers to teach these subjects with a high degree of academic rigour and professionalism. Hence, integrative research and learning cultures are of paramount importance in furthering educational work in intercultural education.

To conclude, the cooperation amongst higher education institutions has an important role to play in creating greater levels of equality through the improvement of educational outcomes for all. In diverse societies, understandings of the relationships between social and natural environments need to be intellectually harnessed at both local and global levels in order to effectively tackle issues of justice in both social and natural environments.

References

Aikman, S. (1997) 'Intercultural Education in Latin America' in Coulby, D., Gundara, J. and Jones, C. (Eds.) *World Yearbook of Education: Intercultural Education.* London: Kegan Paul.

Amin, S. (1989) *Eurocentrism.* London: Zed Books.

BECKWITH, C. (2009) *Empires of the Silk Road.* (Princeton: Princeton University Press)

Bernal, M. (1991) *Black Athena.* Volume 2. London: Free Association Press.

Bernal, M. (1987) *Black Athena.* Volume 1. London: Free Association Press.

Bosworth, C. E. And Asimov, M. C. (2009) *History of Civilisations of Central Asia.* (UNESCO: Paris)

De Waal, T.(2010) *The Caucasus: An Introduction.* (Oxford: Oxford University Press)

Eggleston, J. and Delamont, S. (1983) *Supervision of Students for Research Degrees.* London: BERA.

Griffin, N. (2001) *Caucasus: In the Wake of the Warriers.* (London: Headline Book Publishing)

Gundara, J.S. (2006) 'Intercultural studies, sustainable development and higher education' in Adomssent, M., Godemann., J, Leicht, A. and Busch, A. (Eds.) *Higher Education for Sustainability: New Challenges from a Global Perspective.* Frankfurt am Main: VAS.

Gundara, J.S. (2000) *Interculturalism, Education and Inclusion.* London: Paul Chapman Publishing Ltd.

Gundara, J. S. (1997) 'Intercultural Issues in Doctoral Studies' in Graves, N. and Verma, V. (Eds.) *Working for a Doctorate: A Guide for the Humanities and the Social Sciences.* London: Routledge.

Huntington, S. ( ) *Clash of Civilisations*

Jones, E. (Ed.) (2010) *Internationalisation and the Student Voice.* New York: Routledge.

Kung, H. (1990) *Theology for the Third Millennium.* Peterborough: Anchor Books.

Morris, L.V. (2008) Higher education and sustainability. *Innovative Higher Education* 32: 179–180.

MIO-ECSDE [Mediterranean Information Office for Environment, Culture and Sustainable Development] (1997) *The Thessaloniki Declaration.* http://www.mio-ecsde.org/old/Thess/declar_en.htm.

Nussbaum, M. (2010) *Not For Profit: Why Democracy Needs the Humanities* (Princeton: Princeton University Press)

Phillips, S. and Pugh, D.S. (1994) *How to Get a PhD: A Handbook for Students and their Supervisors (Study Skills)*. 4th edition. Maidenhead: Oxford University Press.

Said, E. (1978) *Orientalism*. New York: Vintage.

Scott, J. (2010) *The Art of Not Being Governed* (New Haven: Yale University Press)

Swietochowski, T. (1995) *Russia and Azerbaijan: A Borderland in Transition*. (New York: Columbia University Press)

Williams, R. (1958) *Culture and Society 1780–1950*. London: Chatto and Windus.

UNESCO-CEPES: (2009). *UNESCO Forum on Higher Education in the European Region: Access, Values, Quality and Competitiveness*. Bucharest: (UNESCO et.al)

UNESCO (2005) *Convention on the Protection and Promotion of the Diversity of Cultural Expressions*. http://portal.unesco.org/culture/en/ev.php-URL_ID=33232&URL_DO=DO_TOPIC&URL_SECTION=201.html.

UNESCO (2001) *Universal Declaration on Cultural Diversity*. http://portal.unesco.org/en/ev.php-URL_ID=13179&URL_DO=DO_TOPIC&URL_SECTION=201.html.

UNESCO (2006): *UNESCO Guidelines in Intercultural Education*. (Paris: UNESCO Education Sector)

Wolf, E. (1983) *Europe and the People without History* (Berkeley: University of California Press)

Educational Issues for Young and Vulnerable Groups

During Periods of Intercultural Conflict and War

This plenary session paper discusses the following issues. Firstly, it deals with issues of human and children's rights and violence in 'peaceable' situations and societies. This is being done because some of these situations become exacerbated and intensified during emergencies and periods of conflict and war. Lot of these issues pertain to individuals and groups in societies. The second, part of the paper discusses the way in which nation states subordinate groups of people and the way many of these people avoid being part of oppressive the national structures. Thirdly, the paper examines the situation during periods of conflict and war and during periods of reconstruction. Since, it is the non-governmental organisations and the UN agencies normally deal with these matters, it is necessary that ministries of education play a role in this field because in many contexts there is little systematically organised documentation and analysis of this work. Since, institutional memories are short knowledge about initiatives in this field is lost through dispersion and disappearance of documents, and high staff turnover. (J. Sullivan-Oweomoye and L. Brannelly: IIEP: Paris: 2009, p. 9). Fourthly, it engages with the issues of violence against educational institutions and learners and educators in particular. Sufficient attention is not paid to the distinct as well as the connections between such violence and as it contributes to the violation the various Human Rights instruments and the Convention of the Rights of the Child. The final section discusses matters of social capital and the ways in which these assets get negated during periods of conflict and the ways in which beingsocial capital may need to be reinvigorated in collapsed or war torn states. The issue of trust and the re-establishment of it is an extremely important issue in strengthening amongst groups fragmented by conflict.

I am very pleased to be here in Zagreb at this joint Conference and to renew my links with friends and colleagues from both a recent and a distant past whom I have not been able to meet. My contacts with Inter-University Centre in Dubrovnik and at the University of Zagreb have lapsed and I hope that they can be renewed not only at the personal level but also institutionally through the International Association for Intercultural Education and the International Centre for Intercultural Education at the University of London. The last piece of work my colleagues and I did for the European Union in South East Europe was coordinated by my colleague Jack Peffers through the ICIS at London University. At that time things in intercultural terms were not optimum for Croatia but now we are in a different place and time and the Republic is a member of the EU and therefore, I hope that our Croatian colleagues, especially at the higher education level, will be able to help other members of the human community who still live under circumstances of conflict, violence and war. It is in that spirit of the contributions that the Croatian colleagues can make to this field through their competences, expertise and experiences that I would like to raise the difficult issues being presented in this paper.

One hopes that this would be possible since there might have been a resolution of some of the bigger issues and that the 'narcissism of small differences' (Freud) would have now receded. The fall out from the collapse of Communism in the 1990's led to the formation of 14 countries. The making and breaking of nations was more dramatic than the impact of the Versailles treaties after WW1. The emergence of nation states at Versailles was a culmination of a long-drawn out process with roots in the middle of nineteenth century, but the events of the late twentieth century were anticipated by no one. (Tony Judt: 2010) The European continent and the countries themselves are still reeling from the effects of these changes and many of the problems confronting the newly established states still remain to be resolved.

Gender, Violence and 'Peaceable Societies'

At a general level there is an enormous range of violence against vulnerable groups in society and these can include members of minority communities who are voiceless as well as boys, girls and women in a number of societies, including democratic and so-called developed states. The incidence of such crimes in safe, 'peaceful' and democratic communities is fairly high and this is especially true of societies where for instance, premarital sex and homosexuality is frowned upon. The range of violence itself is also extensive and these include: sexual assaults, domestic violence, honour killings, violence and killings to do with dowries, bullying at school as well as communities and now including cyber bullying, as well as female mutilation. In many contexts where this violence takes place it is justified on the basis of customs, traditions and sometimes religion. The acceptance of any or combination of these forms of violence is not only a negation of the human rights of women but of the children's rights under the Convention of the Rights of the Child.

Its' occurrence furthermore, at all the social levels makes it common place that violence against girls and women is seemingly acceptable. When social order and stability breaks down, girls, boys and women are the first people who become vulnerable to being victimised. The incidents against them includes verbal, as well as physical abuse. During this process they become scapegoats for other societal problems and this process becomes legitimised. One of the major outcomes of this situation which will be discussed later in the paper is that according to the UN Secretary General rape and sexual violence becomes widely used as a war tactic and this includes countries like Afghanistan, the Central African Republic, Chad, the Republic of Congo and the Sudan. It is useful to note that some of these states claim to be religious but their victims are girls who suffer physical injury, psychological trauma and stigmatisation and as a result of all this suffer from profound and lasting disadvantage in education. The issue of rape in so-called 'peaceful' societies becomes an 'instrument of war with broader consequence, whereby insecurity and fear leads to keeping girls out of school—and the breakdown of family and community life depriving children of secure learning environment.' (EFA Global Monitoring Report 2011: p 24)

In many contexts religion is also involved, but it is always necessary to ensure that religion is not unscrupulously invoked. This issue needs to be critically scrutinised, so that when the Taliban burn schools for girls and forbid girls and women from engaging in educational activities, can this be justified on religious grounds? On purely religious grounds this does not seem to be the case because in the Islamic faith when Prophet Mohammed talked about education, he said that if you educate can only one child—then let be a girl because to educate a girl is to educate the whole family.

In 'peaceable' and democratic states there is a need to establish solidarities amongst women to minimise, for instance, sexual coercion which in Britain occurs amongst 1 out of 3 women. It is therefore, necessary not to accept the normalisation of any forms of violence against girls and women. This is not only a role for women but also for boys and men to ensure that the cultural, traditional and peer group macho cultures are negated and not encouraged.

It is useful to remember that it is not only the old customs, traditions and conservative patriarchal values which lead to violence against girls and women. The 1990s Hip Hop Culture and 'Black is Cool,' led to Black and other women becoming hugely sexualised. This 'raunch' culture which can be considered to be post-feminist was a consumerist version of Feminism (The Pussy Cat Dolls.)This was a way in which young peer groups as part of autonomous cultures used violence against girls and women and who themselves become party to this. This leads to two binary oppositional cultures where in response to girls and women engaging in 'taking all your clothes off'; it has also led to the reaction of 'putting all your clothes on'.

Rutter and Smith (1995) research in a number of European countries demonstrated that autonomous peer group cultures which were not amenable to any adult cultures (parents, teachers and youth workers) posed a grave danger to the lives of these young people. This includes suicide, criminal activity, psychological and physical health and the peer cultures which includes both genders. This piece of research was undertaken in the European context in 1995, and it might be worth considering whether it needs to be undertaken now but in a broader and more international context. The grounds for new work in this field is necessitated because in war torn zones and polities which have been decimated by HIV/AIDs and both parents have been lost present even more serious and deeper problems of autonomous cultures of young people. There is a need to assess both the qualitative and quantitative aspects of these social changes through fragmentation of societies and breakdown of families.

This paper would like to stress that there are no simple norms of acceptable behaviours not only within but between societies and groups of boys and girls, and men and women. The one important issue that is raised here is that women are not to be constructed as 'territories' or objects that are patrolled and controlled by men and treated as victims but as citizens who are capable of fighting their corner to protect their rights.

The understandings in some societies like the US at a general level about issues of feminism are very high. In 1970 there was only one course on Feminism in a higher education institution, but there are now 700 courses. It is however, perhaps worth considering whether such courses should not only be for women but also for men as perpetrators of dominant male norms and embodying macho cultures. This is however, an international issue and such studies and substantive actions as correctives should not only be the preserve of the US, but should apply to all cultures, societies and states.

Many examples of women as activists and not victims come from educated and literate western societies, but this is no longer the case. For instance, in India amongst the uneducated or illiterate rural populations, women are developing resistance to exploitation and subordination. Incidents of violence and rape in both urban and rural Indian contexts have led to mass demonstrations decrying those who commit these crimes; and have included men and women and in both urban and rural contexts. The four men involved in the Delhi bus rape and fatal violence against the 23 year old woman who was training to be a physiotherapist were sentenced to death by the Indian High Court on 13th September 2013. In sentencing the men the judge told the court that the gang rape and 'cold blooded' murder had 'shocked the collective conscience of society.' (The Evening Standard: 13-9-2013) This mobilisation of ordinary citizens has received a great deal of publicity in support of the above victim led in March 2013 to the introduction of death penalty for serious cases of rape. Till now the government in India has been accused of being lax in dealing with such matters and the levels of gender based violence have remained high. In addition to serious punishment this whole issue is so deeply rooted in society that it necessitates long term educational measures and social policy changes.

At the global level the revelations of extremely high levels of crimes against girls and women are indicative of the failure of religious and traditional family values as a safeguard and protection of women and children. The role of law based on con-stitutions, human rights and children's rights convention are paramount and there is a need to make punishment extremely rigorous. A major part of the problem is how most religions support and reinforce patriarchal norms and women believers especially, become 'voiceless' although there are now countervailing secular and feminist ways in which women all over the world are increasingly organising them-selves autonomously.

The women's' resistance and the cultures of resistance which they are creating form the basis of wider political struggles for equality. In India it is groups like the Pink Ladies, in Utter Pradesh who are in the forefront of this struggle. They are the Dalit (Untouchable) women are organising in rural areas to fight the exploitative land lords. They have become powerful enough for men in their own and many other subordinated communities to help them to fight against their historical exploitation by dominant castes and land lords. The Pink Ladies however, acknowledge that edu-cation has a fundamental role in reversing the historical subordination of women on a gender basis (including by patriarchs within their own communities) as well as on a caste basis.

Subordinated Peoples and Nation States:

This section of the paper would now like to engage with the issue of 'critical intercul-tural education' by focussing on how the so-called 'First World Peoples' were turned into 'Fourth World Peoples'.

The legacies of the dominant/subordinate relations are based on the deeply entrenched legacies of the dominant groups using brutal power to give legitimacy of their control of the subordinated groups. These oppressions are based on notions of 'civilising the natives' and need to be negated. (Wallerstein: 2006) The Spanish thinker Sepulveda justified the right to intervene in the Amerindian societies because of their barbarity. Las Casa's on the other hand, purported that evil existed everywhere and that therefore there was no theological justification for interference.

However, this sixteenth century debate has continued for five centuries and the consequent interventions have barbarised both the brutalisers and the brutalised. These concepts also have a longer pedigree than that, especially as the fragments of Europe broke off from the 'Old World' and went and planted themselves as English, French, Spanish or Portuguese colonisers. This meant that there was the imposition of their 'European and Christian' world views which destroyed the cultures and societies of the American-Indian Nations in the Americas, the Inuit peoples in Canada and the Aboriginal peoples in Australasia. Hence, Sepulveda's ideas have destructively carried the day.

Most of the subordinated and marginalised peoples are viewed by anthropologists and policy-makers as archaic vestiges from another historical time. Yet, many of these communities may also be understood as those who have survived as runaways, fugitives and maroon communities who over a few millennia have flown from the oppressions of the state-making projects. They have escaped situations of subordination—slavery, conscription, taxes, corvee labour, epidemics, religious dissent and warfare. (J. C. Scott: 2010) In short many of the nation states were formed by appropriating of these smaller nationalities, their lands and other resources. Many of these people have a history if there is one—of struggling against the state and have used many ways of keeping the state at arm's length and survived through subsistence agriculture which maximises their physical mobility. The settled states describe such groups as being 'uncivilised' and 'barbarians' and as being in a state of nature. Yet, these people see themselves as avoiding harm, servitude and disease which 'civilisation' has to offer and therefore their so called 'barbarism' is a result of their own construction. Such communities are therefore constructing or creatively fabricating identities as a way of evading the state. However, as more and more of the globe is being politically subjugated by the nation state systems these groups are on the verge of being made extinct. At this moment it is therefore, important to take a deep breath and consider how to create greater levels of equitable relationships between the nation states and the marginalised and peripheral groups. (MAP: 1. Scott. P 17) At the present time in south-east Asia there are at least 100 million people who can referred to as minorities, such as, the Akha, Chin, Hmong, Kachin, Karen, Khmu, Lahu, Miao, Wa and Yao who occupy an area of 2.5 million square kilometres stretching from China to north-east India living in the uplands of countries like Burma, Thailand, Laos, Cambodia and Vietnam. There is an urgent necessity of developing intercultural understandings amongst this diverse range of groups and between them and the surrounding aggressive and oppressive nation states. Amongst these excluded peoples by the state systems are the sea gypsies (orang laut: Scott: p. 328) who evade slavers and states within the waterways of the Malay archipelago in Melka region of Malaysia and other mangrove coasts. On the mainland's of the world are the Roma,

Gypsies, the Cossacks, the Masaai, the Berbers, Mongols and other nomadic peoples who practice swidden agriculture and have established zones of refuge. As Scott states: "many, but by no means all, groups in extra state space appear to have strong, even fierce, traditions of egalitarianism and autonomy both at village and familial level that represent an effective barrier to tyranny and permanent hierarchy." (J. Scott. p. 329) Given the type of life these people lead they are not people without history as Braudel states but have 'multiple histories'. They have made the ultimate sacrifice to avoid the oppressive measures of state formation which in common sense terms are referred to as civilisation. As Scott states: "They represent, in the longue duree, a reactive and purposeful statelessness of peoples who have adapted to a world of states while remaining outside their firm grip." (Scott.p.337.) This they have done by purposefully being not pre-anything but as being post-irrigated rice culture, post sedentary, post subject and even perhaps post literate. Scott argues that in the case of South East Asia as the peoples on the plains expand outwards and require more land for paddy, thus pushing the minorities living in the foothills deeper into the hills and forests. These groups are therefore not pre-literate but post-literate; since literacy is given up to deliberately disengage from certain kinds of state forms.

This argument is strengthened from another direction. Wendy Brown in her book *Walled States, Waning Sovereignty* (Zone:2010) argues that borders and modern-day walls are discredited markers of failing sovereignty which are porous and interpenetrative but represents the empty bravado of the modern staatspolitik. This reflection of Xenophobia begins in the head, a psychic war of all against all. The Farmers General Wall built through the middle of Paris in the 1780s to collect octroi from traders has a verse: 'La ferme a juge necessaire/De metre Paris en prison.' These aliens hated but needed (hated because needed) are part of the persistent psychic structures and will not disappear soon. As masks of sovereign autonomies the borders and walls are as much markers of people wanting to come in, as those wanting to leave or stay out.

For all the above groups whose ways of life and culture have now become even more vulnerable there is a need for measures to enhance intercultural understandings and education at least at three levels: firstly, between the many diverse and various groups in this and other regions of the world; secondly, between the dominant national groups and these groups who live on the margins and borders of nation state systems; thirdly, at inter-state and international levels to protect their human and group rights through regional measures and through regional organisations.

In the Nordic region we can cast a similar glance at that part of the world. Many Nordic countries perceive themselves as being mono-cultural societies which were turned multicultural by the arrival of the immigrant communities. What such comments tend to ignore are the longer term and historically based diversities and differences within these societies. The Sami of Lapland or Samiland are seen by the Nordic nations are treated as any other members of their nations states. Yet, these people who have historically lived in north of the Arctic Circle are perceived as 'the others' by the Nordic nation states. As Sam Hall writes:

"the Nordic governments, reputed to be the guardians of the world's conscience, have steadfastly refused to recognise Sami nationality. Legislators carefully avoid any reference to the Sami people, preferring to label them the Sami-speaking population." (S. Hall: *The Fourth World* (1987) p. 138)

What the governments in South East Asia have done to the marginalised groups has also been the case in the Nordic countries. The Sami people are being assimilated into dominant Nordic cultures; their religions suppressed; their resources have been exploited. All this has happened despite the fact that "they never sold their land, nor gave it away, nor lost it in a battle." (S. Hall: p.138)

The long term racism that the Sami have suffered has led the UN General Assembly to meet with the Sami parliaments as well as the Nordic Parliaments and their Rapporteur James Anaya stated in his 7th July 2010:

"the challenges ahead in Sapmi are significant, and that overcoming the harm inflicted by the discrimination and extensive assimilation policies carried out throughout history in the Nordic countries will require serious commitment, political will and hard work." (UN General Assembly, A/Human Rights Council, 15th Session, Agenda Item 3. A/HRC/15/37/Add.6. 7th July 2010)

The Hidden Crises: War Torn States

In the decade to 2008, 35 countries experienced armed conflict, of which thirty were low income countries and conflict in general lasted for twelve years, and this meant that 28 million children of primary school age were out of school—which constitutes 42% of the world total. The youth literacy rates in conflict-affected areas are 79% compared to 93% in other developing countries. Both at the levels of national governments or the UN system there is a failure to protect children in fragile states and there is a failure to recognise the violence affecting education. There is also a need to unlock the role that education can play in peace building. Inclusive education with appropriate linguistic and curricular policies can play a role in providing the vital skills for developing concepts of tolerance, mutual respect.

In the Middle East Queen Rania Al Abdullah of Jordon states, that over 110,000 children in Palestine are out of school and their number is growing as the occupation of their territories grow.—with their lives scarred by conflict, bombs and blockades. In Iraq over half a million children are denied the right to go to primary school. (EFA:

p 23)The recent conflict in Syria leads to extremists strengthening their hold over yet another fragile stat, with devastating effects to children and whether the agreement on the control of chemical weapons will improve the lot of the people, especially women and children is not clear. This is especially since trhe conflict and war will continue and the numbers of refugees will continue to increase. (The Guardian, 17-9-2013 and UNICEF Press Releases) Gordon Brown as the patron of the Global Partnership in Education has presented proposals to the UN to raise $500 million to pay for the schooling of 300,000 Syrian refugees in Lebanon and he fears the numbers might increase to 500,000 by next year. (The Guardian, London, 23-9-2013)

In Pakistan seven times as much of the budget is spent on arms as on education, and the most famous victim from there at the present time is Malala Yousafbhai a teenager who early this month spoke to the UN General Assembly (IMAGE) and opened the £188million library in Birmingham in England. Her claim is that that the only way to 'global peace is through educating not only our minds, but our hearts and our souls'. (The Metro, London: 4-9-2013) However, at the global level these statistics on expenditures for armaments and the military are staggering and in 2009 they reached US$1.5 trillion.

At the basic level this raises the important issue in all communities world wide of the right to education but in 2008 53% girls were still out-of-school and gender parity in terms of EFA goals at least 47 countries will not meet their targets. However, in war torn countries, regions and areas like Somalia, Afghanistan or the Sudan, education plays an important role in emergency situations by providing a basis for stability for children and adults traumatised by conflict and displacement. Schools can provide life-saving information on landmines, HIV/AIDS prevention and health care and attending school can help to lessen the chances of children being recruited into gangs and as child soldiers and avoid to be sexually or economically exploited.

Education can provide essential life and cognitive skills and education for post-war reconstruction. A 35 year old refugee Aza from Darfur states: 'Someone who has not studied compared to someone who has studies is like darkness compared to light.' Hence, in conflict ridden and war torn zones the situation is not very different from the rural areas of stable communities in rural Utter Pradesh. (IMAGE) The Darfur refugees numbering about 200,000 in Chad were asked what the women wanted for their daughters' futures. The overwhelming response was education and one of them said: 'If we are educated, we learn to fight with the pen, not with the sword.' The Janjaweed can take away the cattle but not the education, which women and girls can carry with them, unless of course they are themselves killed.

However, the issue of education raises a very important question of standard setting of the provision and quality of education as well as life skills, in emergencies, because without minimum standards of quality education the period of post-conflict and disaster reconstruction becomes a problem. This is not only an issue in Asia or Africa but also in countries in Europe including south east Europe (Kosovo, Bosnia or Haiti in the Caribbean), as the European Commission heard from civil society organisation from there and other states in 2006.

In 1992 as war broke out in the Balkans there was a breakdown of social controls and 20,000 women were raped in one year and between April 1994 and April 1995; in Rwanda 15,700 women and girls were raped. In Bosnia and Herzegovina, the Dayton Agreement of 1995 sought to create a basis for nation-building through high levels of decentralisation. The resulting fragmentation of the education authority made it more difficult to forge a multi-ethnic national identity. The thirteen separate ministries of of education and schools remained segregated by ethnicity, religion and language. (EFA 2011, Box 3.9, *Global Monitoring Report*) Such fragmentation created several concerns for educational governance and the ICIS was commissioned by UNICEF to attempt to bring about greater levels of coherence and cooperation in the polity. (Peffers, Ferguson, Gundara)

Also education on its own is not enough to bring about peaceable and stable communities, because violence and conflict have long term societal impact. This demonstrates the importance of joined-up inter-agency work to improve, health, sanitation, housing, employment as well as political empowerment measures. Since, many of these situations are patriarchal most of the victims are girls and women who under-utilise these social goods and provisions. Child mortality in Bangladesh is five times greater amongst children whose mothers have no education than amongst mother who have seven or more years of education.

In war torn places the situation is even worse than in Bangladesh. So, for instance, in Somalia girls dropped out of school as it became dangerous to travel to attend schools, hence the issue of safe accessibility to safe schools is also a critical factor. Distance education using broadcast materials, recorded media programmes and packaged materials 'school-in-a-box' can provide an answer in some cases. In the short term learning and teaching in mini-neighbourhood safe centres, or secret schools at homes as education goes underground provide some safety or girls and women, teachers and learners. This however, is not a long term solution because in situations of chaos the school can provide a temporary state of normalcy.

In the absence of men from communities, girls and women have greater workloads to feed families and in the absence or death of both parents' adolescent girls become the head of households. Only when in the longer term the underlying causes on conflict and violence are reduced by building measures to provide security and develop the protective capacities at a collective level of families and communities— do they become safe. In many schools it is not only the boys, who bully girls, but girls have been sexually assaulted by teachers and in war torn zones. In a number of African countries teachers have systematically molested girl students and not only spread aids amongst school populations but has also led to decimating teacher numbers. However, even after peace is established, the UN peace keepers in many countries have themselves exploited girls. For example, after the 1992 Peace Treaty the UN Observer Mission in Mozambique the soldier's recruited 12 to 18 year old girls into prostitution.

Educatonal Violence

Education is seldom a primary cause of conflict there is often an underlying element of political dynamic pushing countries towards violence. Three mechanisms have been identified through which little and poor quality of education; unequal access to education; and the wrong type of education can make societies more prone to armed conflict. (IMAGE) Firstly, the limited and poor quality provision leads to unemployment and poverty and large numbers of young people are denied access to decent quality of basic education, which result in poverty, unemployment and hopelessness and acts as a recruiting agent for armed militia. Where there is a 'youth bulge' this adds to the urgency of building a bridge from education to employment because otherwise they become fodder and recruiting ground for soldiers.

Secondly, unequal access generates grievances and a sense of injustice, and inequalities in education interact with wider disparities and heighten the risk of conflict and led in 2002–2004 to a civil war in Cote d' Ivore. The perceptions that the education of local populations is suffering because of unfair patterns of resource allocation has been a factor behind many conflicts in places ranging from Indonesia's Aceh province to Nigeria's oil rich Niger Delta region.

Thirdly, the use of the school system to reinforce prejudice and intolerance in several armed conflicts, education has been actively used to reinforce political domination, the subordination of marginalised groups and ethnic segregation. The use of education systems to foster hatred and bigotry has contributed to the underlying violence in conflicts ranging from Rwanda to Sri lanka. In Guatemala the education system has been seen as a vehicle for cultural domination, suppression of indigenous languages and wider resentments leading to civil war. As in Bosnia and Herzegovina educational separation through peace settlements can perpetuate attitudes that make societies prone to armed conflict.

There is however, another international dimension to this issue and that is the violence carried out against educational institutions and those involved in education, whether they are student, teachers, trade unionists, administrators and officials. In many conflict situations people and institutions involved in education are considered legitimate targets of war. There is a disturbing increase in the attacks on humanitarian workers and in three years leading to 2011, about 600 aid workers were killed, kidnapped or seriously wounded.(2011 EFA, p 28).

The 5th October of each year has been designated by UNESCO as Teachers Day and to reinvigorate their contribution to education as well as their position in different countries is taken cognisance of. The state of educators in different countries varies enormously, and they are valued in some and maligned in others. Amongst many collapsed states there are large numbers of girls and women who are victimised and the grounds for this include different factors: political, military, ideological, sectarian, ethnic, and religious reasons. Violent attacks include damage and injury through the use of physical force, such as killing, torture, injury, abduction, illegal incarceration, kidnapping, setting of landmines around or approach to educational buildings, assault any kind of weapon, ranging from knives, bombs or military missiles and burnings.

Looting, seizure, occupation, closure and demolition of educational property by force by armed or military groups can be done by rebels, occupying troops, armed sectarian groups or by the state itself. The following examples are a case in point: in Afghanistan in 2006 militants killed 85 students and teachers and destroyed 187 schools, according to the education minister. In Columbia on average 42 teachers are murdered every year and between 2000 and 2006, 310 teachers were murdered; in the Democratic Republic of Congo in 2003 in Djugu, 211 schools of 228 schools were destroyed and it is estimated that 30,000 children were taking part in combat or attached to armed groups. This included girls who provided sexual and other services; on Iraq since the fall of Saddam Hussain on April 2003, 280 academics including 186 university professors were killed, 180 teachers killed between February and November 2006, and armed gunmen in police uniforms killed 100 men from the Ministry of Education. This obviously had dire consequences for the families of these men, especially the wives and daughters. The same has applied to: Liberia, Myanmar, Palestinian Autonomous Territories, Sierra Leone, Sri Lanka, Thailand, and Zimbabwe. In all these cases men and women and boys and girls have been targets, but in the case of place like Afghanistan, it really has been a war against the education of girls. The current negotiations with the Taliban do not bode well for educational or other rights of girls and women in that country.

The gains from war conflict and war are very far in between. For instance, it is stated that girls and women became educated about socialism during the Eritrean or Nepal conflict. But the question is whether this was the best way of girls acquiring this kind of knowledge and to get involved in co-education learning situations?

There is very little systematically collated statistical information on these issues, because information is collected on the basis of terrorism at the international level, but is largely funded by the US Department of Homeland Security, which does not cover state violence and hence for instance women teachers who were caught, imprisoned and hanged by the Taliban state are not recorded and nor are the child soldiers who have been recruited. There are UN records which show that 250,000 child soldiers in 2005 were recruited in different places.

There are different types and complex attacks on education because in some states attacks of education institutions divide groups on sectarian lines like Shia/Sunni in many countries: caste groups like Brahmin and Dalit communities in India; Nubians in the Sudan and the situation in the new state of Southern Sudan has not improved. There however, are also other states which use the education systems to perpetuate differences between diverse groups in societies and this may be done within for instance, the intent to maintain the dominance of the paramount or majority or minority groups in power. Hence, there can be cases in which education systems are used malevolently to separate groups. This misuse of education to divide groups needs to be dealt with by state systems as has happened in East, Central and Southern Europe. It is very difficult to heal these social fragmentations and divides they foster are reinforced in the minds of young people by educators and education systems.

In other cases attacks on educators, education institutions destroy good education systems; hence for instance in Iraq a very good research, higher education and school systems were destroyed. Many of the researchers and educators have been killed or have fled.

Education for All and Millennium Development Goals` cannot be met if the situation in many states is further thwarted by violence and wars. International sanctions which use Human Rights Conventions and the Conventions of the Rights of the Child need to be invoked and given more teeth, so that these international measures can be firmly applied at local and national levels. Teachers and children's' rights also need to be defended by the International Labour Office instruments where teachers as workers are violated and violations against children worse than child labour also takes place.

Conflict and Social Capital

Conflict has been responsible for destroying educational infrastructure and in the recent past this has happened in conflicts not between states, but within states. (IMAGE) Two examples will suffice. In the five year period (2002–2006) the Maoists destroyed 79 schools, 13 district offices and one university in Nepal. (O'Malley: 2007) During the 14 year war in Liberia 80 per cent of the schools were severely damaged. (ISCA: 2006)

Most communities' value education for its intrinsic value to humanity and the possibilities it creates for societal improvement. It may also contribute towards an end to the conflict and education and schooling can become the focus of community engagement. Communities may as locally autonomous entities may share culture, language, tradition, law, class, ethnicity and or geography. They may also have forms of informal or formal group structure and all or a mixture of these features may prompt a community to provide education. The nature of social capital within communities may be enhanced by levels of trust and reciprocity. Bonding social capital may denote ties between people and in the educational environment, by the Parent-Teacher Association or other mechanisms which provide the glue that bonds neighbours.

Bridging social capital may be represented by the ties between the local education authorities and the NGO's which provide the bridge between the community education stakeholders and local, regional or national official education systems. Conflict in many cases disrupts the societal base for these groupings and networks and new ways to promote community participation may need to be found. These may be necessitated by the need to restore or create civic virtue which would provide the glue which holds the different elements of a community together. (Puttnam: 2000: 19).

After conflict and war it is important to rebuild the structures which enhance social capital, but these measures will be different and will have diverse basis in different locations. At the international level agencies like IIEP UNESCO has issued 'Guidebook for planning education in emergencies and reconstruction' (IIEP: 2006); the UNHCR 'Education Field Guidelines' (2003); UNICEF's 'Education in Emergencies: A Resources Toolkit' (UNICEF ROSA: 2006). These resources very helpful and provide strategies for education planners and managers with tool kits, which while working alongside other development partners can help consolidate community reconstruction, and enhance mutual understanding. These tool kits however, can only provide assistance at a secondary level because communities need to have the ownership and develop capacity of stakeholders to construct education structures and schools. They may also help to provide access to excluded poor and illiterate groups as well as, girls or minorities, as well as, keep the sensitivities of the social and political relationships. These measures should be able to play a role in restoring peace and support reconciliation through establishing trust.

The Aga Khan considers that cultural identity tends to enhance social cohesion because otherwise human groups lose an essential point of reference to relate to each other. Furthermore, their identity can help in the development of cohesion is only sustainable if the beneficiaries can gradually master this process. (Khan: 2002) This can also ensure that positive learnings from the past can lead to synergies which help to strengthen and develop networks. They may also help in the reinvigoration of traditional communities and help strengthen bonding and bridging social capital mechanisms.

It is also useful that programmes from the perspective cannot only be technically or economically competent but also need to have an integrated bases which encompasses social and cultural dimensions. It is also necessary that educational activities in local contexts are not viewed and implemented separately from other humanitarian and developmental activities. They need to be contextualised within international frameworks to ensure that they meet minimum standards for education within emergency contexts. This is also needed because in post-conflict situations communities are in a state of flux and have the potential both to draw groups together but also to heighten social and intercultural divisions. Therefore, holistic approaches which combine community structures with resources not merely to provide education but to improve and educational outcomes. The global standard setting instruments need to be devised to ensure that the educational provision and institutions are functioning and performing optimally.

From our own point of view the IAIE, KAME, Intercultura and NAME recognise the changing nature of these conflicts with non-state and multi-national terrorists also intervening and massacring an equally diverse range of innocent people, including children. We will consider the formation of a collaborative and joint body to enhance issues of intercultural education in both conflict ridden and peaceful states. This will happen at the end of this Zagreb Conference

Finally, the education of violence against education systems and the building of the social capital there is a need to create a Convention to make schools safe and as sanctuaries from violence and international bodies like ILO, UNICEF, UNESCO have a fundamental role in making this happen.

Inclusive Education Policies

for Vulnerable Groups in Multicultural Societies

1. Introduction

The basic assumption of this paper is that education on its own cannot solve all societal problems. Educational issues and initiatives for vulnerable groups need to be considered as a part of broader societal context. Multidimensional action is needed to deal with educational issues for all citizens in unequal, complex and socially diverse societies.

At the outset it is important to highlight the essence of the terms 'multicultural' and 'intercultural. (i) The meaning attributed to the term ''multicultural' is that it is used as a descriptive term of a society inhabited by different sociocultural groups. These include those based on linguistic, social class, religious, ethnic, territorial and non-territorial nomadic peoples like the Roma and Traveler groups. Nicholas Hans the comparative educationalist stated that these were the historical basis of the nation states. (ii) The term 'intercultural' is the basis of social interactions; developmental dialogues as well as policies and practices which enable interactions and can help reduce social inequalities. Hence, the term 'multicultural' is a descriptive term and 'intercultural' is about dynamic activities which include a broad vision of knowledge.

The political context of where and how societal inclusions or exclusions take place is important. Education as a process does not take place in absence of the decisions of policy makers and the actions which flow from these decisions. This has become a more critical issue because even in the twenty first century many of the gains of the modern state in the nineteenth century are being reversed: the abolition of slavery and serfdom, the establishment of democracies and the enfranchisement of people, and the establishment of the laws, rules, regulations and constitutional frameworks which guarantee people's human rights. How one might ask have these hard won rights and developments been overridden by the recent rise of xenophobia, narrow ethnicism and nationalism in many European states? In many other parts of the world also, seemingly normal national political forces have unleashed violence at various levels: neighborhoods, communities, localities, regions and nations. Civilised and educated polities have turned into Hobbesian jungles. The rise of ethnicised conflict and/or violence in its wake raises a question about why such situations have arisen from within what were considered stable national, educated and civilised states. Conflict and violence in the past few decades has not been between states, but within nation states and herein lies a much more urgent challenge for all citizens and governments.

This necessitates a reappraisal of the notion of vulnerability and vulnerable groups. As one aspect of state policy the education systems have a role in inhibiting or exacerbating conflict between different groups within a state.

The loss of capacity by a political state to cope because groups or populations have become superfluous to its needs or to provide for them has led to extreme situations. While state systems have tended to impose controls, populations have either resisted, migrated or been reduced to refugees through civil strife and/or economic reasons. Hence, many sections of young people, especially during this period of globalisation, whether wealthy or poor are subject to uncertainty and change. For different reasons many young people can act in irrational, erratic and violent ways. There are numerous examples of wealthy communities and young people being involved for instance, in ethnic or football violence. As Hans Enzensberger (1994) writes about young people in wealthier societies:

> 'Youth is the vanguard of civil war. The reasons for this lie not only in the normal pent-up physical and emotional energies of adolescence, but in the incomprehensible legacy young people inherit: the irreconcilable problem of wealth that brings no joy. But everything they get up to has its origins, albeit in latent form, in their parents, a destructive mania that dares not express itself in socially tolerated forms—an obsession with cars, with work and with gluttony, alcoholism, greed, litigiousness, racism and violence at home.'

In societies which are poorer there are additional problems which the marginalized sections of the population confront. The situation can be made worse by the lack of capacity of any civil authority to govern, and to adequately educate the communities—adults, parents and young people—and adds to the situations of conflict and enhances the vulnerability of many groups in society. However, in countries like Egypt, Tunisia, Libya and Bahrain which have been run by authoritarian regimes and there are extreme problems represented by the 'youth bulge' with young population represent about 60% of the population a more positive aspect of youth power which is peaceful and creative has been exercised by the marginalized and the vulnerable. This should give us a pause for reflection: how have these millions of marginalized, excluded and vulnerable people assumed control as active citizens who understand the power of peaceful action and their democratic and human rights.

At one level some education systems have failed to develop the critical faculties as well as analytical powers which can help to resist the slide into ethnic strife and chaos. Nations use symbols legitimated by the education systems of their invented identities which construct 'us' and 'them, 'belongers' and 'strangers'. Hence, the education system has a major challenge and a role to play in exacerbating or resolving these dilemmas.

The greatest paradox is that national authorities can continue with impunity to violate their own citizens and international conventions they are signatory to, do little to stop these violations. Therefore, these standard setting international instruments need to be given teeth so that the vulnerability of such groups can be reversed at all levels from the local, regional to the international.

2. Parliamentary Action

Issues of xenophobia and racism in European countries and in other parts of the world has relevance for public and social policy and it is for parliamentarians and policy makers to consider these matters judiciously, and to develop agendas in which inclusion, stability and peace have high priorities. A second major concern of parliamentarians and educators ought to be to establish a European wide intercultural parliamentary and policy group which cuts across all political parties. The assumption here is that the persecution of vulnerable groups and the reducing the possibilities of them becoming vulnerable is not the prerogative of any particular political perspective or any one political party.

Educational policies which flow from such considerations need to have a general support within the education system and the population. This obviously would require parliamentarians across party political divides to work together to enhance notions of a multicultural Europe deep into this millennium. The emerging educational policies can draw upon various initiatives in the fields of democratic and human rights.

3. Terminology and Concepts

A taxonomic framework of states which include the various indices of difference and diversity; the ways in which socio-economic inequalities are structured in society; as well as those of domination and subordination are needed. There is a need to develop inclusive public and social policies to ensure that in legal and legislative terms all groups who reside in a polity have citizenship rights. Hence, the focus in educational terms has to be the fact that most societies are not only socially diverse but also embody various forms of inequality which in turn lead many groups becoming vulnerable. The absence of such a perspective can lead to what Balibar (1991) refers to as 'the internal decomposition of the community', which are exacerbated by the 'exclusionary power and powers of exclusionary institutions'. Hence, it needs to develop a inclusive social and public policies which is based on sound intellectual foundations and is firmly grounded in the core functioning of the institutions of the state.

The notion of analyzing socially diverse democratic societies also requires a critical academic engagement. At one level a question can be raised whether societies have historically included vulnerable groups or are they the result of more recent societal changes. There is however another complexity. Even if a society can be seen as having recently acquired vulnerable groups what actions might this necessitate at the level of national governments to formulate inclusive national policies? Part of the solution might lie in creating a fair, just and integrated set of public services, including the education services which can enhance the life chances of all communities, groups and citizens in a society.

The terminological issues also revolve around the Janus headed nature or the nation, which may have features leading to inequality as well as constructions based on modern constitutions. The latter should ensure equality, liberty and fraternity in legal terms and relate to questions of citizenship and promise of greater levels of equality. Young people need to learn that the nation and a society are complex entities and do not and are not subject to singular or simplistic readings. The failure of many schools to do this is a major cause of ethnically based exclusions, conflicts and violence.

4. Public Policies

Exclusions in socially and culturally diverse unequal societies and nations can create vulnerabilities and in turn breed mentalities of exclusivity. These have led to Armageddon in many parts of the world. Member states therefore, ought to safeguard citizenship rights of all groups to ensure not only an equitable resolution of conflicts but to establish prophylactic public and educational policies which strengthen democratic ideas. Such national policies ought to bridge differences and negate the rise of narrow nationalism and xenophobia. In the new millennium civil and political rights need to be validated in all culturally diverse environments to ensure that the civil state is strengthened.

In the socially diverse local and national contexts the increased tensions can lead to tribalisation and fragmentation of communities particularly if particular groups are not reskilled for new jobs. This as Castell (1989) has written would lead to the "globalisation of power flows and the tribalisation of local communities".

The limited notions of ideas of a capitalist and globalising market require further discussion in terms of social democracies and the social market to minimise inequalities and the growth of a large underclass in society. The development of inclusive public and social policies ought to ensure that no groups are made vulnerable through job losses due to the rapid technological changes or economies which liberalise and the consequent rising levels of deskilling and unemployment which have accompanied these changes. There is clear and present danger of certain groups being made vulnerable and poorer. Inclusive democratic processes are far from being actualized in most polities. There are a number of problematic and unresolved issues about ensuring equity and quality in most social democracies for all citizens. Provision of equal access, equal opportunity and equality of outcomes is still not an actualised feature of many European societies. The harshness and inequalities in the market economy are more manifest than equality and quality of social and educational provision. This in turn leads to making the vulnerable groups even more marginalized and not has this become an issue in the older member states of the European Union but is even more stark in the East and Central European countries which joined the EU subsequently after the collapse of Communism.

It is also important that in democratic contexts all groups have a "voice" because without powerfully secular and inclusive demos the reverting back to narrow identities and fragmentation of the polity becomes a more real issue. Education systems have generally so far, not been effective in providing this 'voice' to young people and marginalised communities from which they come.

5. Belongingness

The other issue which should be raised is that of belongingness of all groups in European societies. This however, presents problems because the dominant nationality can construe a society as being "theirs" and as encroached upon by "others" who are not seen to belong. There are obviously specificities of different localities, communities, families and groups which provide a different colour, texture and hue to different localities. There are also differences of local politics, economies, and histories as well as how these intersect and interact with other local, regional, national, European and global contexts which constitute differences in different areas.

The sharing of spaces by the dominant and the subordinate, the minority and the majority, the rich and poor comes together in polities so as to make the functioning of modern democratic state more complex.This complexity includes the way in which material and social goods are produced and distributed. This production includes: political, economic, literary, and cultural as well as the media output. The 'other' is no longer out there, but here, and as Chambers (1994) states: there is an intersection of "histories, memories and experiences". It is important to develop an agenda for public and social policy and to create spaces where societal complexity can be negotiated, both in rural areas and cities. Such an analysis should be inclusive of all groups who live in them. In establishing such a context past and current exclusions would be put to rights, and make it possible to initiate a dialogue between the various groups of those who live in different localities and neighborhoods. The possibility of interaction and intersection of the histories, the cultures and languages enables the construction of a more realistic understanding of the pasts of a community or a society and better inform what may be their present, which may in turn have implications for constructing a less biased and a more meaningful future. For instance, this can include the contributions of all groups and nationalities have made to a nation and a society, its culture, civilization, as well as issues of antipathy, conflicts or cooperation.

Many communities which constitute populations in many societies are not only situated within their localities but have other identities both at national and supra-national levels which lead to an enormous range of heterogeneity to the society and its life. The complexity of all this defies a simplistic definition by either a dominant or a subaltern culture.

Most societies as such embody notions of belongingness as well as of alienation. They have both features of a universalistic nature as well as particularisms and local differences. Yet, non-confederal localisms can become parochial, racist, insular, stagnant and authoritarian. There are thick and textured layers of political, social and economic contexts which intersect with histories.

Most European societies therefore provide possibilities and prospects of a stable future, and yet, can also make the lives of vulnerable communities lonely and confining. The confederal nature of groups and communities requires that integrative thinking and structures should link individual groups and localities. The challenge for the political and educational system is to develop a shared and common value system, in which inclusive rights and responsibilities will be developed as an outcome of the work of schools, social and political institutions.

The challenges for educators at local, regional and national levels are of critical importance in addressing these questions, and their success would ensure citizenship rights of all groups. Such a political and educational initiatives need to establish broadly based educational policies, measures, strategies, actions and institutional changes. Without the development of these strategies and analysis of the negative aspects of education systems the exclusion of vulnerable groups would continue to be perpetuated. If positive policies and actions to counter ethnic conflicts and genuinely promote inclusion are not implemented then the development of good intercultural understandings and relations would be postponed.

There is an urgent need for the formation of a network of institutions and structures to initiate further work: development of internet and other informational networks, disseminating findings, establishing educational and political strategies for different contexts.

6. Political and Citizenship Education and Human Nature

Politically undereducated or ill-educated members of societies are dangerous because they can misrepresent the complexity of humanity and opt for simplistic solutions based on populist politicswhich encourage authoritarian and undemocratic solutions to complex societal issues. Therefore, political and citizenship education is necessary to promote intercultural learning. The skills, knowledge and understandings of the political nature of societies are very little understood, by large numbers of people. The purpose of this type of education is not to be politically partisan or party political but to enhance an understanding of the complexity of the polities in which we live.

In some contexts the rationale for not engaging in political education is that ordinary people are not capable of understanding issues and susceptible to propaganda. Leaders, elites and political sometimes suggest that because human nature is largely negative it is better not to inculcate interest in political issues amongst the masses.

The assumptions being made in this paper are twofold. Firstly, that political awareness, knowledge and understanding is necessary for all people to grasp the inherent complexity of society and their rights and responsibilities within it. Secondly, the assumptions about the negativeness of human nature also require scrutiny and comment.

One issue is that if human nature is considered to be negative then selfishness, conflict and violence are deeply embedded in human consciousness and educational and other socializing influences have no role to play in changing patterns of behaviours and social relations. It was commonly argued that human nature is basically selfish and to expect human beings to be social is an uphill task and that the problems of conflict and violence based on group divides is an evidence of this.

The contention of this paper is that there is insufficient evidence to suggest that 'human nature' has been extensively investigated and definitive statements about human nature can be made. Previous political structures and socialization processes may have been responsible for the perceptions about human nature being negative. It is therefore necessary to suggest that in the absence of sound evidence no firm views about human nature can be made. In other words, human nature may be seen to be neither good nor bad, and human capacity to be social or selfish is an open issue and capacity and potential for both exists amongst people. Human nature as such may neither be Hobbesian nor Rousseauic but have the potential, the proclivity and the capacity to be both.

Individuals may hold not only selfish but also social instincts and nature and nurture can result in social contracts based on equality at individual and group terms. This, however, is not a simple matter because minds are not tabula rasa and the separate stories of inter-group violence are deeply ingrained in the psyches of all groups. They encode both personal and larger historical legacies which make the issue of equitable socialisation very complex.

The role of political and citizenship education is to enable the establishment of a healthier balance between the selfish and the social, personal and the public, conflict and peace, by accepting the sanctity and autonomy of the learner. The development of such autonomous learners would enable them to negotiate some of the complexities of societies. The education system with an appropriate citizenship and political education syllabus would enable the emergence of thinking citizens who would be less likely to seek solutions to conflicts through violence. The education of the young also ought to involve the unpacking of the underpinnings of evil in society. However, this is also a broader task of public and social policy and requires an inter-agency approach. This complex approach is necessary because in as much as truth and veracity are inherently human values so are lying and deception. Broader social and public policy measures are necessary to deny the route to evil, lying and deception, and such policies include the curbing of cruel treatment of children.

In educational terms the common manifestation of children's ill treatment and violence against them leads to the lowering their academic performance, higher levels of truancy, and drift into criminal and violent behaviours.

The differences between boys and girls and men and women ought to receive the consideration of educators by encouraging higher levels of education of girls. The role of the women's movement in Northern Ireland to develop a coalition politics can provide a very important example for developing similar solutions in other parts of Europe. This would optimize not only the life chances of girls and women but also allow them to contribute fully as a human resource to European societies. Girls and women can also play a powerful role in establishing mutual and inclusive inter-group understandings.

Such general educational and political educational issues raise problems about the levels of academic autonomy which exist in education systems. If such systems are insecure they will lead to the use of the education system for narrow nationalistic purposes. Regional and international organizations have been playing an important role in ensuring that they can contribute to curbing these tendencies.

The education systems also have a responsibility to determine the ways and directions in which technology will be developed and used. If it is allowed to be rationalised and instituonalised to perpetuate violence, then technology will reinforce the inherent forces of violence and conflict in society. The role of education and public policies to channel technological developments into peaceful and positive directions is essential to obviating vulnerability, conflict and violence. This is especially true if the global media is to be used positively rather than being used as a vehicle for cheap commercialism and the development of a mindless consumer culture.

7. Vulnerability, Inclusion and Education

The need for inclusive educational strategies is made powerful at the present time because some education systems have failed to deal with the issues of societal diversity. Even when they have undertaken to do something they have often misconstrued these issues. There is a need to work out short, medium and long term strategies of how separate levels of institutions for the majority and the minority groups can lead to desirable levels of integrative processes—without in anyway threatening the group identities of any particular communities either through ill thought out policies or practices.

In many societal contexts while dominant groups might support assimilation, those from minority communities typically favour the cause of autonomy and diversity. A school which accepts diversity on inter-group terms presupposes that pupils, parents and teachers have a shared status based on shared power. However, this is not always the case because in institutional and structural terms the dominant groups do not allow power to slip from their hands. If these policies end up making subordinated groups more vulnerable they may try to set up separate schools. This may not further inclusionary practices or further inter-group understandings between students, teachers, and the local communities located around these neighbourhoods. Conversely some vulnerable groups may fear that failure to accept the dominant value system would leave them open to oppression and persecution in the future. It involves no changes in the social structure and the content of education, nor does it reflect the presence of diverse cultural groupings.

8. Deprivation, Disadvantage and Inclusive Models

The existence of inclusion on social class basis raises issue for those who are poor and disadvantaged. In many social contexts those who are from the lower social classes are considered to be 'culturally deprived' or 'culturally disadvantaged'. The conservatives in this debate tended to argue that inferiority based on genetic factors. The liberals in the debate tend to stress that the disadvantage is really a result of the past discrimination based on sex, race, class and ethnic or territorial grounds which has resulted in the existence of a disadvantaged section of the community. A combination of these forms of discrimination, so runs the argument, may contribute to family breakdown, which may have led to the inadequate socialization of individuals, accumulated intellectual deficit and a resistance to schooling. Educational researchers and teacher-training courses have used such theories to explain poor performances of students in schools: such explanations have formed the basis of various remedial or compensatory school programmes like the Head Start in the United States.

This issue also raises a further complication so that psychological difference can become construed as psychological deficit. In the United States, Jensen (1969) wrote an article from the University of California, in which he argued that intelligence was largely (about eighty per cent) determined by genetics and that differences in IQ reflected genetic differences. In this argument he reversed the postwar psychological theory in addressing the problem of compensatory education. He asserted that since intelligence was largely determined by genetics, the efforts to raise the intelligence of people with low IQ scores by compensatory education programmes were bound to fail. Intelligence, as such, was not defined except by reference to intelligence tests.

Education system need to critically evaluate the negative aspects of the racially based psychological theories and testing which may inhibit educational outcomes of many students by focusing on the negative aspects of single factor analysis.

Jensen focused on the racial differences in IQ scores and gave a genetic explanation: that blacks on average do not possess the same innate intellectual qualities as the whites. Such American research was swiftly supported by Eysenck (1971) who till his death was, an influential member of the Institute of Psychiatry in London.' The arguments found favour with right-wing politicians and those who favoured cuts in educational budgets. This was illustrated by the Black Papers episode in Britain, which brought together practicing teachers under the same umbrella. Their conservative stance under the guise of demanding higher standards resulted in a negative appraisal of the liberal curriculum content and urged the withdrawal of financial support.

The whole position is however, suspect, because any psychological analysis which deals with individual differences and ignores ideology as a problem does not provide a fair analysis but compounds issues of disadvantage.' Criticisms of Jensen and Eysenck were also made because of the data on which they based their hypothesis. It has been shown that the data of Sir Cyril Burt, on which both Jensen and Eysenck relied had actually been fabricated.' Sir Peter Medawar, a biologist and Nobel Prize winner has suggested that 'intelligence' cannot be summarized by a single IQ score. He stated that human capabilities and potentialities are far too diverse for this type of simplification.

The important issue to remember is that Jensen's and Eysenck's work has been picked up without using the details of their arguments. Fascist groups saw these two psychologists as vindicating their racist

ideologies. Eysenck's books form part of the reading list of fascist groups like the British National Party and have been widely used in the training of psychologists in many countries. This research has received further impetus from the work done by Murray and Herrenstein (1994) which advances these arguments with even greater force. In many East and Central European countries there are still residues from the Communist period of these 'defects' being represented in educational terms as 'defectology'.

In fact, the hypothesis of IQ tests scores or 'defectology' needs to be rejected, as does the so-called rigorous testing and measurements which support this thesis. The groups who are labeled because of the genetic inferiority thesis face disaster in educational and social terms. Unless, measures in child or social psychology can be undertaken to improve problems in educational terms which certain young people face, these measures ought to be treated with a great deal of circumspection. This is especially the case if difference between young people can be used to label them as having a deficit and rather than reducing hierarchies in educational terms, leads to differences being reinforced as social hierarchies.

9. Inclusion and Human Rights

The groups which are considered vulnerable need to be integrated within inclusive school systems. There is a need for more inter-group and interfaith contacts between young people and educational institutions need to promote the inclusive values of respect, equality, and acceptance and toleration of different groups, based on genuine inter-group and public values.

Policy makers cannot ignore the important issues raised by the skeptics of human rights or the rationale and the need for the general strategies which enhance ideas of human rights while strengthening processes of democratization, political stability and economic development. At the level of educational institutions it is the task of educators to explore how best to enhance universal and constitutional rights by drawing the underlying basis of such values from different cultural traditions, and demonstrating that universal rights are often locally rooted. Such work must also take account of the rights and needs of the marginalized, oppressed or vulnerable students from both the majority and minority backgrounds.

Hence the context for human rights education is an inclusive one, affecting the experiences of youngsters at school. There are also issues of access: because access to education itself is a human right for all children and this requires the need to make the school safe and secure so that there is no bullying, indiscipline and gender discrimination, which present further barriers to the actualization of access and reduce school exclusions.

Work undertaken in Northern Ireland, under the aegis of Education for Mutual Understanding is an important development. Paradoxically many children there are not aware of their rights as compared to children in India who understand these rights. Better understandings of rights by Indian children are partly explicable because there is a wider understanding of the Indian constitution and the rights which accrue to Indian children as future citizens of India. It however, remains be said that even in the Indian context it is the media and not the school which provides information about the Rights of the Child.

Finally, inter-group conflicts and children and human rights cannot be seen as abstract concepts about which schools can teach through didactic instruction. The process of education, teaching and learning as well as the way in which schools function as democratic institutions is important. The democratic school experience for children carries powerful messages. Democratic, participative and inclusive schools are an important part of the process of the education of children as well their actual democratic experiences within an egalitarian school.

10. Intercultural Bilingual Education (IBE)

Many children can be made less vulnerable in schools if their languages are part of the classroom and school culture. The development of bilingual education which has facets of being intercultural need to be considered in academic terms, but Intercultural bilingual education (IBE) may also help to obviate some of the tensions for the vulnerable linguistic communities.

IBE has relevance for most societies for both majority and minority linguistic communities. It can play the role, firstly to equip all groups to participate as citizens of a society, and secondly to support them in their right to practice and empower their own communities. IBE presents them with the knowledge and means to defend their interests and vulnerabilities against the wider encroaching forces like monolingual globalisation, as well as revitalising and strengthening the vibrancy of various linguistic communities. IBE paradoxically is not about destroying but about developing and enhancing linguistic diversity and repertoires of the various linguistic communities. If IBE is made to constitute the basic structure and content of formal education process it gradually brings in thematic areas from the dominant culture in non-conflictual and non-substitutive way this can assist the process of intercultural understanding. More importantly in the context of majority/minority, dominant/subordinate relations: all the groups would benefit from intercultural bilingual education.

The societal response in teaching the national language to the exclusion of minority or subordinate languages on the grounds that to do otherwise would lead to less political unity or separation does require examination. The enormous resources or skills required to teach other languages may also constitute an impediment. The following rationale is therefore worth considering:(a) Avoidance of language loss as mentioned above; (b) first language provides the child with the best medium to learn at early stages: hence literacy in first language precedes literacy in the second; (c) acquisition and development of first language, assists in successful acquisition of second (dominant, national, minority or majority language). Hence, first language enhances and does not detract from learning second language; (d) IBE enhances the sense of belongingness of a group, its knowledge and values in a school. The use of first language is useful in developing an inclusive ethos. It is less likely to reduce the marginalisation of children with other languages, cultures, histories than those from the school and its curriculum, if its languages and cultures are used in the school.

In general, linguistic dominance prevails and is a major cause of inter-group tensions amongst groups whose languages are being excluded from the educational process. A Europe wide and international collation and replication of good IBE practices can be drawn upon by educators to obviate conflicts between linguistic communities while enhancing good educational outcomes for all the linguisitic communities.

11. Non-centric Curriculum and Disarming History

An inclusive or non-centric curriculum merits consideration in an increasingly integrating Europe. One example in curricular terms which can illustrate this issue is the history curriculum. All children have a right to know and understand their own personal 'story'. This is an important enough issue, because when children do not have access to their parents, family or community history they become obsessed by it. Young people not only need access to these stories but to be able to read them critically. This entails young people being able to critically analyze historical information facts and documents. These historiographic skills would be invaluable to young people in evaluating stories and histories.Members of societies generally think that their understanding of history of their own and other societies corresponds to the reality of events which have taken place. Yet, the norm is that we generally have notions based on falsified histories. Part of the problem lies in the way in which descriptions of events even by participants are by definition partial. As historians become more removed from historical events or periods their narrative becomes more removed from historical realities. It is however, possible to devise certain narratives that are more accurate than others and to remove the excessive levels of ethnocentrism. Many societies have socially centred views of themselves, which distances them from those who are considered the 'others'. At one level they have notions of 'centrism' based on their ethnic community, or as a group which is narrowly defined by its culture.

While ethno-centrism may focus on culture it can be distinguished from racism, which is largely dependent on the attribution to biological heredity of the cultural peculiarities of a group which has highly distinctive physical features. Ethnocentrism as a phenomenon may have an older history and which has preceded racism, because racism became more pronounced in the eighteenth century. The subsequent rise of nationalism has complicated matters further. Political organisation and the use of force have provided the ultimate sanction, especially if the political entity has been able to define its territory and those who belong to it or are excluded from it. The current political and educational systems can help to normalise inter-group relations. This process of normalization is capable of being used very narrowly defined by an authoritarian state at the local or national level. Ordinary citizens and those who work in the institutions of the state can internalize rules of exclusion of groups like the Jews, the Roma or the new immigrant communities. Education systems can sometimes legitimize the most appalling events as normal and for ordinary people to seemingly accept these authoritarian rules. The role of the educational processes to legitimize these actions and to accept gossip as fact cannot be underestimated. Authoritarian systems can in general, bypass the critical functions of education. The best defense for an educational process with a critical edge is within democratic schools and systems, where people do not have to obey rules without questioning them.

Omissions and distortions of history play a major role in allowing gossip or stereotypes to become crystallized. The presentation of various histories by its absence, especially if there is a dominant and subordinate past is an important element in the construction of exclusions: a people without a history or a past. The use of the similar exclusion by dominant group can exacerbate the problems of mutual recognition as has been the experience of groups in various other societies. Additionally, heroes in history are largely warriors and victors of dominant groups. The heroes of peace and their histories are far rarer and this needs to be recorded so that history can be disarmed and not rearmed. Hence, the contributions of Mother Theresa or other figures of peace may be recognized but not play a central role in the national story.

To develop more universalized understandings of history the underlying hypotheses and implicit theories of writers need to be unpicked. An epistemological and methodological break could lead to developing more widely acceptable histories which not only include written sources but also the oral understandings of certain groups. The school level understandings of history can vary vastly across European countries. Therefore, in general: notions of civilisations, the evolutionist schema, and the impact of stereotypes, revoicing and reimaging invisible and subordinated groups do merit attention. The development of critical understandings of teachers, development of appropriate teaching materials and textbooks based on new research and developmental work deserve immediate attention.

Preiwerk and Perrot have carried out a critical analysis of 30 textbooks and this has formed a basis for their own analysis. They conclude:

> 'In short, it is not enough to recognise in ethnocentrism a factor which distorts images on the level of social knowledge, but to see on the level of the specialist's knowledge the fundamental epistemological problems of plausibility of the epistemic subject.'

Such works can be used as a basis to develop other initiatives which critically analyze historical texts.

The usages of terms like 'tradition' or 'modernisation' as applied to study of history have their own parochialism and linearity. Cultures and histories of groups which either become minorities or powerless get constructed as traditional while the dominant and the powerful perceive themselves as the acme of modernity. Such notions detract from the development of a more inclusive, universalised or global approach to understanding history. Liberating the notion of the modern from the 'centric' straitjacket can help in notions of modernity being inclusive. Many studies provide grounds for reappraising the writing of newer historical texts and to tackle other historical 'centrisms'.

The complex and conflictual encounters of the local and the global in economic and cultural terms provides further clues to notions of development of markets, as well as the resistance, retrenchment and development of siege communities. The undemocratic features of the global economies in many contexts have led to the erosion of good local values, stable and sustainable communities as well as local skills and economies. The consequent ethnic conflicts and tensions present complex problems.

There are also cultural syncretism which have taken place as a result of interactions which are cooperative as well as conflictual within Europe. As Raymond Grew writes the development of a global history can be a product of our own time which:

> 'Offers some historical insight into contemporary concerns and therefore into the past as well. And it will do so while substituting multicultural, global analysis for the heroic, national narratives on which our discipline was founded.'

Teachers and schools need to explore the viabilities of syncretic understandings and histories which may exist at local levels to help bring about intergroup learning and understandings. Issues represented by history as a discipline may have resonances with issues of non-centric knowledge in other curriculum disciplines.

12. Teachers, Pedagogies and Teacher Education

One of the problems within education systems for vulnerable groups is the increasing gap and distance between teachers and students. The cultural gaps between teachers and students can have various features and issues of different social class, language, religious, age difference as well as different views about education. Hence, urban teachers working in rural areas need to be able to understand not only the rural or village culture but the aspirations and dreams and the realities that students confront to actualize these aspirations and dreams.

The issues for teachers in general and the intergroup dimensions are twofold: one is what teachers need to know, which has knowledge dimension; and secondly, what teachers are able to do, which has a skills dimension. If teacher education is of high quality then the teachers understanding of knowledge issues and skills is necessarily going to be of a higher order. This is obviously and primarily a role for teacher education institutions.

Those who join the profession ought to bring from their earlier education a sound academic background. This would especially be possible if those who join the teaching profession have an undergraduate degree and that teacher education is a postgraduate qualification whereby teachers can become good professionals through a systematic study of teaching and learning. These studies and especially their intergroup dimensions need to be closely supervised and monitored. Many so called teacher training courses in fact, fail to educate teachers to function effectively as professional teachers in complex school environments. These processes entail not only a command of the subjects taught but also a sound grasp of techniques in teaching these subjects. They also need to have information on research into teaching and an understanding of children's growth and development. In complex European classrooms teachers increasingly have to deal with children would have different learning needs and learning styles? If teachers are sufficiently educated and can also become their own researchers they would be able to deal with these issues systematically.

The status of teacher education institutions and their structure is critical for the role of teacher education itself. If teacher educators are seen as previous school teachers with no higher order skills and knowledge which includes understandings as well as the educational sciences and their research skills which are not of a higher order, then teacher education institutions and the profession will be perceived as having a low status.

Teacher education should essentially be an integral part of the university system and have good established links with schools in the same way as medical schools have good links with hospitals. This situation would create the possibility of cross-fertilisation of ideas from other knowledge systems, and developments within the educational sciences which are firmly located in school practice. The intergroup dimensions of such teacher education would be also help in the nurturing of the continuing educational provision of education and help to raise the educational standards amongst all children. One of the criticisms of intergroup education in some western countries is that it 'waters down' educational outcomes and process. In other words, equality compromises quality. Here, this paper would like to highlight that equality and quality go hand in hand.

Changes within teacher education institutions are necessary because they have customs, procedures and practices which either directly or indirectly discriminate. Such discriminatory practices may not be evident on the surface and can only be eliminated if institutional structures are examined to bring about greater levels of openness to their operationalisation. These discriminatory practices may not only have relevance to intercultural education, but for educational equality, including inter-group and gender equality.

Any policies for intercultural teacher education cannot be effective unless they have support of all staff, and involve measures on (a) student admissions; (b) staff recruitment and promotions; (c) and an initiation of research and curriculum development.

Such changes require an evaluation of their effectiveness, and cannot be of a tokenistic nature. Hence, the implementation of any strategies needs to be properly monitored. While teacher educators can themselves initiate changes these need to be supported by the institutions themselves. This institutional commitment includes the systematic orangisation of staff development, so that teacher educators can update their knowledge, skills and understandings in the field of intercultural education. There is a need for coordinated action to redress issues of inequality and vulnerability in society and only a coordinated effort in all areas of economic and social policy would lead towards greater levels of equality. Targeted action which is well constructed to deal with specific disadvantage is important. However, action in one area, say education, may not be effective if other disadvantages are not alleviated through a long-term strategy and a multi-agency approach. This is therefore, not just a matter of politics but also one of public policy and which has implications for the public domain.

This paper has briefly discussed the complexities involved in the way in which education may exacerbate or contribute to vulnerability which can contribute to the rise in inter-group conflicts. Paradoxically, an educational system through general as well as targeted interventions also has the potential to ensure greater levels of equity and help in the resolution of conflicts. The rise of tensions and violence between ethnic groups may partly be embedded in inequalities which vulnerable groups confront in societies in which education systems operate. In as much as education systems reproduce these inequalities they exacerbate and help to perpetuate conflicts. The role of education in minimising the notions of 'othemess' within communities and societies is essential to maintain peace. Its role in ensuring the belongingness of all groups to a society present great challenges to the school. These challenges about educating for inclusivity in a democratic context, which ensures citizenship rights to all cannot be ignored.

Select Bibliography

Enzensberger, H.M. (1994), *Civil War* (London: Granta Books)

Balibar, E., Wallerstein, I. (1991), *Race, National, Class: Ambiguous Identities* (London: Virago)

Castell, M. (1989), *The Informational City* (Oxford: Blackwell's)

Dunn, J. (1993), *Democracy The Unfinished Journey 508 BC to 1993* (Oxford: OUR).

Chambers, 1. (1994), *Migrancy, Culture, Identity* (London: Routledge)

Jensen, F.N. (1969), *Harvard Education Review,* 39, 1, *1–23.*

Eysenck, H.J. (1971), *Race, Intelligence and Education* (London: Temple Smith)

Kamin, L.J. (1977), *The Science and Politics of IQ* (London: Penguin)Billig, M. (1979), *Psychology, Racism and Fascism* (Searchlight Press, Birmingham)

Herrenstein, R., Murray, C. (1994), The Bell Curve: *Intelligence and Class Structure in American Life* (New York Press).

Gould, S. (1981), *The Mismeasure of Man* (New York: Norton).

Kohin, M. (1995), *The Race Gallery: The Return of Race Science* (London: Jonathan Frredland)

Burnage Report (1986), *Murder in the Playground: The Report of the MacDonald Inquiry into Racism and Racial Violence in Manchester Schools* (Longsight Press).

See Rutter, M., Smith, D. (1995), *Psychosocial Disorders in Young People* (John Wiley & Sons).

Learning in Terror (1988), (London: CRE).

Sagaland Centre for Multicultural Education (1992), (London).

Bookchin, M. (1992), *Urbanisation without Cities: The Rise and Decline of Citizenship* (Montreal: Black Rose Books)

Intercultural Education Policies for

a Multicultural and Democratic Europe

1. Introduction

The basic assumption of this paper is that education on its own cannot solve all societal problems. Educational issues and initiatives for a multicultural Europe need to be considered as a part of broader societal context. Multi-dimensional action is needed to deal with educational issues for all citizens in complex and socially diverse societies.

The political context of where and how societal inclusions or exclusions in Europe take place is important. Education as a process does not take place in absence of the decisions of policy makers and the actions which flow from these decisions. This has become a more critical issue because even in the twenty first century many of the gains of the modern state in the nineteenth century are being reversed: the abolition of slavery and serfdom, the establishment of democracies and the enfranchisement of people, and the establishment of the laws, rules, regulations and constitutional frameworks which guarantee people's human rights. How one might ask have these hard won rights and developments been overridden by the recent rise of narrow ethnicism and nationalism in many European states? In many other parts of the world also, seemingly normal national political forces have unleashed violence at various levels: neighbourhoods, communities, localities, regions and nations. Civilised and educated polities have turned into Hobbesian jungles. The rise of ethnicised conflict and/or violence in its wake raises a question about why such situations have arisen from within what were considered stable national, educated and civilised states. Conflict and violence in the past few decades has not been between states, but within nation states and herein lays a much more urgent challenge for all citizens and governments in Europe. This necessitates a reappraisal of the notion of groups which are marginalised. As one aspect of state policy the education systems have a role in inhibiting or exacerbating inter-ethnic conflict within a state.

The loss of capacity by a political state to cope because groups or populations have become superfluous to its needs or to provide for them has led to extreme situations. While state systems have tended to impose controls, populations, have either resisted, migrated or been reduced to refugees through civil strife and/or economic reasons. Hence, many sections of young people, especially during this period of globalisation, whether wealthy or poor are subject to uncertainty and change. For different reasons many young people can act in irrational, erratic and violent ways. There are numerous examples of wealthy communities and young people being involved for instance, in ethnic or football violence. As Hans Enzensberger (1994) writes about young people:

> Youth is the vanguard of civil war. The reasons for this lie not only in the normal pent-up physical and emotional energies of adolescence, but in the incomprehensible legacy young people inherit: the irreconcilable problem of wealth that brings no joy. But everything they get up to has its origins, albeit in latent form, in their parents, a destructive mania that dares not express itself in socially tolerated forms—an obsession with cars, with work and with gluttony, alcoholism, greed, litigiousness, racism and violence at home.

In societies which are poorer there are additional problems which the marginalized sections of the population confront. The situation can be made worse by the lack of capacity of any civil authority to govern, and to adequately educate the communities—adults, parents and young people—and adds to the situations of conflict and enhances the vulnerability of many groups in society.

At one level some education systems have failed to develop the critical faculties as well as analytical powers which can help to resist the slide into ethnic strife and chaos. Nations use symbols legitimated by the education systems of their invented identities which construct 'us' and 'them', 'belongers' and 'strangers'. Hence, the education system has a major challenge and a role to play in exacerbating or resolving these dilemmas.

The greatest paradox is that national authorities can continue with impunity to violate their own citizens and international conventions they are signatory to, do little to stop these violations.

Therefore, actions to alleviate problems of vulnerable groups can be initiated at supra-national, national, regional and local levels.

2. Parliamentary Action

Issues of xenophobia and racism in European countries and in other parts of the world has relevance for public and social policy and it is for parliamentarians and policy makers to consider these matters judiciously, and to develop agendas in which inclusion, stability and peace have high priorities. A second major concern of parliamentarians and educators ought to be to establish a European wide intercultural parliamentary and policy group which cuts across all political parties. The assumption here is that intercultural relations in a multicultural Europe and the reduction in the possibilities of groups becoming vulnerable is not the prerogative of any particular political perspective or any one political party, since issues of racism and xenophobia are deep in their intensity. Educational policies which flow from such considerations need to have a general support within the education system and the population. For European states this can be a historic moment, at a time when political and governmental structures of many new and older states are being created and developed to build a national and regional European level apparatus to address the futuristic needs of all their citizens in a increasingly globalizing world. This obviously would require parliamentarians across party political divides to work together to enhance notions of a multicultural Europe deep into this millennium. The emerging educational policies can draw upon various initiatives in the fields of interculturalism, democratic and human rights which have been undertaken by the Council of Europe, including the 1997 European Year against Racism. The year 1997 initiated a process to deal with these issues and to establish a more systematic institutional framework to counter racism and xenophobia. These initiatives on their own however, are not sufficient and longer term and sustained strategies are required. There is a need for sustained action to deal with these issues within the political and the educational system from the grass roots, local, national and European institutional levels.

There is urgent need for initiatives in this field because reactionary, xenophobic, racist and fascistic groups provide a backdrop to the current situation in a number of states. Unless there is a serious consideration to develop prophylactic intercultural policies and practices, the threat to multicultural democratic polities can undermine stability of not only those groups which are considered to be minorities but also other groups, which include the dominant groups in society.

3. Terminology and Concepts

Terms like multiculturalism and social diversity are used as descriptive terms, in contemporary discourse, to highlight the presence of 'the other'. If issues of intercultural relations and equality in intercultural public and social policy are to become a reality, then these groups have to be treated as being part of the mainstream rather than marginal to a society. Part of the problem which needs to be addressed is the institutionalized exclusion, xenophobia and racism within the education system.

The first issue is how to define culturally diverse or a multicultural state. A taxonomic framework of states which include: linguistic, religious, social class, nationalities and ethnic groups means that most societies have been historically as well as contemporaneously diverse. They therefore need to develop inclusive policies to ensure that in legal and legislative terms all groups who reside in a polity have citizenship rights. Hence, the focus in educational terms has to be the fact that most societies are socially diverse and if there are vulnerable groups within them then their education has to be undertaken within that broader framework. The absence of such a perspective can lead to what Balibar (1991) refers to as 'the internal decomposition of the community, created by racism'. Development of intercultural measures has to start from negating racism, xenophobia, narrow nationalisms and ethnicisms. Such intercultural learning can only be meaningful if it can help resolve the practice of 'exclusionary power and powers of exclusionary institutions'. Hence, it needs to develop a critical interculturalism which is based on sound intellectual foundations and is firmly grounded in the core functioning of the institutions of the state.

The notion of analysing multicultural democratic societies also requires a critical academic engagement. At one level a question can be raised whether societies have become multicultural or if they have historically been multicultural. Historical facts are subject to distortion whether this is done by national historians, dominant groups or those from specific religious or ethnic backgrounds. There is a myth and a fallacy on part of educators, researcher and the political elites that Europe has only contemporaneously become 'multicultural', because most states have also been historically 'multicultural' and 'multilingual.'

There is however another complexity. Even if a society can be seen as being multicultural would the member states consider themselves as being multicultural or socially diverse and what actions might this necessitate at the level of national governments to formulate inclusive (not assimilation) national policies? Part of the solution might lie in creating a fair, just and integrated set of public services, including the education services which can enhance the life chances of all communities, groups and citizens in a society.

The terminological issues also revolve around the Janus headed nature or the nation, which may have 'ethnic' features as well as constructions based on modern constitutions. The latter should ensure equality, liberty and fraternity in legal terms and relate to questions of citizenship.

Young people need to learn that the nation and a society are complex entities and do not and are not subject to singular or simplistic readings. The failure of many schools to do this is a major cause of ethnically based exclusions, conflicts and violence.

4. Public Policies

Exclusions in socially and culturally diverse societies and nations can create vulnerabilities and in turn breed mentalities of exclusivity. These have led to ethnic Armageddon in many parts of the world. National governments therefore, ought to safeguard citizenship rights of all groups to ensure not only an equitable resolution of conflicts but to establish prophylactic public and educational policies which strengthen democratic ideas. Such national policies ought to bridge ethnic, religious, linguistic and racial differences and negate the rise of narrow nationalism and xenophobia. In the new millennium civil and political rights need to be validated in all culturally diverse environments to ensure that the civil state is strengthened. In the socially diverse local and national contexts the increased tensions can lead to tribalisation and fragmentation of communities particularly if particular groups are not reskilled for new jobs. This as Castell (1989) has written would lead to the "globalisation of power flows and the tribalisation of local communities".

The limited notions of ideas of a capitalist and globalising market require further discussion in terms of social democracies and the social market to minimise inequalities and the growth of a large underclass in society. The development of intercultural public and social policies ought to ensure that no groups are made vulnerable through job losses due to the rapid technological changes or economies which liberalise and the consequent rising levels of deskilling and unemployment which have accompanied these changes. There is clear and present danger of certain groups being made vulnerable and poorer.

Intercultural democratic processes are far from being actualized in most polities. There are a number of problematic and unresolved issues about ensuring equity and quality in most social democracies for all citizens. Provision of equal access, equal opportunity and equality of outcomes is still not an actualised feature of many European societies. The harshness and inequalities in the neoliberal market economy are more manifest than equality and quality of social and educational provision. This in turn leads to making the poor groups even more marginalised.

It is also important that in democratic contexts all groups have a "voice" because without powerfully secular and inclusive demos the reverting back to narrow identities and fragmentation of the polity becomes a more real issue. Education systems have generally so far, not been effective in providing this 'voice' to young people and marginalised communities from which they come.

5. Belongingness

The other issue which should be raised is that of belongingness of all groups in European societies. This however, presents problems because the dominant nationality can construe a society as being "theirs" and as encroached upon by "others" who are not seen to belong. There are obviously specificities of different localities, communities, families and groups which provide a different colour, texture and hue to different localities. There are also differences of local politics, economies, and histories as well as how these intersect and interact with other local, regional, national, European and global contexts which constitute differences in different areas.

The sharing of spaces by the dominant and the subordinate, the minority and the majority, the rich and poor comes together in polities so as to make the functioning of modern democratic state more complex.

This complexity includes the way in which material and social goods are produced and distributed. This production includes: political, economic, literary, and cultural as well as the media output. The 'other' is no longer out there, but here, and as Chambers (1994) states: there is an intersection of "histories, memories and experiences". It is important to develop an agenda for public and social policy and to create spaces where societal complexity can be negotiated, both in rural areas and cities. Such an analysis should be inclusive of all groups who live in them. In establishing such a context past and current exclusions would be put to rights, and make it possible to initiate a dialogue between the various groups of those who live in different localities and neighbourhoods. The possibility of interaction and intersection of the histories, the cultures and languages enables the construction of a more realistic understanding of the pasts of a community or a society and better inform what may be their present, which may in turn have implications for constructing a less biased and a more meaningful future. For instance, this can include the contributions of all groups and nationalities have made to a nation and a society, its culture, civilization, as well as issues of antipathy, conflicts or cooperation.

Many communities which constitute populations in many societies are not only situated within their localities but have other identities both at national and supra-national levels which lead to an enormous range of heterogeneity to the society and its life. The complexity of all this defies a simplistic definition by either a dominant or a subaltern culture and most people have multiple identities.

Most societies as such embody notions of belongingness as well as of alienation. They have both features of a universalistic nature as well as particularisms and local differences. Yet, non-confederal localisms can become parochial, racist, insular, stagnant and authoritarian. There are thick and textured layers of political, social and economic contexts which intersect with histories.

Most European societies therefore provide possibilities and prospects of a stable future, and yet, can also make the lives of minority communities lonely and confining. The confederal nature of groups and communities requires that integrative thinking and structures should link individual groups and localities. The challenge for the political and educational system is to develop a shared and common value system, in which inclusive rights and responsibilities will be developed as an outcome of the work of schools, social and political institutions.

The challenges for educators at local, regional and national levels are of critical importance in addressing these questions, and their success would ensure citizenship rights of all groups. Such a political and educational initiatives need to establish broadly based educational policies, measures, strategies, actions and institutional changes. Without the development of these strategies and analysis of the negative aspects of education systems the exclusion of vulnerable groups would continue to be perpetuated. If positive policies and actions to counter ethnic conflicts and genuinely promote inclusion are not implemented then the development of good intercultural understandings and relations would be postponed.

There is an urgent need for the formation of a network of institutions and structures to initiate further work: development of internet and other informational networks, disseminating findings, establishing educational and political strategies for different contexts.

6. Political and Citizenship Education and Human Nature

Politically under-educated or ill-educated members of societies are dangerous because they can misrepresent the complexity of humanity and opt for simplistic solutions based on populist politics which encourage authoritarian and undemocratic solutions to complex societal issues. Therefore, political, human rights and citizenship education is necessary to promote intercultural learning and understandings. The skills, knowledge and understandings of the political nature of societies are very little understood, by large numbers of people. The purpose of this type of education is not to be politically partisan or party political but to enhance an understanding of the complexity of the polities in which we live.

In some contexts the rationale for not engaging in political education is that ordinary people are not capable of understanding issues and susceptible to propaganda. Leaders, elites and some political parties sometimes suggest that because human nature is largely negative it is better not to inculcate interest in political issues amongst the masses.

The assumptions being made in this contribution are twofold. Firstly, that political awareness, knowledge and understanding is necessary for all people to grasp the inherent complexity of society and their rights and responsibilities within it. Secondly, the assumptions about the negativeness of human nature also require scrutiny and comment.

One issue is that if human nature is considered to be negative then selfishness, conflict and violence are deeply embedded in human consciousness and educational and other socialising influences have no role to play in changing patterns of behaviours and social relations. It was commonly argued that human nature is basically selfish and to expect human beings to be social is an uphill task and that the problems of conflict and violence on ethnic lines are an evidence of this.

The contention of this contribution is that there is insufficient evidence to suggest that 'human nature' has been extensively investigated and definitive or scientific statements about human nature can be made. Previous political structures and socialization processes may have been responsible for the perceptions about human nature being negative. It is therefore necessary to suggest that in the absence of sound evidence no firm views about human nature can be made. In other words, human nature may be seen to be neither good nor bad, and human capacity to be social or selfish is an open issue and the capacity and potential for both exists amongst people. Human nature as such may neither be Hobbesian nor Rousseauic but have the potential, the proclivity and the capacity to be both. The educational and socialization processes therefore have a major role to play in the education of all citizens (whatever their origin) in society.

Individuals may hold not only selfish but also social instincts and nature and nurture can result in social contracts based on equality at individual and group terms. This, however, is not a simple matter because minds are not tabula rasa and the separate stories of inter-group violence are deeply ingrained in the psyches of all groups. They encode both personal and larger historical legacies which make the issue of equitable socialisation very complex.

The role of political and citizenship education is to enable the establishment of a healthier balance between the selfish and the social, personal and the public, conflict and peace, by accepting the sanctity and autonomy of the learner. The development of such autonomous learners would enable them to negotiate some of the complexities of societies. The education system with an appropriate citizenship and political education syllabus can enable the emergence of thinking citizens who would be less likely to seek solutions to conflicts through violence. The education of the young also ought to involve the unpacking of the underpinnings of evil in society. However, this is also a broader task of public and social policy and requires an inter-agency approach. This complex approach is necessary because in as much as truth and veracity are inherently human values so are lying and deception. Broader social and public policy measures are necessary to deny the route to evil, lying and deception, and such policies include the curbing of cruel treatment of children and especially girls and women.

In educational terms the common manifestation of children's ill treatment and violence against them leads to the lowering their academic performance, higher levels of truancy, and drift into criminal and violent behaviours. In many cases such youth themselves become pathologically violent and their parents do not realise that the children perform badly in educational terms and become consigned to the lower echelons of society.

The differences between boys and girls and men and women ought to receive the consideration of educators by encouraging higher levels of education of girls. The role of the women's movement in Northern Ireland to develop a coalition politics can provide a very important example for developing similar solutions in other parts of Europe. This would optimize not only the life chances of girls and women but also allow them to contribute fully as a human resource to European societies. Girls and women can also play a powerful role in establishing mutual and intercultural understandings.

Such general educational and political educational issues raise problems about the levels of academic autonomy which exist in education systems. If such systems are insecure they will lead to the use of the education system for narrow nationalistic purposes. Regional and international organisations have been playing an important role in ensuring that they can contribute to curbing these tendencies.

The education systems also have a responsibility to determine the ways and directions in which technology will be developed and used. If it is allowed to be rationalised and institutionalised to perpetuate violence, then technology will reinforce the inherent forces of violence and conflict in society. The role of education and public policies to channel technological developments into peaceful and positive directions is essential to obviating poverty, conflict and violence. This is especially true if the global media is to be used positively rather then being used as a vehicle for cheap commercialism and the development of a mindless consumer culture.

7. Racism, Xenophobia and Education

The need for intercultural education is made powerful at the present time because some education systems have failed to deal with the issues of societal diversity. Even when they have undertaken to do something they have often misconstrued these issues. In this section of the article a brief interpretation in some of the western countries of what has been called interchangeably as 'multicultural education'. 'multiethnic education' and multiracial education' are discussed. In the 1980's the discourse among educationalist was also fragmented along the lines of those who advocated 'multicultural' policies and those who called themselves 'anti-racist'

While some educationalists maintain that the issue of 'race' tends to be blurred by the term multiculturalism, others hold that it is not relevant category. This paper assumes that racism and xenophobia are important variables on many societies, and that there is sufficient evidence of the pervasiveness of xenophobia and racism and that the term 'multicultural' is better used as a descriptive term.

There is a need to work out short, medium and long term strategies of how separate levels of institutions for the majority and the minority groups on racial, linguistic or religious grounds can lead to desirable levels of integrative processes —without in anyway threatening the group identities of any particular communities either through ill thought out policies or practices.

In many societal contexts while dominant groups might support assimilation, those from minority communities typically favour the cause of autonomy and diversity. One justification for this perspective in many contexts is that the minority communities are often bicultural and bilingual and possess traits of the dominant groups as well as a culture distinctive to themselves. A school which accepts diversity on inter-group terms presupposes that pupils, parents and teachers have a shared status based on shared power. However, this is not always the case because in institutional and structural terms the dominant groups do not allow power to slip from their hands. If these policies end up making subordinated groups more vulnerable they may try to set up schools on religious or ethnic grounds. Such separate schools however, do not necessarily further intercultural understandings between students, teachers, and the local communities located around these neighbourhoods.

A major theory of cultural pluralism views integration as racial assimilation, i.e. the socialisation of minority children with children from the dominant or majority community. If and when some elements of majority or minority communities accept this postulation, they might do so on the grounds that if their culture resembles that of the dominant group they may become more acceptable. Conversely such groups may fear that failure to accept the dominant value system would leave them open to oppression and persecution in the future. It involves no changes in the social structure and the content of education, nor does it reflect the presence of diverse cultural groupings. In many cases minority communities reject this form of assimilation or integration.

8. Deprivation,Disadvantage and Inclusive Models

The existence of assimilation on social class basis raises issue for those who are poor and disadvantaged. In many social contexts those who are from the lower social classes are considered to be 'culturally deprived' or 'culturally disadvantaged'. The conservatives in this debate tended to argue that inferiority based on genetic factors. The liberals in the debate tend to stress that the disadvantage is really a result of the past discrimination based on sex, race, class and ethnic or territorial grounds which has resulted in the existence of a disadvantaged section of the community. A combination of these forms of discrimination, so runs the argument, may contribute to family breakdown, which may have led to the inadequate socialization of individuals, accumulated intellectual deficit and a resistance to schooling. Educational researchers and teacher-training courses have used such theories to explain poor performances of students in schools: such explanations have formed the basis of various remedial or compensatory school programmes like the Head Start in the United States.

This issue also raises a further complication so that psychological difference can become construed as psychological deficit. In the United States, Jensen (1969) wrote an article from the University of California, in which he argued that intelligence was largely (about eighty per cent) determined by genetics and that differences in IQ reflected genetic differences. In this argument he reversed the postwar psychological theory in addressing the problem of compensatory education. He asserted that since intelligence was largely determined by genetics, the efforts to raise the intelligence of people with low IQ scores by compensatory education programmes were bound to fail. Intelligence, as such, was not defined except by reference to intelligence tests.

Education system need to critically evaluate the negative aspects of the racially based psychological theories and testing which may inhibit educational outcomes of many students by focusing on the negative aspects of single factor analysis.

Jensen focused on the racial differences in IQ scores and gave a genetic explanation: that blacks on average do not possess the same innate intellectual qualities as the whites. Such American research was swiftly supported by Eysenck (1971) who till his death was, an influential member of the Institute of Psychiatry in London.' The arguments found favour with right-wing politicians and those who favoured cuts in educational budgets. This was illustrated by the Black Papers episode in Britain, which brought together practising teachers under the same umbrella. Their conservative stance under the guise of demanding higher standards resulted in a negative appraisal of the liberal curriculum content and urged the withdrawal of financial support.

The whole position is however, suspect, because any psychological analysis which deals with individual differences and ignores ideology as a problem does not provide a fair analysis but compounds issues of disadvantage.' Criticisms of Jensen and Eysenck were also made because of the data on which they based their hypothesis. It has been shown that the data of Sir Cyril Burt, on which both Jensen and Eysenck relied had actually been fabricated.' Sir Peter Medawar, a biologist and Nobel Prize winner has suggested that 'intelligence' cannot be summarized by a single IQ score. He stated that human capabilities and potentialities are far too diverse for this type of simplification.

The important issue to remember is that Jensen's and Eysenck's work has been picked up without using the details of their arguments. Fascist groups saw these two psychologists as vindicating their racist ideologies. Eysenck's books form part of the reading list of fascist groups like the British National Party and have been widely used in the training of psychologists in many countries. This research has received further impetus from the work done by Murray and Herrenstein (1994) which advances these arguments with even greater force. In many European countries there are still residues of these 'defects' being represented in educational terms as 'defectology'.

In fact, the hypothesis of IQ test scores or 'defectology' needs to be rejected, as does the so-called rigorous testing and measurements which support this thesis. The groups who are labelled because of the genetic inferiority thesis face disaster in educational and social terms. Unless, measures in child or social psychology can be undertaken to improve problems in educational terms which certain young people face, these measures ought to be treated with a great deal of circumspection. This is especially the case if difference between young people can be used to label them as having a deficit and rather than reducing hierarchies in educational terms, leads to differences being reinforced as social hierarchies.

The groups which are considered vulnerable need to be integrated within inclusive school systems. There is a need for more inter-group and interfaith contacts between young people and educational institutions need to promote the intercultural values of respect, equality, and acceptance and toleration of different groups, based on genuine inter-group and public values.

Policy makers cannot ignore the important issues raised by the sceptics of human rights or the rationale and the need for the general strategies which enhance ideas of human rights while strengthening processes of democratisation, political stability and economic development. At the level of educational institutions it is the task of educators to explore how best to enhance universal and constitutional rights by drawing the underlying basis of such values from different cultural traditions, and demonstrating that universal rights are often locally rooted. Such work must also take account of the rights and needs of the marginalised, oppressed or vulnerable students from both the majority and minority backgrounds.

Hence the context for human rights education is an intercultural one, affecting the experiences of youngsters at school. There are also issues of access: because access to education itself is a human right for all children and this requires the need to make the school safe and secure so that there is no bullying, indiscipline and gender discrimination, which present further barriers to the actualisation of access and reduce school exclusions.

Work undertaken in Northern Ireland, under the aegis of Education for Mutual Understanding is an important development. Paradoxically many children there are not aware of their rights as compared to children in India who understand these rights. Better understandings of rights by Indian children are partly explicable because there is a wider understanding of the Indian constitution and the rights which accrue to Indian children as future citizens of India. It however, remains be said that even in the Indian context it is the media and not the school which provides information about the Rights of the Child.

Finally, ethnic conflicts and children and human rights cannot be seen as abstract concepts about which schools can teach through didactic instruction. The process of education, teaching and learning as well as the way in which schools function as institutions, in the eyes of children and their experiences within them carry their own powerful messages. Democratic, participative and inclusive schools are an important part of the process of the education of children as well their actual democratic experiences within an egalitarian school.

9. Intercultural Bilingual Education (IBE)

The development of bilingual education which has facets of being intercultural need to be considered in academic terms, but Intercultural bilingual education (IBE) may also help to obviate some of the tensions between linguistic communities.

IBE has relevance for most societies for both majority and minority linguistic communities. It can play the role, firstly to equip all groups to participate as citizens of a society, and secondly to support them in their right to practice and empower their own communities. IBE presents them with the knowledge and means to defend their interests and vulnerabilities against the wider encroaching forces like monolingual globalisation, as well as revitalising and strengthening the vibrancy of various linguistic communities. IBE paradoxically is not about destroying but about developing and enhancing linguistic diversity and repertoires of the various linguistic communities.

If IBE is made to constitute the basic structure and content of formal education process it gradually brings in thematic areas from the dominant culture in non-conflictual and non-substitutive way this can assist the process of intercultural understanding. More importantly in the context of majority/minority, dominant/subordinate relations: all the groups would benefit from intercultural bilingual education.

The societal response in teaching the national language to the exclusion of minority or subordinate languages on the grounds that to do otherwise would lead to less political unity, or separation does require examination. The enormous resources or skills required to teach other languages may also constitute an impediment. The following rationale is therefore worth considering:

(a) avoidance of language loss as mentioned above; (b) first language provides the child with the best medium to learn at early stages: hence literacy in first language precedes literacy in the second; (c) acquisition and development of first language, assists in successful acquisition of second (dominant, national, minority or majority language). Hence, first language enhances and does not detract from learning second language; (d) IBE enhances the sense of belongingness of a group, its knowledge and values in a school. The use of first language is useful in developing an inclusive ethos. It is less likely to reduce the marginalisation of children with other languages, cultures, histories than those from the school and its curriculum, if its languages and cultures are used in the school.

In general, linguistic dominance prevails and is a major cause of ethnic tensions amongst groups whose languages are being excluded from the educational process. An international collation and replication of good IBE practices can be drawn upon by educators to obviate conflicts between linguistic communities while enhancing good educational outcomes for all the linguisitic communities.

10. Non-centric Curriculum and Dis-arming History

An inclusive or non-centric curriculum merits cosideration in an increasingly integrating Europe. One example in curricular terms which can illustrate this issue is the history curriculum. All children have a right to know and understand their own personal 'story'. This is an important enough issue, because when children do not have access to their parents, family or community history they become obsessed by it. Young people not only need access to these stories but to be able to read them critically. This entails young people being able to critically analyse historical information facts and documents. These histriographic skills would be invaluable to young people in evaluating stories and histories.

Members of societies generally think that their understanding of history of their own and other societies corresponds to the reality of events which have taken place. Yet, the norm is that we generally have notions based on falsified histories. Part of the problem lies in the way in which descriptions of events even by participants is by definition partial. As historians become more removed from historical events or periods their narrative becomes more removed from historical realities. It is however, possible to devise certain narratives that are more accurate than others and to remove the excessive levels of ethnocentrism. Many socieities have socially centred views of themselves, which distances them from those who are considered the 'others'. At one level they have notions of 'centrism' based on their ethnic community, or as a group which is narrowly defined by its culture.

While ethno-centrism may focus on culture it can be distinguished from racism, which is largely dependent on the attribution to biological heredity of the cultural peculiarities of a group which has highly distinctive physical features. Ethnocentrism as a phenomenon may have an older history and which has preceded racism, because racism became more pronounced in the eighteenth century. The subsequent rise of nationalism has complicated matters further. Political organisation and the use of force have provided the ultimate sanction, especially if the political entity has been able to define its territory and those who belong to it or are excluded from it. The current political and educational systems can help to normalise inter-group relations.

This process of normalisation is capable of being used very narrowly defined by an authoritarian state at the local or national level. Ordinary citizens and those who work in the institutions of the state can internalise rules of exclusion of groups like the Jews, the Roma or the new immigrant communities. Education systems can sometimes legitimise the most appalling events as normal and for ordinary people to seemingly accept these authoritarian rules. The role of the educational processes to legitimise these actions and to accept gossip as fact cannot be underestimated. Authoritarian systems can in general, bypass the critical functions of education. The best defence for an educational process with a critical edge is within democratic schools and systems, where people do not have to obey rules without questioning them.

Omissions and distortions of history play a major role in allowing gossip or stereotypes to become crystallised. The presentation of various histories by its absence, especially if there is a dominant and subordinate past is an important element in the construction of exclusions: a people without a history or a past. The use of the similar exclusion by dominant group can exacerbate the problems of mutual recognition as has been the experience of groups in various other socieities. Additionally, heroes in history are largely warriors and victors of dominant groups. The heroes of peace and their histories are far more rare and this needs to be recorded so that history can be disarmed and not rearmed. Hence, the contributions of Mother Theresa or other figures of peace may be recognised but not play a central role in the national story.

To develop more universalised understandings of history the underlying hypotheses and implicit theories of writers need to be unpicked. An epistemological and methodological break could lead to developing more widely acceptable histories which not only include written sources but also the oral understandings of certain groups. The school level understandings of history can vary vastly across European countries.

Therefore, in general : notions of civilisations, the evolutionist schema, the impact of stereotypes, revoicing and reimaging invisible and subordinated groups do merit attention. The development of critical understandings of teachers, development of appropriate teaching materials and textbooks based on new research and developmental work deserve immediate attention.

Preiwerk and Perrot have carried out a critical analysis of 30 textbooks and this has formed a basis for their own analysis. They conclude:

> In short, it is not enough to recognise in ethnocentrism a factor which distorts images on the level of social knowledge, but to see on the level of the specialists knowledge the fundamental epistemological problems of plausibility of the epistemic subjects

The usage of terms like 'tradition' or 'modernisation' as applied to study of history have their own parochialism and linearity. Cultures and histories of groups which either become minorities or powerless get constructed as traditional while the dominant and the powerful perceive themselves as the acme of modernity. Such notions detract from the development of a more inclusive, universalised or global approach to understanding history. Liberating the notion of the modern from the 'centric' straitjacket can help in notions of modernity being inclusive. Many studies provide grounds for reappraising the writing of newer historical texts and to tackle other historical 'centrisms'.

The complex and conflictual encounters of the local and the global in economic and cultural terms provides further clues to notions of development of markets, as well as the resistance, retrenchment and development of siege communities. The undemocratic features of the global economies in many contexts has led to the erosion of good local values, stable and sustainable communities as well as local skills and economies. The consequent ethnic conflicts and tensions present complex problems.

There are also cultural syncretisms which have taken place as a result of interactions which are cooperative as well as conflictual within Europe. As Raymond Grew writes the development of a global history can be a product of our own time which:

> Offers some historical insight into contemporary concerns and therefore into the past as well. And it will do so while substituting

multicultural, global analysis for the heroic, national narratives on which our discipline was founded.'

Teachers and schools need to explore the viabilities of syncretic understandings and histories which may exist at local levels to help bring about intercultural learnings and understandings. Issues represented by history as a discipline may have resonances with issues of non-centric knowledge in other curriculum disciplines.

11. Teachers, Pedagogies and Teacher Education

One of the problems within education systems for vulnerable groups is the increasing gap and distance between teachers and students. The cultural gaps between teachers and students can have various features and issues of different social class, language, religious, age difference as well as different views about education. Hence, urban teachers working in rural areas need to be able to understand not only the rural or village culture but the aspirations and dreams and the realities that students confront to actualize these aspirations and dreams.

The issues for teachers in general and the intercultural dimensions are twofold: one is what teachers need to know, which has knowledge dimension; and secondly, what teachers are able to do, which has a skills dimension. If teacher education is of high quality then the teachers understanding of knowledge issues and skills is necessarily going to be of a higher order. This is obviously and primarily a role for teacher education institutions.

Those who join the profession ought to bring from their earlier education a sound academic background. This would especially be possible if those who join the teaching profession have an undergraduate degree and that teacher education is a postgraduate qualification whereby teachers can become good professionals through a systematic study of teaching and learning. These studies and especially their intercultural dimensions need to be closely supervised and monitored. Many so called teacher training courses in fact, fail to educate teachers to function effectively as professional teachers in complex school environments. These processes entail not only a command of the subjects taught but also a sound grasp of techniques in teaching these subjects. They also need to have information on research into teaching and an understanding of children's growth and development. In complex European classrooms teachers increasingly have to deal with children would have different learning needs and learning styles. If teachers are sufficiently educated and can also become their own researchers they would be able to deal with these issues systematically.

The status of teacher education institutions, and their structure is critical for the role of teacher education itself. If teacher educators are seen as previous school teachers with no higher order skills and knowledge which includes understandings as well as the educational sciences and their research skills which are not of a higher order, then teacher education institutions and the profession will be perceived as having a low status.

Teacher education should essentially be an integral part of the university system and have good established links with schools in the same way as medical schools have good links with hospitals. This situation would create the possibility of cross-fertilisation of ideas from other knowledge systems, and developments within the educational sciences which are firmly located in school practice. The intercultural dimensions of such teacher education would be also help in the nurturing of the continuing educational provision of education and help to raise the educational standards amongst all children. One of the criticisms of intercultural education in some western countries is that it 'waters down' educational outcomes and process. In other words, equality compromises quality. Here, this article would like to highlight that equality and quality go hand in hand.

Changes within teacher education institutions are necessary because they have customs, procedures and practices which either directly or indirectly discriminate. Such discriminatory practices may not be evident on the surface and can only be eliminated if institutional structures are examined to bring about greater levels of openness to their operationalisation. These discriminatory practices may not only have relevance to intercultural education, but for educational equality, including inter-group and gender equality.

Any policies for intercultural teacher education cannot be effective unless they have support of all staff, and involve measures on (a) student admissions; (b) staff recruitment and promotions; (c) and an initiation of research and curriculum development.

Such changes require an evaluation of their effectiveness, and cannot be of a tokenistic nature. Hence, the implementation of any strategies needs to be properly monitored. While teacher educators can themselves initiate changes these need to be supported by the institutions themselves. This institutional commitment includes the systematic orangisation of staff development, so that teacher educators can update their knowledge, skills and understandings in the field of intercultural education.

There is a need for coordinated action to redress issues of inequality and vulnerabilty in society and only a coordinated effort in all areas of economic and social policy would lead towards greater levels of equality. Targeted action which is well constructed to deal with specific disadvantage is important. However, action in one area, say education, may not be effective if other disadvantages are not alleviated through a long-term strategy and a multi-agency approach. This is therefore, not just a matter of politics but also one of public policy and which has implications for the public domain.

This article has briefly discussed the complexities involved in the way in which education may exacerbate or contribute to vulnerability which can contribute to the rise in intercultural conflicts. Paradoxically, educational systems through general as well as targeted interventions also have the potential to ensure greater levels of equity and help in the resolution of conflicts. The rise of tensions and violence between ethnic groups may partly be embedded in inequalities which vulnerable groups confront in societies in which education systems operate. In as much as education systems reproduce these inequalities they exacerbate and help to perpetuate conflicts. The role of education in minimising the notions of 'othemess' within communities and societies is essential to maintain peace. Its role in ensuring the belongingness of all groups to a society present great challenges to the school. These challenges about educating for inclusivity in a democratic context, which ensures citizenship rights to all cannot be ignored.

Bibliography

Enzensberger, H.M. (1994), *Civil War* (London: Granta Books)

Balibar, E., Wallerstein, I. (1991), *Race, National, Class: Ambiguous Identities* (London: Virago)

Castell, M. (1989), *The Informational City* (Oxford: Blackwell's)

Dunn, J. (1993), *Democracy The Unfinished Journey 508 BC to 1993* (Oxford: OUR).

Chambers, 1. (1994), *Migrancy, Culture, Identity* (London: Routledge).

Jensen, F.N. (1969), *Harvard Education Review*, 39, 1, 1–23.

Eysenck, H.J. (1971), *Race, Intelligence and Education* (London: Temple Smith)

Kamin, L.J. (1977), *The Science and Politics of IQ* (London: Penguin)

Billig, M. (1979), *Psychology, Racism and Fascism* (Searchlight Press, Birmingham) _—"

Herrenstein, R., Murray, C. (1994), The Bell Curve: *Intelligence and Class Structure in American Life* (New York Press).

Gould, S. (1981), *The Mismeasure of Man* (New York: Norton).

Kohin, M. (1995), *The Race Gallery: The Return of Race Science* (London: Jonathan Frredland)

Burnage Report (1986), *Murder in the Playground: The Report of the MacDonald Inquiry into Racism and Racial Violence in Manchester Schools* (Longsight Press).

See Rutter, M., Smith, D. (1995), *Psychosocial Disorders in Young People* (John Wiley & Sons).

Learning in Terror (1988), (London: CRE).

Sagaland Centre for Multicultural Education (1992), (London).

Bookchin, M. (1992), *Urbanisation without Cities: The Rise and Decline of Citizenship* (Montreal: Black Rose Books)

Globalisation and Intercultural Education

Introduction

Globalisation represents an interactive process through which economies, societies and cultures have been integrated at the international level. The intercultural dimensions may be represented by the ways in which languages, cultures and social mores have either become integrated or are excluded from this process. The importance of this topic arises because of the ways in which societal differences and diversities globally can be understood in the context of intercultural education.

The international context: globalisation, diversity and uniformity

The recent people's uprisings in a number of countries in North Africa and the Middle East have demonstrated the global connectivity and the emerging democratic and political imagination of citizens in many of these countries both in territorial and extra-territorial terms. These horizontal revolts have deep causes but as social networks were facilitated by Facebook, YouTube and Twitter.

These acts of connectivity were not nurtured by the national education or school systems. During the period of the authoritarian Egyptian government intercultural relations between Shias and Sunnis and Copts and Muslims were antagonistic but they have improved after the fall of the government in Egypt. While education may not be the primary cause of conflict, perceived injustices linked to identity, faith, ethnicity can tip the balance in favour of peace or conflict. For instance, limited or poor quality provision which leads to unemployment and poverty during a period of 'youth bulge' can act as a forceful recruiting agent for armed conflict; unequal access generates grievances and sense of injustice; school systems can be used to reinforce prejudice and intolerance and used to reinforce political domination. The UNESCO EFA Monitoring Report states that 'the use of education systems to foster hatred and bigotry has contributed to the underlying causes of violence from Rwanda to Sri Lanka.' (UNESCO: GMR Paris: 2011)

It is however, not clear from the recent awakening of the people and the impulses for peaceful revolt in North Africa and the Middle East what are the causal under-pinnings of these events and what role 'informal' citizenship education has played in the development of this intercultural and collective political consciousness and civic action. These revolts at the regional and potentially global levels may represent a new dawn of citizens taking part in new political possibilities which challenge the bru-tal authoritarian and corrupt regimes. They represent the desire for justice, dignity and self-respect after being subjected to decades of subordination by paternalistic regimes of people's democratic aspirations in diverse polities.

There are other complex problems at the international levels to create level play-ing fields between the 'west and the rest' and this Eurocentric perspective has a long pedigree which is indicated by a recent publication (N. Ferguson: 2011). The west is perceived as being part of modernity and the 'the rest' as being tradition bound but there a longue duree perspective dating from ancient times by Samir Amin which provides a powerful voice which counters the Eurocentrism of many scholars (S. Amin : 2011). In this Janus faced context, the west projects itself as being in the fore-front of globalisation and as having universal values and the 'rest' are perceived as being bound by tradition.

There are a range of actions of global hegemonic and neoliberal economic global activity which have led to negating rights of citizens within and outside the boundar-ies of nation states. There are however, international instruments which set standards and are designed to protect the rights of peoples at the universal level.

The Universal Declaration of Human Rights in Article 26.1 provided for the right to education for everyone and is one of the building blocks of human rights more generally. Article 26.2 states that education shall be directed to the full development of human personality and the strengthening of respect for human rights and pro-mote friendship amongst nations, racial and religious groups.

This constitutes a good definition for intercultural education but it remains far from a reality because at least one billion people have largely been bypassed by the positive aspects of globalisation. The right to education from the Universal Declaration is translated into a more precise form in the International Covenant on Social and Cultural Rights and the International Covenant on Civil and Political Rights. In the 1980s and 1990s the human rights agenda broadened with recognition of development rights, environmental rights and more a precise formulation of chil-dren's rights. The UN Convention on the Rights of the Child devotes two articles,

28 and 29 to the rights to education and the aims of education is not just limited to the provision of basic and primary education in poor countries but also quality education to all, which by definition has to be intercultural in both the richer and poorer countries.

The UNESCO document 'Education and Cultural Diversity' stresses that the organisation will encourage issues involving value issues in multilingual and multicultural societies to be included in national Education for All action plans. This focus would make the Dakar Framework for Action more intercultural by including provision for the nomadic, traveller and gypsy populations. In the Americas it ought to include the Inuit, Maya and Quechua peoples. The importance of EFA for industrialised countries in many parts of the world is to ensure that the educational content is appropriate to the increasingly intercultural future of the international context.

An optimistic view is that there are states, including some in Europe, who believe in multilateralism and would like to strengthen democratic legitimacy within international institutions. The attempts by the European Union to embed national sovereignties in multiple layers of rules, norms and regulations are an attempt to 'obviate the violent history of the first half of the 20th century as the result of unbridled exercise of national sovereignty'. As a result of integrative processes intercultural relations in Europe have improved public and social policies including education. The mobility of academics and students through programmes like Erasmus, Socrates and Tempus has led to better intercultural understandings across national borders. In addition to this the decrease in inequality between and within richer and poorer countries can help reduce pressures on constructing a fortress Europe. Within Europe high levels of inequalities between the immigrant and poorer communities have a potential for intercultural conflict and violence. Quality and equality of educational provision can overcome some of the conflicts that can arise.

Some of the oppositional tendencies in the world referred to earlier are mirrored in the way in which intercultural relations and understandings at one level are being enhanced but at another level intercultural conflicts on the basis of racial, religious, linguistic, class and nationality are being exacerbated.

At the global level many of these issues are not only a result of contemporary globalisation but also a result of historical legacies of the empires of the nineteenth century. The failure of international initiatives of the United Nations agencies in bridging gaps in many societies can fragment them, as has recently happened to the Sudan with the democratic secession of Southern Sudan. The gaps between many people remain because even though increased multiculturalism of polities creates possibilities of better intercultural relations, it also increases the prospects of intercultural conflicts.

Issues and concepts

One of the problems arising from the complex range of issues causing intercultural conflicts is that there is very little agreement about the use of terms or a framework of analysis.

In the British context, some academics argue that the term 'multiculturalism' has been racialised. Many anti-racist policies in education, for instance, tended to stress discrimination against those who were immigrant minorities but ignored, for example, the poorer sections of the dominant and majority communities.

The essentialist rhetoric of such policies has led to some communities being designated as 'the other' and furthered the creation of binary oppositions (e.g. the majority/ minority; immigrant/citizen; white/black; the belongers/the non-belongers). These oppositional definitions as well as the hierarchical positioning of groups within societies have detracted from developing inclusive institutions based on intercultural policies.

The British state colluded with the racialisation of multiculturalism because it was viewed as a way of ensuring that social diversity was seen as merely a result of post-World War II migration, particularly for people who were coming from the 'new' Commonwealth. Statements, made in the 'School Curriculum' document by the Department of Education and Science in 1965, that 'our society has become multicultural', could only be explained as a way of camouflaging the more complex societal diversities. If one uses the taxonomy of linguistic, religious, social class and territorial indices of diversity then British society has historically been multicultural. The situation is now different because after the devolution of power to Scotland and Wales, through democratic means, we can no longer throw a cloak of monoculturalism or monolingualism over the British state.

Intercultural educational perspectives till recently have been informed by a century old history of international and local perspectives. Within this diachronic dimension, the dominant cultures of Britain and other European states are themselves the products of centuries of past and present interactions between peoples, their cultures and the state. The colonial empires of the European states are an important part of these interactions. Thus, contemporary patterns of social and cultural inequality are underpinned by the historical legacies of imperialism and colonialism.

Deficit and disadvantage models have continued to inform intercultural educational measures. In Britain this meant that those from social classes 4 and 5, using the Registrar-General's classification were considered 'culturally deprived' or 'culturally disadvantaged'. The conservatives in this debate have continued to postulate inferiority based on genetic factors. The liberals have tended to stress that the disadvantaged were the result of past discrimination on sex, race or class group. The IQ debate on both sides of the Atlantic has further continued to generate controversy.

Future for Intercultural Studies

Concepts and analyses need to be developed which draw upon the historical and contemporary aspects of diversity and which are relevant in developing an inclusive curriculum, and integrate intercultural citizenship education. Within complex socially diverse societies where technological changes may be leading to high levels of unemployment, greater stress needs to be placed on democratic institutions. The need to deepen democracy entails a critical appraisal of issues of societal concern and the development of community participation as well as curricular and pedagogic changes to enhance such collaboration.

Also, it is not only what children are taught and what they learn but also their actual experiences at school, which contribute to their understanding of their rights and responsibilities as future citizens. So, a democratic school ethos is important and this needs to be experienced through active citizenship and engagement in the context of the wider community. The role of youth work, further and other formal and non-formal life-long learning are all important. An African saying states that 'it takes the whole village to educate a child', and this is truer today in the period of increased globalisation.

Barriers to equity

We face a dilemma because the old solidarities based on social class as antecedents of class divided society, whilst providing a clear role for different groups in society created the divisions between classes that have been the subject of confrontations over the last 150 years. Now that there is no preordained class basis to solidarity, the younger generation is faced with much clearer patterns of polarisation by being divided into winners and losers without any class reference. This poses a new challenge for intercultural education because of the exclusivity of identities. Of course the reverse is also true if the winners refuse to acknowledge any debt to society especially as groups from different backgrounds do not share solidarities or a set of resemblances. Intercultural education, therefore, has a complex role of addressing the sense of exclusions and loss amongst all young people. The previous policies, which privileged one or the other group, will prove to be counterproductive by exacerbating differences and reducing features of commonality amongst different groups. This therefore presents a challenge of rethinking of policies like affirmative action so that they do not exacerbate differences and have divisive implications but develop policies that include the disadvantaged from all communities.

If some groups are excluded from or marginalised within the education system and schools due to lack of social cohesion, should the state stay neutral or should it intervene? In other words should the state be fair or impartial? Rawls using the difference principle argues that the better off should not have special advantages than the worst off. So, to accord equity, the state is 'fair' but not impartial. In a democratic state, citizens should have access to education and knowledge in order to equalise their life chances. If the state remains impartial it cannot create level playing fields in educational terms. It can only do so by intervening.

Centric knowledge

At an even broader level these issues raise problems of centric knowledge, which according to the Concise Oxford Dictionary (1990) is defined as 'having a (specified) centre'. This is especially the case because a curriculum centred on knowledge of dominant groups does not serve the needs of socially diverse polities. A non-centric curriculum is needed in most civilizational, national regional and local contexts in the new era of globalisation.

One of the problems in the implementation of intercultural education is that the languages, histories and cultures of subordinated groups in Europe are not seen as having equal value with those of dominant European nationalities. Such an entitlement to a non-centric or inclusive curriculum is perhaps one of the greatest challenges to actualising the development of an intercultural education.

This UNESCO agenda should enable countries in Africa, Asia and the Americas to address issues of societal diversity through intercultural education policies. To maintain safety and security within their diverse polities, states in these continents need to develop curricula that avoid centrisms of their own. Devising the necessary basis of knowledge in a national and civilisational context presents curriculum planners with a difficult but essential challenge. Shared knowledge and habitus can assist in the process of the development of a common value system in the public domain.

A non-centric curriculum would enable teachers, students and other learners to develop the inclusive and shared value systems which are necessary for the development of democratic societies. As Amartya Sen states the attempts to choke off participatory freedom on the grounds of religious fundamentalism or so-called 'Asian values' misses the issue of legitimacy of peoples participation in what they want.

One aspect of the curriculum, which illustrates the issue of knowledge centrism, is the teaching of history curriculum. The teaching of history from a non-militaristic and triumphalist perspective needs to be developed at a much wider level internationally. Such curricular developments should not only be part of mainstream education, but also build on the basic education and the acquisition of languages and literacies. Such an integrated system would enhance the intercultural competencies of active African, American, and Asian citizenship within multicultural democracies. Subjects like history and social sciences particularly need to be appraised for their relevance to the contemporary needs of cosmopolitan societies.

This is especially the case because 130 to 145 million people, at least, live outside their countries of origin. These figures would be higher if undocumented migrants were included. Over 21 million refugees live in other developing countries. Hence, the development of an inclusive curriculum is necessary for the maintenance of stable and democratic processes of national integration, modernisation and development. Such issues ought therefore to include relevant consideration of participatory pedagogies. In marginalised communities learning and teaching should be progressive and not constrained by a traditional African, Asian and American-centric curriculum, which tends to inhibit questioning. This in turn allows Euro-centrism in knowledge to prevail at the global level.

To install the 'voice' of the disenfranchised in the curriculum will require a great deal of delicacy, diplomacy, persistence and sophistication, particularly if the desired changes are not to be relegated to the margins of academic life. Reactive, rhetorical and rebellious responses in curricular terms are not only inadequate but also counterproductive. While action is needed across all European, American, African and Asian societies, those in the poorer parts of these continents have greater levels of difficulties, and may require support from international agencies. Hence, the more affluent and experienced educational agencies like the European Commission and UNESCO, and its regional centres, can also be helpful in lending them non-directive support for educational change and development.

Secularism and religious Armageddon

The tensions between secular and religious ideologies in a globalising world perhaps raise the gravest warning to multicultural and multi-faith polities and need to be addressed by educators and curriculum planners in a non-nationalistic and creative manner. While religion and personal beliefs may belong to the private domain there are issues from religious systems and knowledge, which can impinge on the national and global minds and the development of critical and democratic citizens of the future. It is a matter of fundamental importance that the role of religion in multi-faith, constitutional and democratic states is clearly defined to avoid being led to fundamentalist and dogmatic notions of 'truth' fuelled by faith.

The importance of Gandhi and his protégé Nehru is that they had a genuine intercultural understanding of western and Indian civilisations. They personified a creativity and determination which is currently lacking in many political and educational leaders. The ex-President of Tanzania Mwalimu (teacher) Nyerere was usually simply called teacher and who through his policies unified the multicultural Tanzanian society. In educational terms he promoted the successful use of the non-dominative language Kiswahili as a language of instruction and has helped develop a sense shared national identity. There is an urgent need to enchant the disenchanted from the local to the global level with inclusive, democratic and active citizenship engagements.

In Nigeria Wole Soyinka regrets the way in which the proselytising religions are eroding local traditions and faiths like the Orisa, but also disrupting education within schools and universities. In the West African context, the implementation of intercultural policies and practices may be one way of avoiding religious strife in educational institutions. In many multicultural and multifaith communities the school and the classroom can act as important peace building institutions.

The role of media and intercultural relations

The media have an important role to play in enhancing intercultural relations because of their power to educate. During the current period of globalisation the media have been constrained by market forces as far as programming is concerned. For many people in the world the media may be a more influential source of information than the classroom As stated earlier in North Africa and the Middle East the people's power has largely been a result of the social use of the media horizontally across communities.

The mainstream media has tended to focus on the exotic, travel and wildlife programmes instead of programming about development, poverty, intercultural issues, politics, history, economics or the environment. These issues receive perfunctory treatment as part of news and current affairs programmes or else they are dealt with from Western-centric, orientalised perspectives. While clearly not unknown in the context of Europe and the US, 'disasters' are typically seen as African, Asian and South American events. Even the earthquake and Tsunami (a Japanese word) which devastated much of Japan in early 2011 were seen to occur in a land far away.

Televisual audiences are largely committed to entertainment and do not watch documentary programmes, which either lecture or hector them. Viewers prefer a story, a good narrative and strong characters. At least two sets of actions may be necessitated. Firstly, the media and communication industries need to adopt a strategic and integrated approach, which are discourse and content strengthened. On issues of intercultural understandings, the educators at all levels have a major role to play in not only using the media but also in educating viewers who are critical to distinguish between hype, rhetoric and productive or progressive discourse. In Britain the Teachers Television digital channel has played an important role in connecting good teaching practices at the classroom and school level as well as involving parents in the process of teaching and learning.

The Role of Intercultural Teacher Education

Teacher education institutions have a major role to play in enhancing intercultural education because as multipliers the teachers educated by them affect the lives of many generations of those they teach.

In many countries around the world teacher educators need to revisit the Carnegie Foundations' Report of 1986, which recommended making the teaching profession a high status profession and on a par with other professions. Most higher education institutions both educate and train doctors, architects and lawyers but only train teachers. This is an important issue because there is a difference between 'training' and 'education'

In order to get the best educated and professionally qualified teachers, their education should be undertaken at universities or institutions with comparable standards. Teachers therefore, as autonomous professionals should join a teacher education institution after an undergraduate degree, and have a professional education similar to those in other professions. Of course the circumstances will vary in different countries.

A high level of professionally and rigorously educated teachers who have a post-graduate accredited qualification is essential to raise the competences of the teaching profession. As a part of this accreditation there is a need for intercultural dimensions of courses to be built into the teacher education process. This in itself raises some complex issues. During this period of globalisation students from minority communities who have done well at university tend to join other professions and not the teaching profession. Yet to make intercultural teacher education effective both teacher education institutions and schools need to have a diverse student body and teaching members of staff. In intercultural terms teacher skills ought to include expertise in interpersonal relations, the conduct of conversations, moderation of difficult discussions, dealing with conflicts and working with parents. Teachers confront the most complex task of tackling student racism and autonomous peer cultures. The need for communicative skills can only be met if teachers have the necessary experience and skills and understandings which cut across student-teacher and school-community divides.

Teachers can acquire knowledge, skills and understandings to deal with racism during their initial teacher education, which needs to be further refined on a continuing basis as part of their professional development. The complexity of the processes, of racism and class-based exclusions as well as the lethal mixture of these with religious divides demands a high level of skills and professionalism. It also demands institutional policies and support within schools. Teacher education institutions have a fundamental role to play in unpicking these complex issues and enabling all teachers to deal with them competently.

Communities of development and hope

One of the main reasons for developing an inclusive democratic framework is the fact that 10,000 distinct societies live in 200 states and may be denied equity and protection. The International Commission on Education for the 21st Century set up by UNESCO placed the issue of learning to live together not only as one of the four pillars of education for the future but as the greatest challenge facing education.

However, unless there are concerted efforts to develop democratic engagements and build 'communities of development and hope' intercultural conflicts are bound to increase. The creation of active citizens in poorer communities can only take place if there are deeper intercultural engagements both within and outside educational institutions.

Democratic and shared political cultures go hand in hand with greater levels of legitimate economic activities for all communities. Income inequalities are associated with increases in education and social inequality. From amongst the OECD countries Britain has the largest income gaps and the highest proportion (19.4%) of young people aged 16–19 who are neither attending school or employed. Many of these young people are not only functionally illiterate and manifest antisocial behaviour but are also a threat to the security and lives of others. The thwarted ambitions of these young people form the basis of grave intercultural conflicts. A massive effort is necessary to create the preconditions for safer and securer communities in most other countries of the world. These efforts which are locally rooted in learning communities need to develop intercultural public values which reach outwards towards the global community.

Further Readings

Amin, S. (2011) *Global History: A View from the South*. London.: Pambazuka Press

Amin, S. (2011) *Ending the Crises of Capitalism or Ending Capitalism*. London: Pambazuka Press

Ferguson, N. (2011) Civilization: The West and the Rest. London: Allen Lane.

Gundara, J. (2000) *Interculturalism, Education and Inclusion*. London: Paul Chapman Publishing Ltd.

UNESCO *Guidelines on Intercultural Education*. Paris: UNESCO, Education Sector.

UNESCO: (2011) *The Hidden Crisis: Armed Conflict and Education*. EFA Global Monitoring Report. Paris: UNESCO

Intercultural and International Understandings:

Non-Centric Knowledge and Curriculum in Asia

As the President of the International Association of Intercultural Education I am very honoured to be invited to deliver this Keynote address at the Opening Session of the 2013 KAME International Conference alongside Professor Duck Ho, President of Hanyung University and Professor Yun Kyung, President of the Korean Association of Multicultural Education. Professor Kyung and I last met in London when we signed a Memorandum of Understanding between KAME and IAIE. I really look forward to our joint collaboration based on this MOU as well as NAME, whose President Professor Kevin Kumashiro, with whom IAIE has also signed a Memorandum of Understanding in Vera Cruz, Mexico. I was not able to attend the Conference and the MOU was signed by Professor Gunther Dietz on the behalf of the IAIE and Professor Christine Sleeter on behalf of NAME. The are both participating at this Conference and I hope that KAME, NAME and the IAIE will be able to establish a more concerted way of developing work in this field at the international level, so that we can hope to have an impact on education systems to deal with issues of difference, diversity and equity more seriously, especially since currently many education systems still continue to construe difference and multiculturalism as deficit. Professor Banks can provide us all with invaluable advice to make this field more vibrant in the 21st century.

1. Education for International Dialogue and Understandings.

I am previleged to be participating in this august Conference being organised by KAME on the very important theme of 'Reconstructing Education, Culture and Identity in a Global Age.' I feel very humbled to be delivering this Keynote paper on intercultural and international education which examines the issue of multiculturalism and social diversity in Asian societies in the early decades of the Global Age of the 21st Century, since there are so many experts in this field at this Conference. Broadly based public and social policies enacted by governments provide the framework within which educational policies are located. However, with increased globalisation it is critical that these policies should be considered at international and regional levels to enhance intercultural and international dialogue and understandings.

I was very pleased to be invited by the Korean UNESCO National Commission to carry out a feasibility study for the setting up of the Asia-Pacific Centre of Education for International Understanding (APCEIU), with Dr. Swee Toh, which was inaugurated in August 2000 and has been functioning as a Centre at Ichon. This decision of the Korean National Commission for UNESCO was very farsighted since the Republic of South Korea is part of the Asia-Pacific region and has 63% of the world's population, many mega-cities and some of the oldest cultural and faith systems in the world. I thought that this decision was far sighted because of the geopolitical and strategic reasons which are of critical importance for the Republic; as are issues of peace, stability and amity with regional powers like China and Japan.

These issue becomes important at the present time since Pyongyang has been rattling sabres in the last few months. (IMAGE 2; CARTOON; BY: JENNINGS. The Guardian cartoon, Jennings, 8-4-2013) These issues are not only of regional importance for the Republic of South Korea, Japan and China but also have an international dimensions and calls by the U.N. Secretary General Ban Ki-moon for avoiding any 'small incident' which could lead to an 'uncontrollable situation.' (The Guardian, London, 11-4-2013). The Secretary of State John Kerry's visits to China, Japan and South Korea representing the U.S. as a super power with troops in the region stated that 'we have lowered our rhetoric significantly' (The Guardian, 13-4-2013) as well as calls for restraint and a united front against North Korea's nuclear manoeuvres by the G8 Meeting in London on 11th April 2013 (The Guardian, 12-4-2013) demonstrates the critical nature of the crises at the regional and international levels..

President Park Guen-hye needs to develop confidence building steps, 'such as resumption of aid and cross-border dialogue' (Justin McCuerry, The Guardian, London: 8-4-2013) to turn her desire for 'Trustpolitik' into a genuinely binding bilateral relationship which is built on trust. The DMZ plays a dividing role between the North and South Korea, but straddling the demarcation line in Panmunjom are several blue huts, where officials from both sides have historically held talks aimed at building the foundations for rapprochement. These should perhaps not be seen as cold war relics but a setting for establishing genuine dialogue and understandings which will enhance trust, and this requires both sides to shed nationalistic rhetoric.

APCEIU and KAME both have a highly skilled and diplomatic role in engaging with Chinese and Japanese academics, scholars and educators to establish skills, knowledge and understandings which can feed into this political process to build on structures of regional safety and security. These are complex issues because there are many layers to the historical as well as current geopolitical issues. So, for instance, at the underlying level the integrity of the Korean border may not be the real bone of contention during the current crises between North and South Korea. (IMAGE 3; SENKAKU ISLANDS0 The real issues are perhaps more related to the fossil resources which lie under the sea half way between China and Japan and the islands which are referred to as Senkaku by the Japanese and Diaoyu by the Chinese. Timothy Mo suggests that this oil resource is a long term energy security for China and Japan, and the crisis is being played out by using the integrity of the Korean border. (Timothy Mo, The Guardian, p, 36, The Guardian, 11-4-2013)

2. Intercultural Dialogue and Education.

The North East Asia region obviously has regional responsibilities for peace and security as mentioned above. However, this region also has Asia wide responsibilities to enhance international and intercultural dialogue and understandings at national and regional levels. The two organisations have organisational competences to enhance the educational aspects of this work. There are huge divides between the richer, urban and more developed N.E. Asia Region and the largely poorer, more rural and underdeveloped S. E. Asian region. The Republic of Korea is a global power because of the new technologies which it is pioneering and as an industrially developed society. Zygmunt Bauman suggeasrs that in South Korea most of the 'social life' is electronically mediated, or even turned into an electronic life or cyberlife, which is conducted in the company of a computer, iPod or mobile (Bauman: 2007). At the other extreme on the Asian continent are some of the poorest and hugely exploited peoples. Despite the fact that Asian nation states are no longer colonised, have modern constitutions and are signatories to various instruments of Human and citizenship rights, these are not always observed in many cases. (W. Kymlicka and B. He: 2005)

As I said at the Inauguration Symposium of APCEIU on 26th August 2000: '... in the twenty first century many of the gains of the modern state in the nineteenth century are being reversed; the abolition of slavery and serfdom, the establishment of democracies and enfranchisement of people are being replaced with 'fortress states' and ethicised mentalities, turning civilised and educated polities in Hobbesian jungles.' (Gundara: 2000)

Institutions like APCEIU and KAME can help in the process of creating international and intercultural understandings, in reducing narrow nationalism in the two regions across the Asian continent; explore possibilities of multidimensional action to maintain peace and stability; help in educational processes to resolve conflicts, enhance educational equalities, reduce exclusions from education, and reduce environmental degradation and the depletion of natural resources, all of which tend to exacerbate inter-ethnic conflicts.

Also many immigrants, asylum seekers and refugees from south and south East Asia have moved to Korea and Japan and enhanced the multiculturalism which would require intercultural educational measures. These include undocumented labour as well as those who manage to escape from the north. There are also socially the phenomena of Korean and Asian marriages (Koasian) which form part of new identities within the polity. Hence, the relevance of international understanding and intercultural education exists at both international and national level within Korea and Japan.

The experiences of many Asian countries indicate that culture has been a force for coexistence and for conflict. It has acted as a bridge making intercultural understandings possible as well as embodying a potential for dissonance. In many polities the majority cultures have tended to control resources in areas where minority communities reside and isolate them from social development of their communities and the markers of identity and cultural differences within Asian nation states.

In south-east Asian contexts there are significant internal cleavages based on ethnicity, race and religion. With the collapse of the ideas of 'modernisation' and increasing neoliberal globalisation stronger communal identities have emerged. This is especially the case where the revolution of expectations in neoliberal economies cannot be met and a there is a subsequent rise of ethno-nationalisms. There are numerous fault lines on ethnic and religious basis across the Asian continent and a few examples of this are: the Han versus the minority nationalities in China; Rakhine Buddhists and Rohingya Muslims in Burma: Hindus and Muslims in India; Sinhalese and Tamils in Sri Lanka; and Shias and Sunnis in Pakistan. In many of these and states like Laos, Thailand the governments purposively 'misrecognise' issues to deal with minorities and classify many of the smaller 'indigenous' people as being 'backward', and as threats to security. In Japan there is hardly any recognition of the issues of multiculturalism, especially as they relate to historical minorities like the Ainu, Burakumins, Okinawans and the Koreans. These different situations and policies in different nation states necessitate intercultural policy measures at local, national and regional levels.

In Fiji within the Pacific Ocean region a very different situation exists, since the government is implementing multiculturalism by force to create a future state without racism and to eradicate the narrow identities of the diverse groups in Fiji. (MRG International: 2013) This position however, detracts from the development of trust through dialogue amongst local groups and communities, as well as through educational measures which include civic and community and life long learning measures.

Conversely, intercultural understandings and coexistence amongst peoples in East Asia have relied tradionally for instance on Confucianism. In political terms and in both regions there are constitutional safeguards through forms of governance which include federalism; forms of autonomy; self-governance and consociationalism. In many Asian societies local communities have developed 'vernacular communitarianism' to deal with issues of multicultural;ism at the local level. Yet, since this entails harmony, deference and patrernalism it has been appropriated by authoritarian Asian political leaders and as 'state communitarianism' is used to justify suppression of political dissent and labelled as 'Asianvalues.' (See, Chua Beng Huat, in W. Kymlicka and B. He (2005) pp. 170–195)

The challenges of societal diversity cannot be dealt with by imposing dominant Asian or Eurocentric or nationalistic norms using education systems. This is especially true of the issues of knowledge within Asian societies which need to develop inclusive knowledge systems and avoid the dangers of various forms of 'centrisms' in the curriculum because these can be inimical to the maintenance of safety, peace and security in diverse polities. A regional and universal basis of knowledge which are recontextualised in Asian societies presents curriculum planners in education systems with a difficult but essential challenge.

A non-centric curriculum can enable educators and learners to develop inclusive and shared value systems which are important for democratic Asian societies like the Republic of South Korea. Particular attention needs to be given to the teaching of history from a non-triumphalist perspective so that the past is used to develop greater levels of mutualities amongst the citizens of the states especially in the Asia-Pacific region. However, such curricular developments need to be part of mainstream education but ought to build on basic education and acquisition of languages and literacies. Some of the initiatives might require the development of school-community links and measures to minimise conflicts in socially diverse schools; educational strategies to improve the educational attainment of children from immigrant families as well as children, especially from the poorer sections of the majority community. This can be facilitated through developing bilingual and multilingual strategies as well as innovative development of the curriculum.

Intercultural relations in the N. E. Region and their positive and negative aspects might illustrate the complexity for the state in articulating national policies which reflect the multicultural nature of their societies. Development of appropriate responses would necessitate a state-craft which ensures that all citizens, indigenous minorities, immigrants and refugees have legal rights and responsibilities. Educational measures in wealthier as well as poorer states need to be devised and implemented to reduce educational inequalities.

National policies should ensure that democratic solutions in complex societies are based on inclusive non-violent value systems and on shared and common understandings in the public domain. National policies to bridge ethnic, religious, linguistic and racial cleavages can obviate the rise of extreme forms of xenophobia. It is partly the failure of state-craft that is responsible for the rise in communalism, xenophobia and racism because such phenomena are not natural to groups in society, and preventative policies are preferable to reactive strategies. The stress on jus sanguinis (based on blood) and jus soli (on soil) notions of citizenship in societies (J. Kristeva: 1991) and the privileging of the ties of blood and soil undermine not only the civic concept of national societies but exacerbate tensions in local areas, particularly in the way in which local territories become contestable spaces because the non-belongingness of certain groups is emphasised. Part of the initiatives to avoid the binary opposition of belongs/non-belongers is to avoid the construction of new communities as embodying 'deficits' and being portrayed as 'the others' who cannot belong.

Notions of public safety and policies to defend human rights and the plural social environments in societies are of fundamental importance to the civil state (etat de droit). This can help the development of a civil society with a strong civic culture and encourage active citizenship amongst all young people. The school as an educational institution has a formative role in developing a constitutional and peace oriented and inclusive ethos amongst all young people. These can help to ensure that all children in a state: learn together, play together, grow together and then stand together through shared public and societal values. Yet many current Asian education systems in all regions continue to stratify groups rather than develop framework citizenship, human rights, a civic culture of inclusiveness and similarity at public level. Groups and communities can retain their different identities at personal levels and private domains of their lives.

3. Neoliberal Economic Globalisation

The transnationalisation of the neoliberal economic forces raises deep questions of governance and regulatory processes. It is necessary to ensure that the polity retain enough control over its political economy to obviate inequity: breakdown of communities, high levels of unemployment and the development of siege mentalities and communities; a disaffected, 'ethnicised' and disenfranchised underclass. Even the well managed Korean economy where dangers of poor deregulation were perceived and planned against, the government was pressurised by the IMF to liberalise the economy faster to suit investments by Wall Streeters. (J. Stiglitz: 2002; 102–4) Such authoritarian measures led to 'privations and hardships suffered by the working classes in countries like Japan, South Korea, Taiwan and Hong Kong...' although they were benign 'compared to wholesale social terror unleashed on populations of the Soviet Union and China.' (F. Fukuyama: 1992: 107, 123) .

As Castells states the 'globalisation of power flows and the tribalisation of local communities' becomes increasingly juxtaposed (M. Castells: 1989). At national levels the doctrinal hegemony of the market has fragmented groups and increased tensions in mixed communities. Refugees and asylum seekers created by political and economic devastations are caught in "Catch 22" situations both in the countries of origin and in the receiving countries. Neither provides a safe haven, yet paradoxically borders remain permeable (L. Bash and J. Gundara: 2012).

In a climate of scarce resources the refugees become the new victims of exclusion and violence at the lower strata of local life. The rapid depletion of resources in Asia; environmental damage and the lack of public health measures can wreak havoc and lead to deteriorating ethnic relations. The impact of the depletion of primeval forests and forest fires in South East Asian countries has hitherto marginalised self sufficient communities and ethnic groups. Perhaps even more vulnerable are the older nomadic and traditional communities, who survive in the forests and increasingly in the twilight zones of local areas and Asian conurbations.

In some of the South and South East Asian countries the increased neoliberalisation of economies have weakened the national governments. Consequently, the increasingly impoverished majority populations tend to scapegoat and oppress the weakest and the 'others'. There are subordinated and marginalised people in this region who are viewed by anthropologists and policy-makers as archaic vestiges from another historical time. Yet, many of these communities have escaped from situations of subordination for over a few millennia to avoid slavery, conscription, taxes, corvee labour, epidemics, religious dissent and warfare. (J. C. Scott; 2010) In short many of the nation states were formed by appropriation of these smaller nationalities, their lands and other resources. The very bleak future of these hostile communities residing in impenetrable forests are likely to vanish as forests are cut down and the insurgencies of groups are ended. (T. Myint-U: 2011)

Many of these people have a history, if there is one, of struggling against the state and have used many ways of keeping, the state at arm's length and survived through subsistence agriculture to maximise their physical mobility. The settled states describe such groups as being 'uncivilised' and 'barbarians'. Yet, these people see themselves as avoiding harm, servitude, and disease which civilisation has to offer. Such communities are therefore creatively fabricating identities as a way of evading the state. However, as more and more of the globe is politically subjugated by nation state systems these groups are on the verge of being made extinct (IAMGE 4; MAP OF SOUTH EAST ASIA. ;Scott.p. 17). At the present time in south-east Asia there are at least 100 million people who can be referred to as minorities, such as the Akha, Chin, Hmong, Kachin, Khmu, Lahu, Miao, Wa and Yao who occupy an area of 2.5 million square kilometres stretching from China to north-east India, living in the uplands of countries like Burma, Thailand, Laos, Cambodia and Vietnam.

There is an urgent necessity of developing intercultural understandings at the political levels between these diverse peoples and the nation states. The above Asian nation states like those on other continents remain oppressive and aggressive and have attacked the zones of refuge these communities have created in extra-state space with traditions of egalitarianism and autonomy to avoid tyranny and permanent hierarchy. In light of this we might need to consider Fernand Braudel's assertion about these mountain people that their history is to have none, to remain always on the fringes of the great wave of civilisation. (J. Scott: p. 329) One might recast this argument radically and say that they have multiple histories which they can deploy singly or in combination depending on circumstances and since they travel light their history travels light with them.

Scott argues that in South East Asia the peoples on the plains expand outwards and require more land for paddy, thus pushing the minorities living in the foothills deeper into the hills and forests. These groups are therefore not pre-literate but post-literate since literacy is given up deliberately to disengage from certain kinds of state forms. What can academics and activists working in the fields of interculturality/multiculturality, and international agencies do to contribute to the seemingly intractable problems presented by these extremely marginalised 'voiceless' minority communities on the Asian continent? International and intercultural issues during neoliberal economic globalisation require an enormous amount of long term and creative commitment to de-limit the damage being inflicted to at least 100 million people.

4.i Education, Training and Public Values

Many of the South East Asian nation states have inherited state structures from the colonial period and need to be re-appraised by democratising them and establishing measures of equalising the huge socio-economic disparities. However, the globalising neoliberal economic forces have weakened these structures further and the systems are geared towards meeting the needs of the market.

In the field of education the economic forces are driving institutions to tailor major activities towards training personnel for the market. The error that is being made is that education is being conflated with issues about training and both these concepts are used interchangeably and synonymously. Educators should reflect on this because training specifically targets the job market and incorporates a significant component of the acquisition of skills which have direct application to the field of work. The role and function of education is different since economic systems are only one aspect of social systems; and the applied economic and work dimensions are subsidiary to the process of education in society writ large.

Education, knowledge and value creation with a societal focus on 'humanitas' and inculcation civic virtues have an intellectual dimension. Thease values and virtues can lead to civic engagement and active citizenship, which can help the younger generation to lead fuller lives, because the intellectual and educational values using the ancient concepts of 'paidea' and 'bildung' have deep goals and values. It is not surprising that many young people are disenchanted with schooling which relegates them to replicated and routine roles and jobs. There is therefore a need to examine the Asian versions as well as intercultural versions of these Greek and German ideas to 're-enchant' and 're-invent' a humanistic paidea as Andreas Kazamias and Martha Nussbaum have suggested. (Kazamias: 2009; M. Nussbaum: 1997)

In traditional Korean society the 'Seonbi' as a public philosopher played an important role of remaining critical of those who governed. Seonbi (IMAGE 5;PORTRAIT OF SEONBI0, who lived from 1482 to 1519, was a virtuous Neo-Confucian scholar from the Joseon period of Korean history and was forced to drink poison. He played a role similar to that of the critical role that Socrates (IMAGE 6; DAVID'S PAINTING OF SOCRAETES DEATH; DRINKING HEMLOCK) played and died by drinking hemlock. This cup of hemlock has an historical intercultural legacy for those who maintain a critical stance under unjust regimes. Seonbi in Korea and Socrates in Ancient Greek society provide us was intercultural and comparative examples of re-inventing the critical role of scholars as autonomous individuals in influencing public policy. There is very little trust or understanding of the values of virtue and ethics which traditional knowledge systems from Asian and Greek contexts can provide to contemporary public institutions.

4.ii. Asian States: Equity and Democratic Structures

The basic issue of political representation and active participation in national and local politics is to ensure that rights and responsibilities and civic values in democratic society are indispensable and that all voices are heard. The development of a federal system after independence in India led to the linguistic nationalities acquiring a voice in the governance of their states in a democratic manner. There is also an issue of how to devise integrative public policies. For instance, to provide access to social and economic institutions, should the underlying policy be based on social class or on the presumed "specific" identity of excluded groups to avoid them being labelled as special beneficiaries? Policies to bring about equity in education ought not to privilege one group against another, and yet no optimum ways of equalising equity within the education systems have yet been developed. This necessitates a critical reappraisal of affirmative action or positive discrimination measures. (D. Gupta: 2009).

In a secular nation like India the designation of the status of groups being constructed as permanent minorities especially those that are not disadvantaged like the upper caste Brahmins, wealthy Sikhs and Parsees can become counterproductive. This becomes a problem if communalist and elitist opportunists misuse their status; while those who need the resources the most continue to remain excluded and marginalised. Likewise, educational policies of positive discrimination directed towards lower castes, tribal and other small indigenous groups have to be complex and sensitive and not stereotype these communities as being special beneficiaries or to position them in a situation of permanent and structural marginalisation.

5. Eurocentrism and Knowledge

This section of the keynote address deals with the issue of how the so-called 'First World Peoples' were turned into 'Fourth World Peoples.' The legacies of the dominant/subordinate relations are based on the deeply entrenched legacies of the dominant groups using brutal power to give legitimacy of their control of the subordinated groups. These oppressions are based on notions of 'civilising the natives' and need to be rejected. (Wallerstein: 2006). The Spaniard thinker Sepulveda justified the right to intervene in the Amerindian societies because of their barbarity. Las Casas, on the other hand, purported that evil existed everywhere and that therefore there was no theological justification for interference. However, Las Casas lost the debate and the legacy of the intervention in other societies after the 16th century has continued for five centuries. Oppression and subordination through colonisation has barbarised both the brutalisers and the brutalised.

The colonisation of the world especially after 1492 led to the Europeanisation of the globe and de-universalisation of knowledge. Eric Wolf (Wolf: 1983) in this book challenged the notion of many anthropologists that the colonised societies were static entities. He explained that in the course of the global expansion of capitalism those who were considered as 'peoples without history' were in fact part of the European expansion from 1400–1800, and part of the process of interconnectedness between societies. The European colonisation also has a more ancient pedigree in terms of the way in which European historiography during the 19th century constructed the knowledge about the non-European 'Other.'

The issue of knowledge and curriculum design are critical to the way in which a state constructs itself. Inclusions and exclusions of knowledge have implications for ethnic conflict or peace and stability in a state. The assumption being made here is that a 'centric' curriculum is inimical to the strengthening of Asian civilisations at the global level. It can in fact, weaken the nation states by privileging dominant discourses, especially since westernisation and Eurocentric knowledge continue to assume greater levels of ascendency.

Asian education systems confront a double challenge. On the one hand there is the European domination of knowledge and on the other there is the problem of modernisation, development and national integration and a challenge to develop a curriculum relevant to the implementation of these policies (J. M. Blaut 1993) and A. G. Frank: 1998). In terms of Eurocentrism, these hegemonic understandings are informed by the colonialism and imperialism of Europe. As Edward Said (1993) writes:

> Without significant exception the universalising discourses of modern Europe and the United States assume the silence, willing or otherwise, of the non-European world. There is incorporation; there is inclusion; there is direct rule; there is coercion. But there is only infrequently an acknowledgement that the colonised people should be heard from, their ideas known.

The interpenetration of cultures and civilisations has universal impact and needs to be analysed at the broadest possible level. Yet, discourses from the colonised peripheries and the subordinated nationalities are still treated as being marginal even in the post-colonial contemporary Asian contexts. Furthermore, dominant nationalities in Asia rather than using Asian and universal democratic means to devise a national curriculum impose the knowledge inherited during colonialism from Europe.

Martin Bernal indicated how in the 18c and 19c Europeans (IMAGE 7; PARTHIAN WORLD; MAP; M. Bernal: 1987) developed a historiography which denied the earlier understanding that the Greeks in the Classical and Hellenistic periods had learnt as a result of colonisation and interaction between the Egyptians, Phoenicians and Greeks. Part of the reason for this new historiography has been that with the rise of racism and anti-Semitism in Europe, the European Romantics and racists wanted to distance Greece from the Egyptians and the Phoenicians and construct it as the pure childhood of Europe. It was unacceptable from their perspective that the Europeans would have developed any learning and understandings from the Africans or the Semites.

The notion of a northern European culture separated from the world south of the Mediterranean is largely a mythical construction. The contributions to knowledge in the ancient period from this immediate region include Mesopotamian astronomy, the Egyptian calendar and Greek mathematics, enriched by the Arabs. As Samir Amin (1989) states:

> The opposition Greece the West/Egypt, Mesopotamia, Persia the East is itself a later artificial construct of Eurocentrism. For the boundary in the region separates the backward North African and European West from the advanced East; and the geographic unities constituting Europe, Africa and Asia have no importance on the level of the history of civilisation, even if Eurocentrism in its reading of the past is projected onto the past the modern North-South line of demarcation passing through the Mediterranean.

The debate about how and where 'civilisation' arose is an interesting one for educationalists and students, but it is only a part of a wider concern with the intellectual straightjacket that Eurocentric and other centric education systems can impose. In this sense it is always necessary to consider ways in which the curriculum, both formal and informal, can be modified or changed. As long as history is studied from the perspective of one or another narrowly nationalist claim to truth, rather than from one or another paradigm of historiography, education will remain trapped in the tramlines of nationalist tautology. And within this question of communalism, racism, xenophobia and ethnicisms will have propagandistic but not educative value. In the teaching and devising of the curriculum educationalists should therefore consider several alternative definitions of knowledge. These alternative definitions ought to include considerations which are democratic and involve consideration of social justice and equality in education. This can be done to enhance the quality of education for all and not lower standards as is normally suggested by elitists .

6. Non-Centric Civilisational basis for knowledge

Developing a non-centric basis of knowledge presents all curriculum developers with the obvious dilemmas of the rootedness of cultures and civilisations as well as their inter-connectedness. Curriculum developers as well as academics, educators and other policy-makers need to examine these complex notions and to analyse the myths, feelings, understandings and concepts surrounding them in order to develop rational ways of dealing with the resultant dilemmas. Education has normally been seen as a secular or religious phenomenon but the division and divisiveness caused by this separation has been very damaging. However, if civilisational knowledge can be pooled differently to draw the best from each phase of human history, then a more syncretic understanding from across civilisations and periods of time could inform the educational process differently.

In the first phase between 5 century BC and seventh century AD universalist concepts of humanity were established by great religions like Zoroastrianism, Buddhism, Christianity and Islam and the Confucian and Hellenistic philosophies. However, as Amin (1997) states:

> this declaration of a universalist vocation did not establish a real unification of humanity. The conditions of tributary society did not permit it, and humanity reformed itself into major tributary areas held together by their own particular universalist religion-philosophy (Christendom, Dar Es Islam, the Hindu world, the Confucian world). It is still the case, however, that tributary revolution, like all the great revolutionary moments in history, projected itself forwards and produced concepts ahead of its time.

Although these earlier movements form an important part of the emergence of universalist norms and values they also continue to present unresolved dilemmas at a global level. Hans Kung (1991), for one, outlines his major project for encouraging an ethical quest at the global level: through dialogue amongst religions to establish peace amongst religions and nations.

The second phase of the development of knowledge especially in the Mediterranean region was the Renaissance. During the 11th and 12th centuries it was the collaboration between scholars from progressive Catholics, Muslim and Jewish faiths working on Greek scientific and other texts which led to the translation of these Greek texts from Arabic to Latin and contributed to the Renaissance. Hence, what underpins interfaith dialogue is not rhetoric about it but actual projects like these involving scholars like Maimondes, (IMAGE 8 STATUTE OF MAIMONEDES), Avincina, Avveroes and Al Kundi in sites like Toledo, Spain.

The third phase during the modern period likewise has made a contribution to universalism through philosophy of the Enlightenment. This social vision of society was based on notions of a social contract and the French Revolution sought a nation based not on ideas of blood and ancestors but of free men (sic). The abolition of slavery and ideas of secularism went beyond mere religious toleration although the rights of women were not recognised. However despite the fact that the nation was not an affirmation of the particular, but of the universal, such universalist objectives have not been achieved. In the American Revolution, a nation largely based on immigration, the right to be 'different' was recognised. Nevertheless, there has been little, defence of the right to be 'similar' within a constitutional state, especially of the descendants of slaves and the indigenous Americans. Hence, inclusive social and political frameworks have not been optimally developed.

Fourthly, the rise of socialism in the 19th century further contributed to notions of radical transformation especially through Soviet Bolshevism. The price paid by socialism in respecting difference and not building inclusive rights to be 'similar' has been very evident in the dissolution of Yugoslavia which brought ethnic cleansing to Europe 50 years after Fascism was defeated. The Soviet Union and all the states associated with communism likewise did not develop equalities and inclusive citizenships with common and shared values.

Fifthly, the post-colonial states likewise faced great challenges of maintaining unity with divisiveness being foisted on them by the colonisers. Most of them have tried to maintain national unity despite tendencies towards fragmentation. The Bandung principles (1955) of non-alignment which avoided polarities need to be revisited for better inter-state relations. Following the 1955 Conference in Bandung the 29 member states formed the Non-Aligned Movement (NAM) to avoid becoming part of the bi-polar world. This independent voice of those who had emerged from the shadow of colonialism was a powerful organisation of poor countries. (IMAGE: 9; PHOTOGRAPH OF NEHRU AND CHOU ENI LEI)

The super-powers in the post WWII period undermined many of the initiatives of NAM especially in relation to the creation of international institutions to nurture greater levels of economic equalities. Hence, no post-war economic restructuring took place to correct the huge economic disparities between the so-called developed world based on capitalism and the so-called developing countries, for whom the victory of the Second World War was hollow. This was despite the very heavy price that the 'developing' countries paid to defeat Fascism during WWII. (M. Mazower: 2012; 244–272)

In the absence of economic changes the most powerful economic agreement within NAM at Bandung was on issues of cultural cooperation and this was an attempt to curb the cultural chauvinism of imperialist powers. UNESCO sponsored a critical study of racism and racial attitudes in different cultures. This work included monographs by Claude Levi-Strauss and Marie Jahoda and it reinforced the idea of race was an 'ideological fiction'. The 29 NAM members at Bandung condemned 'racialism as a means of cultural suppression' and stressed the need for the study of national cultural history as well as developing measures of cultural cooperation.

They issued Five Principles of Peaceful Coexistence which argued that imperialism had prevented cultural cooperation and directed the cultural history of people, including that of Europe. It is important to remember how the NAM spearheaded by leaders like Nehru, Nasser, Suharto and Chou En Lei contributed to the making of knowledge a universal project and not a prerogative of the 'civilised' European and American colonial powers. It is important to remember for this Conference that it was the work of NAM countries which led to the work on cultures, education and scientific cooperation in the post WWII period which became the substance of work of UNESCO. (Prasad: 2007)

Hopes for the genuine underpinning of universal values therefore lay in the collective wisdom of the earlier religious epoch; the Renaissance as an intercultural enterprise; the Enlightenment philosophy; their reinterpretation by the socialist movements; and from progressive elements from amongst the post-colonialist liberated states and Non-Aligned Movement. The educational and political challenge for democratic ideas is to hold notions of respecting difference but at the same time ensuring the right to be similar. Such an approach could begin to break the polarisations between particularism and universalism. This establishment of a common set of resemblances amongst citizens of Asian states can largely be accomplished by their education systems.

7. Issues at the Regional Level

The dominant-marginal perspective in educational discourses needs to be constantly challenged and often redrawn. The issues being presented here are historically significant and of the gravest importance for the future of education as well as the political and social structures of most nations. It requires a combination of pedagogical patience and persistence. There has to be a constant and fundamental reappraisal of the histories and national identities into which we have all been inducted with such care. The answer does not lie in trying to establish either a liberal or a 'back-to-basics' curriculum founded in centric, narrowly nationalist and empire-based intellectual milieu which has done so much to contribute to our present predicament. An important issue which requires rational consideration is how to engage in processes of national integration, modernisation and development which are democratic and inclusive. At this level curriculum development issues ought to include relevant considerations of participatory pedagogies.

In many marginalised communities learning and teaching ought to be seen as flexible processes which involve both younger and older people in life long learning situations. Such participatory pedagogic situations would enliven the curriculum, rather than deaden it. Hence, both formal and non-formal learning strategies are needed, an both of them should also have the potential for life long learning.

For most education systems the challenge is to engage in a wide ranging establishment of connections with other cultures and civilisations which are part of the fabric of contemporary realities for young people and the future generations of Asian citizens. Currently, the regional differences at societal levels between NEA and SEA are extremely wide and the role of particularistic curriculum in worsening ethnic tensions and strengthening siege communal mentalities cannot be underestimated.

It is a question of disentangling, decoding, identifying the operation and structures of those discourses which help to sustain the present relations of intellectual power and subordination in our societies. Eurocentrism is of particular significance in relation to knowledge, since it has an implicit theory of world history. It is also a global political project with far reaching universal ramifications. From this perspective the so-called western thought and philosophy emerges from Greece and is based on 'rational principles' while the 'Orient' does not move beyond 'Metaphysics'. (S. Amin: 1997: 19) The curricular question is how can the Asian education systems help to liberate universalism from the limits of Eurocentrism? The current habits of thought within some education systems inhibit such a development and this tends to reinforce notions of a fortress mentality. This mentality exists not only in Europe but has its equivalents in Sino-centrism, Islamo-centrism and Indo-centrism and these substitutions only continue to perpetuate issues of knowledge exclusion and dominance. Asian centrisms therefore can allow Eurocentrism to dominate at the global and universal levels.

8. Politicisation of Religion and Secularism

Economic globalisation as Eric Hobsbawm states: 'dismantled all lesser boundries and the secular theology created a void, a worldwide of purely individual agents maximising their benefits in a free market'. This was given force by rthe phrase used by Mrs. Thatcher that 'there is no such thing as society.' (E. Hobsbawm: 2013. p. 221). This vacuum created by global neoliberal fundamentalism and its power which led to the destruction of the social fabric. It helped to nurture religious fundamentalism,by polarising the religious and the secular. It also led to the consequent loss of ancient wisdoms which were embodied in the spiritual wisdom represented by the Sufi's (IMAGE 10; SUFI ART) in Islamic faith (and Orisa in West African spiritual culture. This detracted from the broader societal context where spiritual contributions to cultures and civilisations could interact with other sources of knowledge.

Wole Soyinka in writing about the destructive role of the missionising religions in Africa states:

> In the end the product is conflict, and the destruction of cultures.
> Let this be understood by the champions
> Of theocracies where religion and ideology meet and embrace.
> Orisa admonishes them; you will not bring the
> World even close to the edge of combustion. The essence of Orisa
> is the antithesis of tyranny, bigotry, and
> Dictatorship—what greater gift than this respect, this spirit of
> accommodation, can humanity demand from the
> World of the spirit? (W. Soyinka: 2012: 129–168).

For instance, in following on from what Soyinka writes as a result of global influence of Wahabbism at a global level, Islam has become constructed as Arabo-centric all over the Asian continent, and the broader universal context of Islam moored in many parts of the globe has been ignored. This in its wake has led to violence in some states and replacement of western corruption with clerical corruption in many faith communities. The role of particularistic curriculum in worsening ethnic tensions and activating siege communal mentalities cannot be under estimated. The great Moghul emperor Akbar (1556–1605) as a Muslim was interested in other faiths like Hinduism, Christianity, Jainism, Parsi faiths and wanted to syncretise them to form a single faith Din Ilahi. This initiative was ahead of its time, and it did not take root. Had it succeded it might have helped to depolitcise the use of religion in the Indian subcontinent.

To reinstate 'the voice' of the disenfranchised would require a great deal of delicacy, diplomacy, persistence and sophistication, particularly if the desired changes are not to be relegated to the margins of academic life. Reactive, rhetorical and rebellious responses are not only inadequate but counterproductive. While action is needed across all Asian societies, those in the poorer parts of SEA have greater levels of difficulties and may require support from international agencies. The more affluent and experienced educational agencies in NEA region can also be helpful and lend support for educational developments in poorer parts of the SEA region.

Schools and higher education institutions play an important role in the formation of secular values important for the public domain. In trying to develop the Nehruvian notion of a secular and inclusive university, there is the general issue of the role of religions within the Asian education systems generally. The Chicago Fundamentalist Project coordinated by M. Marty and R. Appleby has documented the role of religion on a range of issues including education. Discussions have also been undertaken by UNRISD (J. Haynes: 1995) and issues arising from different types of religious groups (culturalist, syncretist, fundamentalist and community oriented) have been analysed. Mark Juergensmeyer in the title of his book wonders if the confrontation of political religious nationalism confronting the secular state is 'The New Cold War?' (M. Juergensmeyer: 1993). However, at the educational level the impact of politicised religion has policy implications for education in the region and requires a more detailed study to enable development of inclusive, democratic and secular educational policies and strategies.

The emergence of the Islamic Umma as well as the Roman Catholic Church at a transnational level present aspects of consensus, domination and dissent. The Hindu cultural chauvinism and the shift towards a purer Buddhist Sangha raise problems for the Indian, Thai and Sri Lankan states. The corruption of the secular apparatus of the state systems in different states (India, Indonesia, Malaysia, Philippines, Pakistan) presents demands for 'pure', 'just' and 'xenophobic' states in Asia. Christian and Islamic fundamentalism has permeated many African and Asian societies

What is the role of religious educational institutions and curricula in the public domain especially when they demand an uncritical adherence to the texts or about issues of religious justice? (R. Khuri: 1998; R. Hefner and Horvatich (1997). These issues also have a bearing on inter-group and inter-ethnic relations inside education systems as well as regional and the wider social fabric of societies and do not only have relevance to universities in the west.

The increased power of organised religions questions ideas of a non-centric curriculum. In multicultural Asian institutions, how can believers of one faith learn about other faiths, as well as non-believers learning about believers and vice versa? In other words it is a complex Kuhnian understanding of teaching about the faiths and the knowledge derived from them, which is not merely religious instruction. This can provide a way forward, out of the sterile and the formally or strictly divided notions of the secular and the religious intellectual (western and Asian) discourses. This poses complex issues not just for educational policy, but curricular reform and teacher education. To replace obscurantism with rationality is not a simple or a linear path but a more complex strategy and journey. Others like Inayatullah argue for an alternative social science which is not based on the nation-state as models of analysis but on new knowledge by "creating layered sovereignty". (S. Inayatullah: 1998)

Rabindranath Tagore drew his own cosmopolitan views from older Bengali traditions and 'consciously melded them with western cosmopolitanism.' (M. Nussbaum: 1993; 53, 128). He established the Visva Bharati University in a rural area near Calcutta where a comprehensive vision of knowledge and understanding continues to exist since its founding in 1921. As a rural university functioning to educate for an increasingly urbanising world it is perhaps a model worth exploring for the implementation of a non-centric curriculum. Its connections with rural India also have implications for other Asian societies which need to educate local peasantry in rural areas not only in literacy, and basic education but also educating them against bigotry. As Brenda Gourley (THES: 27-2-1998) writes:

> Universities indeed had their conceptual origins in such fabled places as Alexandria with its great library, the Greece of the academy and the lyceum, in the Persia of the Sassanids, and the Gondishapur, in India of Das Guptas and the Nalanda, in the golden ages of Confucian China, in the Muslim worlds of Harun-al-Rashid and the House of Wisdom, in the late medieval Europe of Bologna, and many more.

Education and university systems provide in the region the potential of being intellectually open institutions that transcend narrow ethnic and nationalistic barriers. Many of them are already institutions which are not bigoted in narrow religious terms or exist in a sea of corrupt materialism but are rich intellectually and spiritually. Such a shift may provide more grounds for integrated knowledge systems in the region. It also bodes well for good inter-group and inter-ethnic relations in most societies in the region.

9.i Multiple Identities and Inclusive Asian Curriculum

Most post-colonial Asian states have not yet developed an optimum understanding of integrating the nation based on an ethos of inclusive multiple identities into the national cultures of Asian societies. Many states hark back to anti-colonial, dominant and majoritarian knowledge as legitimation of their polities. Knowledge systems and curricula for both formal and non-formal education therefore are excluding and ignore the complex basis of knowledge and histories based on multiple identities of many Asian societies. The recounting of anti-colonial struggles which exclude the contributions of minorities cannot be equated with broadly based and inclusive national struggles and post-colonial national identities. These inclusions are important to obviate the the separate culturalist developments which use Charles Taylor' notion of 'politics of recognition'. (C. Taylor: 2011). These calls can then be used to demand a separatist 'curriculum of recognition.'

Representation of the national culture based merely on anti-colonial, economic development and class politics is not a sufficient basis to constitute national culture in city state like Singapore. The superficialities of multiracialism or "Asian Values" are no substitute for a serious consideration of the complex values and histories of its peoples.. Religious leaders like the Dalai Lama do not think that the United Nations Universal Declaratons on Human Rights can be replaced by 'Asian Values' as suggested by certain political leaders.

The focus on particularism of identities constitutes a major challenge in nation building especially in the post-colonial states of south and south east Asia. On the issue of ethnicity as Benedict Anderson (1983) states:

> The politics of ethnicity have their roots in modern times, not ancient history, and their shape has been largely determined by colonial policy. (It is no accident that uncolonised Siam has the least violently ethnicised politics in the region).

Their imbrication with class and religion as well as the differences between the 'alien' and the 'indigenous' make for complex curricular implications within the south east and south Asian education systems. The best defence for an educational process with a critical edge is within democratic school systems, where people do not have to obey rules without questioning them.

9.ii Historical Knowledge

Omissions and distortions of history play a major role in allowing gossip or stereotypes to become compounded. The presentation of many local Asian histories by their absence especially their pre-modern national past is an important element in the construction of the exclusions of Asian groups as peoples without a history or a past. The use of a similar exclusion by dominant Asian groups of non-dominant Asian communities exacerbates the problems of mutual recognition, as has been the case in many countries.

The genocide of subordinated Asian peoples and enslavement are glossed over in many history books. Subjugated groups like the outer island collectivities in Indonesia, the Dalits, or tribal peoples in India are seen as having no great past, and their identities are not represented by the powerful legitimising symbols within the currently constructed national states.

Those who plan the history curricula face a very complicated task. On the one hand, they need to engage with the identities of groups like the Burmans, the Vietnamese, the Hindus or the Bengalis. On the other hand, within the state education systems, they need to develop a coherent and inclusive story of and for the whole nation. The question, therefore, for curriculum designers is what aspect of histories to select and on what principles to make that selection.

To develop more universal understandings, the historical underlying hypothesis and the implicit theories of writers needs to be dissected. An epistemological and methodological break could lead to developing more widely acceptable histories which include not only the written sources but also the oral understandings of certain groups. Since school level understandings of history vary so vastly not only between countries but also within countries, abstract solutions cannot be suggested here. Nevertheless, in general notions of civilisations, the evolutionist schema, the impact of stereotypes, revoicing and reimaging the invisible and the subordinated groups do merit attention. The development of the critical understanding of teachers and the development of appropriate teaching materials and textbooks based on new research and developmental work deserve immediate attention.

The changes in Hong Kong over the last few years illustrate the question of the historiography of the island. Colonial powers normally granted colony independence. In the case of Hong Kong it was handed back to China, thus, control being assumed by one state from another. So, neither in 1841 when Britain assumed control over Hong Kong, nor in 1997 were the residents of Hong Kong consulted about their wishes. (K. Lowe: 1991) Both China and Britain colluded in denying a voice to the people of Hong Kong including those who fled from China as political refugees. Whose history of Hong Kong will represent its controversial pasts: will it be a history of its land, its rulers, its institutions or its peoples? How will its colonial past or its capitalist present be seen by the Marxists histories? These are complex historiographical issues.

From the point of view of intercultural and inter-ethnic relations in Hong Kong, there have been immense contributions by Indian Bohras, Parsees, Sikhs and Jews. But their histories have been ignored and their citizenship rights undermined because only the Chinese can acquire rights as Chinese nationals. How can a China-centred government ignore a history of a dynamic multicultural urban city-state?

More generally, the usage of terms like 'tradition' or 'modernisation' as applied to the study of history tends to have parochialism and linearity. Non-western civilisations are constructed as traditional, while the west is seen as the acme of modernity. Such notions detract from the development of a more universalised or global approach to understanding history. Liberating the notion of the modern from the Eurocentric straitjacket can help with notions of modernity being universalised. The work of Samir Amin, Gunther Frank, Immanuel Wallerstein and Eric Wolf (1982) has explored notions of western 'dominance' through the development of capitalism. These provide grounds for reappraising the earlier historical texts, with a view to developing more relevant new texts for schools in all Asian states.

9.iii Silk Route and Cultural Syncretism

The encounters of the local and the global in economic and cultural terms provides further clues to notions of the development of the arts, culture and markets, as well as the resistance, retrenchment and the development of siege communities. In the Asian continent this has been reflected by the ways in which the Silk Route provides evidence of syncretisms as well as retrenchments. The routes of invasion also became the route of art and trade. Alexander the Great conquered vast territories right through Persia and north Afghanistan. From 1–4 centuries A.D. there developed a syncretic Greco-Buddhist culture and arts—the sculpture of Buddha from the Gandharan civilisation in Taxila is an example of the syncretism of the arts in this region and has as much importance at the present time as it did in the ancient times. Over a decade ago the Taliban in Afghanistan blew up the Bamiyan Monuments of Buddha which UNESCO has been trying to reconstruct. Hence, the fundamentalists of today view such ancient monuments as a threat and in the absence of intercultural understandings and education, there is the possibility of intercultural conflicts becoming deeper which can only be described as Saul Bellow as the 'moronic inferno'. Columns of Peace built by Emperor Ashoka (272–232 BC) who built these after he began to adhere to Buddha's message of non-violence also represent a message that the fundamentalists of today would not want to hear and therefore could face destruction.

The Silk Route also took the messages and images of Buddha as far east as China, Korea and Japan. Korea as part of the East Asian civilisation shared in the way in which Confucianism and Mahayana Buddhism became rooted in the region. Chinese cultural influence in the region subsided in the 19th century as the Europeans and Americans began to dominate it. However, Korean society on the Asian peninsula provided a bridge between the Asian continent and Japan. Hence, in historical terms it is important to remember that Korean society has a multicultural history in the way in which it influenced and was influenced by Japanese and Chinese cultures. For instance, the Korean kingdom and period of Baekje Asuka influenced Japanese painting, architecture, design and sculptures. The Japanese imported Korean artists and sculpturers. The sculptor Baekje carved Kudara Kannon sculpture. Many paintings in various Buddhist temples were done by Korean artists (E. Fenollosa: 1912).

As a spiritual tradition Shamanism represents an ancient tradition in modern Korean society although it is probably being marginalised by modernity, the Buddhist, Confucian and Christian traditions. However, it plays a role in solving human problems through the meeting of humanity and the spirits and has counterparts in other northern cultures of Siberia, Mongolia and Manchuria. Professor Kim has suggested that Shamanism and traditional Korean culture has its own artistic aesthetic and unique quality.

Hence, while the Asian continent might be rife with examples of the conflict of civilisations, it also has an enormous contribution to make to human civilisation through the examples of syncretisms of cultures and civilisations. It can lend an enormous depth to the work of Unesco on the Alliance of Civilisations. (Gundara: 2011)

As Raymond Grew writes, the development of a global history can be a product of our own time which:

> Offers some historical insight into contemporary concerns and therefore into the past as well. And it will do so while substituting multicultural, global analysis for the heroic, national narratives on which our discipline was founded.

10. i. Ethnicity and War: Disarming History

There are no easy ways of disarming history because most assumptions also lead to counter assumptions and arguments. The more the world becomes democratised, the more possible it is for ordinary men, women and children to be involved in the institutions which sustain nations. One of the major institutions which sustains some nations is war. One of the dangers of this has been that the battles are not conducted by professional armies and soldiers and ordinary men, women and children have also become victims. In cases like Afghanisatan and Pakistan where territorial national boundries are not clear communities have become victims of warfare. The role of Taliban in destablising these two soceities can however spread to other countries in the region (A. Rashid: 2012)

Many symbols are used to legitimise wars and these symbols strengthen the religion of nationalism and when some nations use notions of the "flag and the faith", the cult of the flag does not remain secular but acquires more narrowly nationalistic meanings.

Hence, disarming history would require complicated measures, and, as Ehrenreich states, the advance of war-related enterprises of the twentieth century has also brought about human resistance to war:

the passions we bring to war can be brought just as well to struggle against war. There is a place for courage and solidarity and self-sacrifice other than in the service of this peculiarly bloody institution, this inhuman "meme", a place for them in the struggle to shake our links free of it.

The disarming of history would, among other things, require the demystification of the fictive pasts of nations. Where these pasts are based on 'ethnicised' histories which demand revenge, then the constructions of acceptable and inclusive and non-violent histories are more complicated. In the case of India and Pakistan the Arabicization (replacing the earlier Persianisation) of Urdu and the Sanskritisation of Hindi reinforce not only communal cleavages within India but also cleavages at the inter-state level between India and Pakistan. These can be mobilised in continually feeding conflict by constructing an imagined and glorious history which excludes neighbours and reinvents the past. On the Indian subcontinent, such developments reverse the role that the early modernisers like Jinnah and Nehru played by suggesting that these societies had complex historical legacies. But in both cases Nehru and Jinnah have incurred the wrath of traditionalists with sinualarised interpretations of the past..

The Mahajir, Shia and Sunni conflicts in Pakistan and the Hindu/Muslim relations in India are like tinderboxes. On the slightest pretext there is an ethnic or religious explosion. The modernisers and educators in Bangladesh, India or Pakistan have inadequately coped with these inter-ethnic tensions. The use of textbooks, religious schools, mosques and temples are mobilised by traditional elites using new technologies to propel ancient and exclusionist myths and glories. While modernisers hark to secular state ideals, the traditionalists stress the certainties of the past in India. Pakistan seeks the Islamic route and Bangladesh the muted secular path. The political interventions of this kind reverse the ancient notion that an hour of learning is worth more than a year of prayer which is common in Islamic cultures.

Islamic knowledge draws on a wealth of cultures which include: Semitic, Hellenistic, Iranian and Indian. The Ulema (scholars) who have ilm (knowledge) have helped to clarify complex issues from the Quran in the Hadiths. In drawing from the Hellenistic tradition, the role of Aristotelian philosophy especially in the areas of reason, the logic and the laws of nature has been profound. The potential therefore of syncretic Islamic knowledge in progressively informing the curriculum is extensive. In many madrasas (schools) Aristotle was considered to be the first teacher, but the notion of reason was subsequently undermined by the faithful. To restore these very important aspects of Islamic knowledge and its earlier syncretism a constructive dialogue with the faithful is necessitated. The very powerful concept of knowledge is recognised by the notion that "kings are rulers of people but scholars are rulers of kings".

10. ii. Re-contextualisation and Social Science

In the post-World War II period if was North American social scientists wrote about issues of modernisation and development. At one level this was very important, because it tried to connect the 'modernised' world with the 'modernising' world. As the 1996 Report of the Gulbenkian Commission on the Restructuring of the Social Sciences recalls:

> The key thesis was that there exists a common modernising path for all nations/peoples/areas (hence they are all the same) but that nations/peoples/areas find themselves in different stages on their path (hence they were not quite the same).

This type of development in social science which used concepts of social change, status discrepancy or analytical concepts like class or quantitative methods to study development seemed appropriate. However, North American social science did not focus on the longue duree,the historical tradition (of the Annales as in France).

There has developed a challenge to universal normatism of North American social sciences from the African-American and feminist constituencies who have challenged these dominant knowledge systems by questioning its presuppositions. These new modes of analysis call for the use of scholarship, analysis and reasoning to engage in reflection concerning the place and weight in our theorising about difference (race, gender, sexuality and class).

The recontextualisation of the social sciences therefore ought to include consideration of a pluralistic universalism akin to the Indian pantheon of past and present social realities. Such a development would represent an important recognition of the multicultural realities which have a bearing on both the historical study of the pasts and the social scientific study of the present.

These initiatives can lead to the development of a more intercultural social science which can re-engage with the complexity of different types of localisms, as well as those at the level of the state and develop these into more global forms of knowledge. A recontextualised social science of this kind which does not leave out the analysis at the state level has the merit of carrying with it many of the disciplines whose focus is the state. It may also have the merit of developing a common social science, which cuts across humanity. The key task is to explode the hermetic language used to describe persons and groups as "others" and that they are objects of social science analysis, as opposed to being subjects with full rights and legitimacies.

The inclusion of these historical pasts and contemporaneous presents has more possibilities of developing comprehensive knowledge systems. Such an inclusive social science would also make it more objective. The alternatives of Sino-centric, Indo-centric, Islamo-centric or Eurocentric knowledges are more likely to be fragmentary if 'other' knowledges remain excluded.

Social sciences which are involved with power politics, or are hegemonic or dominant will be increasingly contested and it is important that polarities and political contestation is obviated to enable the development of more inclusive social scientific studies. These can enable us to have a better grasp of the local and the global and in reshaping them into being more inclusive.

Selected Bibliography

The Guardian, London: 8-4-2013; 11.4.-2013; 12-4-2013; 13-4-2013.

W. Kymilka and B. He (2005) *Multiculturalism in Asia* (Oxford: Oxford University Press)

T. Myint-U (2011) Where China Meets India: Burma and the New Crossroads of Asia (London: Faber and Faber)

Z. Bauman (2007) *Consuming Life* (Cambridge: Polity Press)

J. Gundara (2000) 'Diverse Communities, Inclusiveness and Education for International Understanding', *International Symposium Commeemorating the Inauguration of the Asia-Pacific Centre of Education for International Understanding*, 26–29th August 2000, Seoul and Ichon.

V. Naidu, M. Sahib and J. Osborne (2013) *Fiji: the challenges and opportunities of diversity* (London: Minority Rights Group International)

J. Kristeva (1991) *Strangers to Ourselves* (New York: Columbia University Press), pp.95–104.

J. E. Stiglitz (2002) *Globalization and its Discontents* (London: Penguin Books)

F. Fukuyama (1992) *The End of Hiistory and the Last Man* (London: Hamish Hamilton)

M. Castells (1989) *The Informational City* (Oxford: Blackwell) p. 350

L. Bash and J. Gundara (2012) 'Contesting Boarders: a challenge to some paradigmatic assumptions of intercultural and comparative education', *Intercultural Education*, Vol. 23, No. 5, Oct. 2012. Pp. 383–395.

J. C. Scott (2009) *The Art of Not Being Governed* (New Haven and London: Yale University Press)

A. Kazamias, in R, Cowen and A. Kazamias (Eds) (2009) *International Handbook of Comparative Education* (Dordrecht: Springer).

M. C. Nussnaum (1997) *Cultivating Huamnity: A classical defense of Reform in Liberal Education* (Cambridge, Mass. And London: Harvard University Press)

D. Gupta (2009) *The Caged Phoenix; Can India Fly?* (Washington D.C.: Woodrow Wilson Centre Press and Stanford, CA: Stanford University Press)

I. Wallerstein (2006) *European Universalism: The Rhetoric of Power* (New York and London: The New Press)

E. Wolf (1983) *Europe and the People Without History* (Berkeley: University of California Press)

J. M. Blaut (1993) *The Colonisers Model of the World: Geographical Diffusionism and Eurocentric History* (New Yoerk and London: Guildford Press)

A. G. Frank (1998) *Re-orient: Global Economy in the Asian Age* (Bekeley: University of California Press)

E. Said (1993) *Culture and Imperialism* (London: Chatto and Windus)

H. Kumg (1991) *Global Responsibility: in search of a new world ethic* (London: SCM Press)

M. Bernal (1987) *Black Athena: The Afro-Asiaric Roots of Classical Civilisation* Vol. 1, (New Brunswick, N. J.: Rutgers University Press)

S. Amin, (1989) *Eurocentrism* (London; Zed Books) p. 24

S. Amin (1997) *Capitalism in the Age of Globalisatioon* (london: Zed Press) p. 80

V. Prashad (2007) *The Darker Nationa: A Peoples History of the Third World* (New York and London:The New Press)

M. Mazower (2012) *Governing the World: The History of and Idea* (London and New York: Allen Lane)

M. E. Marty and R. Scott Appleby (1993) *Fundamentalisms and Scoiety: Reclaiming the Sciences, the Family and Education* and *Fundamentalisms and the State: Remaking Politics, Economics and Miltance.* (Chicago and London: The University of Chicago Press)

J. Haynes (1995) *Religion, Fundamentalism and Ethnicity: A Global Prespective* (Geneva: UNRISD) p.7

M. Juergensmeyer (1993) *The New Cold War? Religious Nationalism Confronts the Secular State* (Berkeley, Los Angles and Oxford: University of California Press)

M. Bookchin: (1995) *Re-Enchanting Humanity: A defense of the human spirit against antihumasnism, misanthropy, Mysticism, and Primitivism* (London: Cassell)

W. Soyinka (2012) *Of Africa* (New Haven and London: Yale University Press)

A. Rashid (2012) *Pakistan on the Brink: The future of Pakistan, Afghanistan and the West* (London and New York: Allen Lane)

S. Inayatullah (1998) 'Imagining and Alernative Politics of Knowledge: Subverting the Hegemoney of International Relations Theory in Pakistan', *Contrmporary South Asia*, Vol. 7, Issue 1. pp. 27–43.

B. Gourley, in *Times Higher Educational Supplement* (London: 27-2-1998)

C. Taylor (2011) *Dilemmas and Connections: Selected Essays* (Cambridge, Mass. And London: The Belknap Press, Harvard University Press)

B. Anderson (1983) *Imagined Communities: Reflection on Origins and Spread of Nationalism* (London: Verso)

K.. Lowe (1991) 'Hong Kong's Missing History', *History Today*. Vol. 41, Issue. 12.

E. Hobsbawm(2913) *Fractured Times: Culture and Society in the Twenieth Century* (London: Little Brown)

R. Grew: (1983) 'On Prospect of Global History', in B. Mazlish and R. Bultjens (Eds.) *Conceptualising Global History* (Boulder, Colorado: Westview Press)

B. Ehrenreich (1997) *Blood Rites: Origins and History of the Passions of War* (New Yiork: Metropolitan Books) pp. 204–224

J. Gundara (2010) 'Interculturalism, Dialogue and Cooperation: Some Research Issues for the UNU-IIAOC', Paper presented to the Scoping Conference for the International Institue for Alliance of Civilizations, United Nations University, Barcelona, 1st to 3rd June 2010 (Barcelona, Spain)

I. Wallerstein, *et. al.* (1996) *Report of the Gulbenkian Commission on the Restructuring of the Social Sciences.* (Stanford, C.A.: Stanford University Press)

Critical Intercultural Education:

Challanges for the Nation State Systems

Introduction

This Conference affords the participants an important opportunity to explore issues in relation to the broad fields of critical and intercultural education at an early moment in the 21st century and to provide a less hazier (or perhaps an even hazier) perspective at intellectual, academic and political levels. This paper, intends to examine some of the background political issues which are considered to be significant for critical and intercultural approaches to education. Such issues confront nation states in Europe and other parts of the world, including the states which are riven with conflict and violence.

The breakdown of the Yugoslav state brought back to Europe 'ethnic cleansing' 50 years after Fascism was defeated on the European continent and the aftermath and legacies of it still continue to reverberate. In the most recent past we have witnessed the breakdown of the Arab state structures. This corrosion throughout the region—starting from the Atlantic to the Arabian Sea has engulfed countries such as Egypt, Algeria, Tunisia, Libya, Bahrain, Jordon, Pakistan, and Yemen, the division of the Sudan, between the Muslim north and the Christian south; also the prospective division of the Ivory Coast between the Muslim north and the Christian south; and the complete disintegration of Somalia. The ousting of both President Mubarak and President Ben Ali of Tunisia by a popular uprising are an indication of the popular democratic, secular and also an understanding of citizenship rights by poor and largely illiterate young peoples. The preceding intercultural conflicts and the resultant reversion to essentialist sectarian identities has led to conflicts between: Shias and Sunnis; Arabs and Kurds; Copts and Muslims; and resulting in what Amin Malouf calls "killer identities." (Soumaya Ghanboushi: 'A quagmire of tyranny', *The Guardian*, 29-1-2011). However, during these popular uprisings by the people the intercultural understandings between different groups have been remarkably improved and very different from earlier intercultural conflicts under authoritarian regimes.

In our own time the need to consider at the broadest political level the requirement to negate intercultural conflicts points to the continuing and urgent necessity to enhance intercultural understandings. In this respect the role that education can play as part of broader social and public policies cannot be underestimated.

At an educational level there are also important issues which this conference can help educators and teachers to critically appraise and understand issues represented by intercultural education. In institutions such as Sodertorn Hogskola, which have a diverse student body and include large numbers of immigrant students, the need for the teaching of the humanities and the social sciences at undergraduate level are extremely important. This ought to be informed by the type of studies and work undertaken by the liberal arts colleges in the U.S. which provide a sound, broadly based education and informs students about critical learning across the range of humanities and social science disciplines. This soundly based liberal arts education would help the Vice-Chancellor, Rebecka Lettervall, to then have all students, both Swedish and immigrants, to learn about democratic society as well as "some of the goals of critical thinking and world citizenship" as discussed by Martha Nussbaum in her book (*Not For Profit*: 2010, p. 126).

One of the reasons for this reflection is that the work undertaken within 'Multicultural' and 'Intercultural' Education has by and large not enabled students to acquire a better understanding of the societies and the polities in which they have to live and function.

In addition, many of the so-called 'multi-cultural' and 'intercultural' initiatives have neither led to equalities of opportunity nor to initiatives to improve their educational outcomes. It is possible that in the liberal market-oriented states the use of the rhetoric of helping those who are an under-class and have been disadvantaged by the vagaries of the economic system has not succeeded in improving the life chances of many of their students. This is largely because much of the education policy and practice has not been constructed on evidence-based research. If and when research has been undertaken then much of it has not been put into practice or been effective.

Secondly, most of these educational initiatives have been directed at immigrant groups and populations by the local and national state systems. The basic assumptions have largely been that the states, as they operate the educational and social policy systems, are optimal and well functioning entities. From this perspective they only need to resolve the educational problem of the so-called 'ethnic' minority and immigrant populations. This paper would like to question this basic assumption concerning nation state systems, because it seems that by and large educators, rather than viewing these state systems critically and problematically, view groups such as immigrants as the problem. The immigrant based focus may be, in and of itself, perhaps be misplaced and there is an urgent need for a total reappraisal of the ways in which future repertoires of policies, work, thinking and action should be established in this field.

The issue which most societies confront is how to ensure that the educational provision leads to all citizens being engaged in a learning process which Paolo Friere (1972, Chapter 2) suggests is creative and becomes part of transformable knowledge. This engagement for the liberation for all the groups in society which also bridges social class inequalities should help in bridging the major barriers and help to remove instruments of oppression.

The Political Dimension in Europe

The political dimension of these issues is illustrated by two current (April 2011) European leaders. The first is Chancellor Angela Merkel of German and secondly, the British Prime Minister David Cameron. The German Chancellor, Angela Merkel, declared to young members of the Christian Democratic Union: "This multicultural approach, saying that we simply live side by side and live happily with each other, has failed." (Quoted by Slavoj Zizek, *The Guardian*, 26-1-2011) As a product of the Communist East German (GDR) regime, she does not have the experiences of the learnings, understandings and accommodations made in the various Landers of the Federal Republic of Germany before the merger of the two Germanys. Hence, her conclusion is that immigrants should adopt the dominant *Leitkultur* does not accord with the experiences in the West German Landers. In response to this Zizek recommends the adoption of an emancipatory *Leitkultur*. In other words there is nothing wrong with dominant culture if it is not restrictive yet the positive values of the immigrant communities are seen not have any place in the German nation state. In this respect Zizek does not even consider the reappraisal of the intercultural democratic values for rejuvenating inclusive and intercultural future for a modern democratic Germany.

The British Prime Minister, David Cameron, has gone further than Merkel, saying that not only have multicultural policies failed but that they have been connected with the issue of threats to the security of the British nation state. His statement was welcomed by the British neo-fascist English Defence League together with Cameron's European allies, the Latvia For Fatherland Party and the racist Polish Law and Justice Party. (*The Guardian*, London 5-2-2011 and *The Observer*, London, 6-2-2011) The problem for David Cameron in educational terms is that instead of supporting secular, comprehensive and common school system for all students, which would strengthen national unity and security of the British state in his terms, his government is setting up separate and divisive religious schools funded by the state. So, no contradiction there then!

This paper would also like to argue that with an increasing focus on free market economic systems and education systems a major error is being committed. This error is that education and training are increasingly being viewed interchangeably and synonymously. This is certainly not the case since training specifically targets the job market and incorporates a significant component of the acquisition of skills and which is largely based on applied aspects of knowledge. The role and function of education, on the other hand, is very different since the economic dimensions and aspects of work are subsidiary to the whole process of education writ large. This is because the economic systems are aspects of a social system and society—and these are complex organisms. Education, knowledge and value creation with a societal focus on 'humanitas' and generating citizens who can lead full lives because the intellectual and education values inculcated through ancient concepts of 'paidea' and 'bildung' have deep goals and roots. This is necessary at the present time because many people amongst the younger generations are disenchanted with the narrowly defined schooling which relegates them into routine roles. As Andreas Kazamias states there is a need for the "reinvention" or "reenchantment" of humanisitic paideia through the cultivation of what may be called "Promethian Neo-Humanism" (Kazamias: in Cowen and Kazamias (2009) p. 1079) One can go further and say that the paideia and bildung need to be interculturalised so that these concepts are validated across group divides in multicultural communities and societies.

In this sense education in democratic societies is by definition a 'critical' activity and if it was not 'critical' it cannot not be referred to as education. Hence, while a school or a university educates students to be critical citizens, the religious institutions like churches, temples and mosques conversely 'instruct' their believers into a belief system. Hence, at the outset of this paper I would like to suggest that it is vital that the notion of 'Critical Education' enhances the processes of teaching and learning at the present time. If the education that has so far been imparted is not critical then educators have been miseducating or merely instructing learners. In social democratic states therefore, education is an open ended activity and educators use critical pedagogies. It is however, possible that in liberal market and certain authoritarian states where either training or propaganda are used that there would be a need in fact to develop initiatives for critical education.

In turning to intercultural education, if the Conference ends up asserting that it is not an acceptable paradigm, then would the argument be that what is needed is monocultural education? The question then is how viable is this assumption given that most societies are not only socially diverse because of the presence of immigrant groups but because of the historically based indices of difference and diversity based on a combination of linguistic, religious, social class, nationality based differences.

Briefly therefore, in social democratic states perhaps, the more acceptable formulation could be a symbiosis or concordance between concepts posed as 'contrasts' in the title of the Conference. Hence, the paper would like to argue that there is a greater mileage in exploring the development of a 'Critical Intercultural Education.' Hence, intercultural education would not be based on rhetoric but on evidence; it would not accept either the state or the target groups in an unquestioning way but critically appraise the role of both. Hence, teaching and learning and teachers and learners would have a genuine partnership. The state at local and national or even global levels would be as open to a critical gaze are those who are those who are subjects of the educational process.

Subordinated Peoples and Nation States:

This paper would now like to engage with the issue of 'critical intercultural education' through a focus on how the so-called 'First World Peoples' were turned into 'Fourth World Peoples'. The legacies of the dominant/subordinate relations are based on the deeply entrenched legacies of the dominant groups using brutal power to give legitimacy of their control of the subordinated groups. These oppressions are based on notions of 'civilising the natives' and need to be negated. (Wallerstein: 2006) The Spanish thinker Sepulveda justified the right to intervene in the Amerindian societies because of their barbarity. Las Casas, on the other hand, purported that evil existed everywhere and that therefore there was no theological justification for interference. However, this sixteenth century debate has continued for five centuries and the consequent interventions have barbarised both the brutalisers and the brutalised. These concepts also have a longer pedigree than that. Obviously, fragments of Europe broke off from the 'Old World' and went and planted themselves as English, French, Spanish or Portuguese colonisers. This meant that there was the imposition of their 'European and Christian' world views which destroyed the cultures and societies of the Amer-Indian Nations in the Americas, the Inuit peoples in Canada and the Aboriginal peoples in Australasia. Hence, Sepulveda's ideas have destructively carried the day.

Most of the subordinated and marginalised peoples are viewed by anthropologists and policy makers as archaic vestiges from another historical time. Yet, many of these communities may also be understood as those who have survived as runaways, fugitives and maroon communities who over a few millennia have fled from the oppressions of the state-making projects. They have escaped situations of subordination—slavery, conscription, taxes, corvee labour, epidemics, religious dissent and warfare. (J. C. Scott: 2010) In short many of the nation states were formed by appropriation of these smaller nationalities, their lands and other resources. Many of these people have a history, if there is one, of struggling against the state and have used many ways of keeping the state at arm's length and survived through subsistence agriculture which maximises their physical mobility. The settled states describe such groups as being 'uncivilised' and 'barabrians' and as being in a state of nature. Yet, these people see themselves as avoiding harm, servitude and disease which civilisation has to offer and therefore their 'barbarism' is a result of their own construction. Such communities are therefore constructing or creatively fabricating identities as a way of evading the state. However, as more and more of the globe is politically subjugated by nation state systems these groups are on the verge of being made extinct. At this moment it is, therefore, important to take a deep breath and consider how to create greater levels of equitable relationships between the nation states and the marginalised and peripheral groups. (MAP: 1. Scott. P 17) At the present time in south-east Asia there are at least 100 million people who can be referred to as minorities, such as the Akha, Chin, Hmong, Kachin, Karen, Khmu, Lahu, Miao, Wa and Yao who occupy an area of 2.5 million square kilometres stretching from China to north-east India, living in the uplands of countries like Burma, Thailand, Laos, Cambodia and Vietnam. There is an urgent necessity of developing intercultural understandings amongst this diverse range of groups and between them and the surrounding aggressive and oppressive nation states. Amongst these extruded peoples by the state systems are the sea gypsies (orang laut: Scott: p. 328) who evade slavers and states within the waterways of the Malay archipelago in Melka region of Malaysia and other mangrove coasts.

On the mainland's of the world are the Gypsies, the Cossacks, the Berbers, Mongols, the Masai, the Tuareg and other nomadic peoples who practice swidden agriculture and have established zones of refuge. As Scott states: "many, but by no means all, groups in extra state space appear to have strong, even fierce, traditions of egalitarianism and autonomy both at village and familial level that represent an effective barrier to tyranny and permanent hierarchy." (J. Scott. p. 329) Given the type of life these people lead they are not people without history as Braudel states but have 'mutiple histories'. They have made the ultimate sacrifice to avoid the oppressive measures of state formation which in common sense terms are referred to as civilisation. As Scott states: "They represent, in the longue duree, a reactive and purposeful statelessness of peoples who have adapted to a world of states while remaining outside their firm grip." (Scott.p.337.) This they have done by purposefully being not pre-anything but as being a post-irrigated rice culture, post sedentary, post subject and even post subugation.

Scott argues that in the case of South East Asia, peoples on the plains expand outwards and require more land for paddy, thus pushing the minorities living in the foothills deeper into the hills and forests. These groups are therefore not pre-literate but post-literate; since literacy is given up to deliberately disengage from certain kinds of state forms.

This argument is strengthened from another direction. Wendy Brown in her book *Walled States, Waning Sovereignty (Zone:2010)* argues that borders and modern-day walls are discredited markers of failing sovereignty which are porous and interpenetrative but represents the empty bravado of the modern staatspolitik. This reflection of xenophobia begins in the head, a psychic war of all against all. The Farmers General Wall built through the middle of Paris in the 1780s to collect octroi from traders has a verse:'La ferme a juge necessaire/De metre Paris en prison.' These aliens hated but needed (hated because needed) are part of the persistent psychic structures and will not disappear soon. As masks of sovereign autonomies the borders and walls are as much markers of people wanting to come in as those wanting to leave, escape or stay out.

For all the above groups whose ways of life and culture have now become even more vulnerable there is a need for measures to enhance intercultural understandings and education at least at three levels: firstly, between the many diverse and various groups in this and other regions of the world; secondly, between the dominant national groups and these groups who live on the margins and borders of nation state systems; thirdly, at inter-state and international levels to protect their human and group rights through regional measures and through regional organisations.

Since we are in the Nordic region we can cast a similar glance at this part of the world. Many Nordic countries perceive themselves as being monocultural societies which were turned multicultural by the arrival of the immigrant communities. What such comments tend to ignore are the longer term and historically based diversities and differences within these societies. The Sami of Lapland or Samiland are treated by the Nordic as any other members of their nation states. Yet, these people who have historically lived in north of the Arctic Circle are in fact perceived as 'the others' by the Nordic nation states. (MAP: 2 North Circle and Samiland, Hall)

As Sam Hall writes:

> the Nordic governments, reputed to be the guardians of the world's conscience, have steadfastly refused to recognise Sami nationality. Legislators carefully avoid any reference to the Sami people, preferring to label them the Sami-speaking population. The Sami people are being assimilated into dominant Nordic cultures; their religions suppressed; their resources have been exploited. All this has hap-

pened despite the fact that "they never sold their land, nor gave it away, nor lost it in a battle. (S. Hall: *The Fourth World* (1987) p. 138.)

What the governments in South East Asia have done to the indigenous groups by marginalising them has also been the case in the Nordic countries. The long term racism that the Sami have suffered has led the UN General Assembly to meet with the Sami parliaments as well as the Nordic Parliaments and their Rapporteur James Anaya stated in his 7th July 2010:

> the challenges ahead in Sami are significant, and that overcoming the harm inflicted by the discrimination and extensive assim-ilation policies carried out throughout history in the Nordic countries will require serious commitment, political will and hard work. (UN General Assembly, Human Rights Council, 15th Session, Agenda Item 3. A/HRC/15/37/Add.6. 7th July 2010)

It needs to be stressed at this point that this is not only a political and legal matter at international and national levels but fertile ground and basis to enhance intercul-tural understandings to obviate intercultural conflicts through workable solutions and practical measures. As a part of this process critical intercultural education has an important role to play in bringing about greater levels of equalities.

The Hidden Crisis: Armed Conflict and Education

The 2011 UNESCO Global Monitoring Report states that all of the Education for All targets set for 2015 will be missed by a wide margin. Certainly, from 1999 to 2008, 52 million children have been brought into primary schools and there has been some improvement in bridging gender gaps. However, hunger is holding back progress. 195 million children under five experience malnutrition, and this results in irreparable damage to cognitive development and long term educational prospects.

In sub-Saharan Africa 10 million children drop out of primary school every year. About 17% of the world's adults—796 million people still lack literacy skills. Nearly two-thirds of these are women. Obviously, financial constraints are a major hurdle and new and innovative ways of funding are needed. For instance, it would take the diversion of just 6 days of military spending by aid donors to close the US$16 billion the Education for All external financing gaps.

Countries affected by armed conflict represent the hidden crisis in education and demands an international response. Most of these armed conflicts are reinforcing inequalities and ethnic differences based on linguistic, religious and territorial differences. Educational strategies to readdress these therefore have to be, by definition intercultural and have a critical dimension because groups engaged in armed conflict harbour deep hidden hatreds and imaginations and are not amenable to superficial solutions.

Over the decade to 2008 there were 35 countries which experienced at least 48 armed conflicts with 30 in the low income and lower middle income categories and the average duration of conflict lasting 12 years. (IMAGE: Girl's EYE through bullet in Glass) These are not conflicts between states as has been common in the past, but armed conflicts within state boundaries. In these conflict-affected countries 28 million children of primary age were out of school—this is 42% of the world total. Literacy levels in these countries are 79% for young people compared to 93% in other poor countries. In these situations state and non-state parties target civilians and school children are viewed by combatants as legitimate targets. This is a clear violation of international law and the monitoring of the human rights violations need strengthening and impose sanctions on repeat offenders. In this respect girls and women are systematically violated. There is therefore a need for an International Commission on Rape and Sexual Violence with the International Criminal Court directly involved in assessing the case for prosecution.

One of the factors which adds to the failure of education and increases the risk of conflict is the increasing 'youth bulge.' Youth are neither getting access to good intercultural education and nor are they receiving skills so that they can escape poverty and unemployment. With 60% of the population in many conflict-affected countries like Guinea, Liberia, Ivory Coast and Sierra Leone aged less than 25, require education of good quality so as to overcome economic despair which contributes to violent conflict. While good intercultural education can be a force for peace, in many of these contexts the school systems are used to reinforce social divisions, intolerance and increase prejudice which in turn lead to war. Only good intercultural education can help to build mutual trust and these needs to begin within the classroom.

National governments and the international community are failing to uphold human and children's rights. State and non-state parties target children, teachers, civilians and schools with total impunity and rape and sexual violence are an important part of this arsenal. Equal treatment in education for girls and boys is not only a human right but can also unlock gains in other areas and especially help women to improve child and maternal health and make choices and take greater control over their lives. Even countries such as the Philippines and Turkey, which are close to providing Universal Primary Education, fail to reach the highly marginalised populations and gender gaps remain deeply entrenched.

In countries like Iraq, Pakistan and Afghanistan aid and funding for education is directed towards strategic priorities such as fighting counterinsurgency and this aid needs to be demilitarised. Both at international and national terms those countries which are in conflict tend to receive far less funding for education; there is a culture of impunity in relation to the violation of human rights and the attacks on children, teachers and schools. They are in fact in the front line and seen as legitimate targets. In Thailand, for instance, in the southernmost three states the insurgents target schools and teachers in a hitherto peaceful region: and the 140,000 Karen refugees from Myanmar (Burma) have no entitlement to education.

Education has the potential to nurture peace and governments and donors need to prioritize the development of intercultural and inclusive education systems. These critically assessed intercultural and inclusive educational measures need to include policies on injustices linked to identity, faith, ethnicity, languages and linguistic diversity. The official school curriculum also needs to consider the subjectivities of knowledge and legitimise knowledge of the subordinated and excluded groups. In countries like Bangladesh and Kenya the quality of education to different groups are measurable. Differences between the students from the richer and the poorer families are very evident and where there are ethnic differences the schools do not help to reduce these learning and educational inequalities.

The intercultural understandings in post-conflict countries are also variable. Hence, in Bosnia and Herzegovina a country of 3.8 million people the Dayton Agreement of 1995 recommended nation building through a process of decentralisation. There are 13 separate ministries of education and it is difficult to forge an intercultural and inclusive national identity. Hence, in this instance the lack of a strong federal ministry of education hampers the development of a multi-group identity which can lead to peace and security, since most schools are segregated by ethnicity, religion and language. Under a single school roof there are two schools—one operates in the morning and the second in the afternoon for a different ethnic group. Once in the classroom children continue to be taught from three separate curricula that differ for subjects such as history, culture and language and contribute to reinforcing prejudice. (R. Ferguson, J. Gundara and Jack Peffers: UNICEF Bosnia and Herzegovina Project.) The need for an intercultural and non-centric curriculum is actually reflected in this country, since they can only use the IBE curriculum.

In Cambodia the education system is only now beginning to address the issue of genocide and in Rwanda where the education system reinforced divisions there is no attempt to teach the country's history. Making schools non-violent environments would be extremely good for education, especially if the normalisation of violence is negated.

At an international level UNESCO and UNICEF need to play a more interventionist role and The Peace Building Commission needs to integrate education into the wider peace building strategy with a budget of $500 million to $1 billion. This is vital to make flourishing multicultural societies which are peaceful are also able to ensure that critical intercultural understandings become deeply engrained.

Some International Legal Instruments

The indigenous peoples in many nation states are involved in armed conflicts within the state systems. Others as stated above who are outside them need their rights to be protected. Since, national constitutions may not preserve their rights it is important that and their human and educational rights are protected by international legal instruments. These however, raise complex issues because of the complex issues of jurisdiction and also since most of the people are extremely marginalised in both the so-called developed and developing countries. Their human and educational rights have been set out in ILO 'Indigenous and Tribal Peoples Convention' (No. 169) which includes a comprehensive list of rights which include rights to education, their own schools, training and educational institutions, languages, lands and freedom from genocide and 'ethnic cleansing'. The 13th September Declaration of Indigenous peoples rights (UN Resolution No. 61/297) was not signed by UK and the United States, which has also not signed the Rights of the Convention of the Child (along with Somalia). Just recently, the UK has withdrawn from ILO! This is as though the societal inequalities for the poor and the working peoples have been eliminated.

The Indigenous and tribal peoples face privations as their natural resources which include forests and minerals are being exploited. There are large numbers of children who are trafficked into child labour and sex trade. While organisations of Indigenous Peoples do exist, it is not clear how effective they are in dealing with any of the massive violations by the member states of the Convention of the Rights of the Child and other international legal and binding instruments which they are all signatories to.

At the first level, the right to quality education and the promotion of their own languages, cultures in their own educational institutions and special measures are necessitated because of their deeper disadvantages. This for instance, has happened with the Indian communities in Quebec who live on welfare and have no vocations, because they have lost their skills of hunting and fishing and they do not need to work to earn a living through traditional work. A head teacher in a Quebec reservation who was my doctoral student has called this a "Golden Cage." Secondly, the isolation and marginalisation of these groups' means that educational provision cannot be provided unless the issues of health, vocational skills, as well as adequate and avenues for work are available. For many of the indigenous and nomadic people this can include veterinary services for their livestock. Educational provision needs to be part of a social policy provision and autonomy for the group right to choose how to lead their lives.

At the next level, the International Working Group on indigenous peoples' education also states that their children need the "same education as all other children." It is at this level that complexities about critical intercultural education are raised and this paper will try to combine these rights and special needs in the context of "intercultural education for all children."

The importance of law is suggested by the late Lord Chief Justice Tom Bingham of England. He died last year of lung cancer without having smoked a single cigarette. The last sentence of his book reads:

What makes for Good and Bad government? I would answer no doubt predictably: the rule of law. The concept of the rule of law is not fixed for all time. Some countries do not subscribe to it fully, and some only subscribe only in name, if that. Even those who do subscribe to it find it difficult to subscribe to it find it difficult to apply all its precepts quite all the time. But in a world divided by differences of nationality, race, colour, religion and wealth it is one of the greatest unifying factos, perhaps the greatest, the nearest we are likely to approach rto a universal secular religion. It remains an ideal, but an ideal worth striving for, in the interests of good government and peace, at home and in the world at large. (T. Bingham, (2010) *The Rule of Law (London: Penguin Books) p. 174.*

Historical Struggles, Diasporas and Common Legacies

There is a very complex picture of the historically oppressed peoples and those who were oppressed during diasporas. In some cases there are solidarities between groups and at other levels there are intercultural conflicts. Hence, the question is: Do the past and common struggles for equality, human and citizenship rights provide any basis for progressive struggles to work together and learn from each other? William Katz has uncovered the unacknowledged history of the shared and common struggles of the African and Amer-Indian peoples from New England to Brazil. This history of relationship and collaboration between the reds and blacks remains largely unwritten. (See W. L. Katz: Black Indians: A Hidden Heritage (New York: Simon Pulse: 2005) (IMAGE 4: OF COVER.)

There is another set of issues raised by Diasporas. The year 2008 commemorated the bicentenary of the abolition of the slave trade, especially the trading in peoples of

African origin, who were transported by force to the Americas in large numbers and to the Arabian Peninsula in smaller numbers. One of the challenges posed at the present time is how to create better intercultural relations, instead of intercultural conflicts and equality of citizenship, not only for the descendents of slaves but for the many millions more who are currently denied citizenship and human rights. The indigenous peoples and the nomadic and travelling peoples are in the forefront of these exclusions.

How can educators functioning in modern state systems establish commonalities and mutualities with those who have experienced differing kinds of oppressions? As an example, the liberation of slaves led to the recruitment of indentured labour, largely from India to work in the plantation economies in the Indian Ocean and Pacific Ocean and the Caribbean region. Are there possibilities of connecting the struggles of these two peoples to attain equality, not only in the Americas, Australasia and Europe, but also feeding into the struggles of the first peoples in the countries where they were transported? Amerindian and Aboriginal peoples also suffered oppression and continue to wage isolated struggles without making connections with others who have fought similar battles.

There is also the massive movement of women who eke out a living in the globalized capitalist economies in the world. For every female executive there are multitudes of poorer women who migrate for work in factories and farms or as cleaners, caregivers, maids and sex workers. This feminization of poverty represents a fundamental denial of citizenship and human rights and the women from indigenous people are the most exploited. How are these millions upon millions of people accorded their rights, and what can be learned from previous oppressions and struggles out of which new solidarities, similarities, and mutualities of interest can be established?

Post Colonial Solidarities

This contribution has pointed out the dichotomies which exist in most societies at the present time and the need to deal with inequalities into greater levels of equality; to turn the negative aspects of unities and diversities into more productive and creative aspects of these disconnected and polarised aspects of difference which are construed as deficits and unities which are interpreted as being assimilation. Hence, the notions of unities ought to include basic and fundamental rights of peoples and citizens and which vest them with rights and responsibilities.

This paper has so far raised some of the challenges for critical intercultural education and for all societies to educate active citizens in cohesive democratic contexts where people continue to struggle against hierarchies, inequalities and disenfranchisement. It has also raised the issues of divides amongst peoples along gender, faith, social class and racial divides which the dominant groups and political institutions have failed to tackle in practical terms and exclusions from educational provision at the local, national and the global levels.

At the core of all these issues are ways in which the academe needs to universalise knowledge and shift away from dominant and 'centric' knowledge systems which have continued to provide singular and dominant versions of humanity and its histories. During this period of global transitions these separate realities and developments need to acquire multiple as well as universal legitimacies so that cohesive futures are based on more inclusive and realistic understandings of humanity.

Conclusion

There is therefore, a serious and urgent need to consider in critical intercultural terms how the knowledge of the diversity of peoples can be validated for the mainstream schools. This would benefit them and their educational outcomes as well as those of the dominant group children in society. This is not a matter of 'political correctness' but an issue of substantive aspects of knowledge within countries which are being ignored or denied.

The development of an intercultural curriculum would also entail a major intellectual challenge, as was the case when UNESCO commissioned the History of Africa in an eight-volume series. For the most part, the series has not been integrated within the main body of universal historical knowledge. There are also other important UNESCO projects on slave trade, the silk route, the culture of peace, and education for international understanding, and these have implications for developing intercultural education within the mainstream of national educational systems (Gundara 2003: 10).

This paper has raised questions in relation to linguistic and curricular issues in complex communities and examples of exclusions of minority groups whose languages, history, literature and knowledge are not adequately represented in the national curriculum. The aim to include the knowledge of all groups in a society presents an important challenge in providing equity and equality in educational terms. To conclude, the question we need to ponder on is this: How do you select from the vast pool of knowledge, and using what criteria, to ensure that the mainstream curriculum is inclusive of the best knowledge of all groups and which connects to the local and community knowledge systems?

In the arts as in other areas there is a syncretism of knowledge and images. This Gandhara image of Buddha 4th A.D (GANDHARA IMAGE). demonstrates the syncretic Indian and Greek influences which existed from 1st to the 5th centuries. However, if these intercultural learning, experiences, knowledge and influences are not built upon, what we confront are massive damage to intercultural understanding by intercultural conflict as this image of the the destruction of the Bamiyan Monument (IMAGE OF BAMIYAN)by the Taliban in Afghanistan demonstrates.

References

Aikman, S. (1999). *Intercultural Education and Literacy*. Amsterdam, Philadelphia: John Benjamin Publishing Company.

Asser, H., Trasberg, K, and Vassilchenko, L. (2004). Intercultural Education in the Curriculum: some comparative aspects from the Baltic and Nordic countries. *Intercultural Education*, 15(1), 33–43.

Beteille, A. (2007). The School and the Community. *Journal of Educational Planning and Administration*, 21(3), 191–201

Bingham, T. (2010) *The Rule of Law*. (London: Penguin)

Bourdieu, P. (1991). *Languages and Symbolic Power*. Cambridge: Polity Press.

Bradley, D. (2003). Lisu, in Thurgood, G. and LaPolla, R.J. (Eds). *The Sino-Tibetan Languages* (pp.222–235). London: Routledge Language Family Series.

Brown, W. (2010) *Walled States, Waning Sovereignty*. (Cambridge, Mass. Zone Press)

Chinai, R. (6 February 2007). Goa Wrestles with Language in Schools. *India Together*. http://indiatogether.com/states/goa.htm Accessed 16 January 2009.

Cohen. P. (1991). *Monstrous Images, Perverse Reasons Cultural Studies in Anti-Racist Education*. Working Paper No. 11. London: Centre for Multicultural Education, University of London.

Dreze, J., and Sen, A. (2002). *India Development and Participation*. New Delhi: Oxford University Press.

Ferguson, R. Gundara, J. Peffers, J. (2009) Report on Education in Bosnia and Herzegovina (UNICEF Report)

Freire, P. (1972) *The Pedagogy of the Oppressed*. (Middlesex: Penguin)

Garner, R. (August 26, 2008). Black History to be taught in School as Part of Curriculum. *The Independent*. http://www.independent.co.uk/news/education/black-history-to-be-taught-in-school-as-part-of-curriculum-908620.html Accessed 16 January 2009.

Government of India (2001). *Report of Working Group on Adolescents, 10th Five Year Plan* (2002–2007). New Delhi: Planning Commission.

The Guardian, London: 26-1-2011; 29-1-2011; 5-2-2011

Gundara, J. (1986). Education for a Multicultural Society, in Gundara, J., Jones, C., and Kimberley, K. (eds). *Racism, Diversity and Education*. London: Hodder and Stoughton.

Gundara, J. (2003). *Intercultural Education: World on the brink?* London: Institute of Education, University of London.

Gundara, J.S. (1982). 'Issues of Linguistic Diversity', in Russell, R. (ed). *Urdu in Britain* (pp. 7–15). Karachi: Urdu Markaz.

Hall, S. (1988) *The Fourth World: The Heritage of the Arctic and its Destruction.* New York: Vintage Press)

Katz, L. W. (2005) *Black Indians: A Hidden Heritage* (New York: Simon Pulse)

Kazamias, A. (2009) in Cowen, R. and Kazamias, A. *International Handbook of Comparative Education* (Dordrecht: Springer Press)

Luciak, M. (2006). Minority Schooling and Intercultural Education: a comparison of recent developments in the old and new EU member states. *Intercultural Education*, 17(1), 73–80.

Nieroda, J. (Spring 1995). Education for Social Solidarity and Revolution: A Closer Look at Intercultural Bilingual Education in Peru. *Languages, Communities and Education*, Spring, 55–64.

Nussbaum, M. (2010). *Not For Profit.* (Princeton: Princeton University Press)

The Observer, London, 6-2-2011.

Pal, Y. (2005). NCERT Fourth National Steering Committee Meeting. http://ncert. nic.in/sites/publication/schoolcurriculum/minutes_4thmeeting_SC.htm

PROBE TEAM (1999). *Public Report on Basic Education in India.* New Delhi: Oxford University Press.

Robinson, C. (January 2004). Out-of-School Adolescents in South Asia: A Cross-National Study. UNESCO Literacy and Non-Formal Education Section, Cross-cutting project-empowering adolescent girls to become agents of social transformation.

Said, E. (1993). *Culture and Imperialism.* London: Chatto and Windus.

Scott, J. C. (2009) *The Art of Not Being Governed.* (New Haven: Yale University Press)

Schaeffer, S. (2003). Language development and Language Revitalisation: an educational imperative in Asia. Plenary Paper, SIL International. http://www.sil.org/asia/ldc/plenary_papers/sheldon_shaeffer.pdf Accessed 16 January 2009.

Sjögren, A. (ed.) (1997). *Language and Environment.* Botkyrka, Sweden: Multicultural Centre.

Swain, M. (1996). Discovering Successful Second Language Teaching Strategies and Practices: from programme evaluation to classroom experimentation. *Journal of Multilingual and Multicultural Development*, 17(2–4), 89–104.

Trapness, L.A. (2003). Some Key Issues in Intercultural Bilingual Education Teacher Training Programmes—as seen from a teacher training programme in Peruvian Amazon Basin. *Comparative Education*, 39(2), 165–183.

Visram, R. (2002). *Asians in Britain: 400 Years of History.* London: Pluto Press.

Wright, T.P. (2002). Strategies for the Survival of Formerly Dominant Languages. *Annual of Urdu Studies*, 17, 168–186.

Xaxa, V. (March 26, 2005). Politics of Language, Religion and Identity: Tribes in India. *Economic and Political Weekly*, 1368–1370.

The Third World Project:

Imperialism, Interculturality in the Post World War II Period

The colonial and imperial control over the Asian and African countries lasted for a few centuries. This control ceased after the ending of the Second World War and was a result of the uniting of nationalist forces within the various countries. Once these generally progressive governments took political control they had to reconcile the diverse range of socio-economic and other interest groups within their national boundaries. The preservation of national territorial integrity came at a price of compromises with the conservative and traditional forces and these led initially to the dilution of attempts to institute progressive changes in order to bring about greater levels of equity and justice.

Within a few decades of national liberation these nations had compromised most of the attempts to institute socialism and the change of societal structures. The failure to do so resulted in disastrous situations for these states. Emerging democratic structures were replaced by authoritarian regimes relying on armed forces and security services to keep control over the masses. Instead of secular ideals fundamentalist religions came to the fore; inclusive modern constitutional frameworks were negated and replaced by ideologies of 'blood and soil' or ethnicity, caste and 'race'. Human rights of many minorities and subaltern classes were denied. Issues of social class were more deeply entrenched and the role of the elites in the governance of many societies was not reduced.

This paper will outline the ways in which the Third World Project was articulated and implemented at national levels and internationally through the United Nations; as well as the way it was undermined by reactionary nationalist forces in collaboration with the neoliberal global economic forces and institutions like the IMF and the World Bank. The early attempts to institute the new international economic order fell by the wayside.

Some of the academics from this tradition have argued that there will be a 'Clash of Civilisations' based on a long history of differences and distinctions largely imposed by the colonising nations. What academics like Samuel Huntington ignored was the long history of colonial oppression which has had a brutalising effect both on the dominating groups, as well as the colonisers. The Spanish thinker Sepulveda defended the right of the colonisers to intervene in Amerindian societies because of their perceived barbarity. Las Casas, on the other hand argued that evil existed everywhere and that therefore there was no theological justification for interference. However, it was Sepulveda's argument which carried the day and as a result people in many parts of the world were brutalised. There is very little talk of the need for an 'Alliance of Civilisations': an initiative of the United Nations to bring about inter-cultural understandings and of which there is a paramount need at the present time.

National Liberation Movements and Bandung

The colonisation of the world by Europe after 1492 began to diminish in the middle of the twentieth century, constituting an extremely important phase of civilizational development through national liberation movements. The colonial powers 'supplanted' the local rulers in the colonised territories in various parts of the world. This supplantation in territorial terms created categories of colonisers being viewed as 'superior' and the colonised as being 'inferior'. It took the colonised a very long time to free themselves from being colonised. The colonised used the rhetoric and ideologies of equality, freedom and liberty which was used by the supplanters for themselves as the governing class. The colonised used these ideas to argue for equality of all citizens in democratic national contexts and not just for the privileged governing classes. The actualisation and implementation of these ideas by the colonised peoples have not been easy because their societies embodied many traditional and hierarchical societal structures, which had been reinforced by the colonisers to make their governance and control over the colonies much easier.

Hence, in the late twentieth century many of the federative ideals to create a reasoned harmony within the body of citizens have been reversed. A part of these negations result from the paradoxical legacies of the colonialism. One of the conditions of the colonisation of North and South America led to the emergence of societies which 'developed a sense of initiative and at a minimum the capacity to invent civil societies less constrained by European monarchies.' (Serna, p. 168).

It is likely that the history of 'world revolution' on the scale of multiple continents needs to be understood as having origins in the period from 1770 up to the decolonisation after the Second World War. The process began late in the nineteenth century and gained momentum during the WW1 and WW2 in a series of uprisings and the organisation of national movements. In the most recent past the young people again arose against authoritarian regimes in the second decade of the twenty first century in the Maghreb region. They also challenged the neo-colonial and neoliberal globalisation. They were however, ruthlessly quashed and manipulated fairly swiftly by the conservative and fundamentalist religious powers in this region.

One hypothesis is that the origins of the non-Eurocentric and French perspective of the French Revolution is a series of rebellions which lies in the 'hydrarchy' of modern times amongst the maritime proletariat who emerged in the seventeenth and eighteenth centuries as multiracial seamen traversed the world on the decks of ships. They were badly treated by the ship owners and this led to the sea farers organising across racial and nationality divides and these crews were the future leaders behind many coming seditions, the sparks from which ignited larger rebellions in the second half of the eighteenth century as harbours of disaffection in Europe, America and Asia. If one considers this proposition as being true then the phenomenon of revolution needs to break from a 'strictly French perspective, a Eurocentric logic, or even simply Atlantic point of view…and explain the interest in thus thinking about the origins of the global revolution in the eighteenth century.' (Serna, p. 169) While the French Revolution does indeed possess some unique characteristics, these can be taken as an outcome of history which goes back to the sixteenth century which was a nodal point with the invention of the future of French political system.

After 1945, decolonisation shed a cruel light on the contradictions of a France which embodied universalism and fraternity of the young people in the decade of the 1960's and especially in 1968, when the government turned both colonialist and xenophobic. Like other colonial powers France was drawn into insurmountable difficulties as a country espousing human rights, since it was the rhetoric and philosophy of 1789 which informed the thinking of liberation movements aimed at expelling the colonists who had usurped their lands. It had also experienced ignominy of collaboration and was once again seen to have inspired the model of liberation, albeit against itself. However, the year 1789 saw a new kind of Revolution and was an important moment for world history, not only because it promulgated universal principles, but also because in France emancipation was directly informed by regions that had liberated themselves from their respective metropoles. This phase of supplantation was based on using ideas and not dominating peoples and their territories.

Compared to the French, in the British context the situation was somewhat different. It was the case of the English nation supplanting the other but smaller nationalities. Those who supplant other groups, in turn, need to perpetually guard against their own supplantation. This process can be seen in Britain with the successive supplantation of the Celts, Angles and Saxons, the Danes, through to the

Normans. This 'internal colonialism' in an industrial European context has been described as a relationship of a 'core English nation' and the Celtic 'peripheral regions' (Hechter: 1997 p. 342–351) This has involved the domination of the Irish, Scots and the Welsh people and territories by the English nation and has lasted for about five centuries. The colonial exploitation of the peasantry was inaugurated by the English in Ireland and later led to a similar subjugation of the peasantry in colonial India leading to the famous famine in Bengal. (S. Amin: 2011, p. 53)

While the larger British nation eventually predominated and became involved in massive external imperial colonization (Davis: 1999) it did not completely erase the identities of the Scots, Irish and the Welsh peoples within the islands. The situation is now being reversed with the minority nations ('regions') partially retrieving their sovereignties with the establishment of Assemblies in Cardiff and Belfast and the Scottish Parliament in Edinburgh. This loosening of the control over the various polities in these islands illustrates the changing nature of the received wisdom about the sovereign territorially bound nation state (Robins: 1998) and of intercultural understandings and conflicts which consisted of English racism against the Celtic peoples.

The fear of being supplanted exists amongst the English even at the present time, and the current fear is represented by immigrants both from within the European Union as well as, from the poorer and war and conflict ridden countries. Jack Straw, while Labour home secretary, argued that English nationalism was potentially very aggressive, very violent". William Hague considered it "the most dangerous of all nationalisms." (The Guardian: London, 23 October 2014) The Scottish votes in September 2014 to 'stay together' within the British nation is opposite of the nervousness embodied by the dominant English nationalism. The Scottish polity has provided, by contrast a different model—a confident modern national identity, which is based on strong civic identity and has been built on Scottish institutions of law, education, trade unions, the church and political culture at local levels. Hence, Scotland represents a different model of national; life than those who demand separation and is being used by other subordinated peoples in many nations. Hence, Scotland at the present time embodies the advantages of intercultural understandings and stress on positive aspects of a shared past history and not the negative story of the past.

The English nation had taken measures against its own supplantation and early in the 18th century by consolidating the control by the English of these islands. This perhaps helped to lay the foundations for the external empire. It had achieved a union with Scotland and had conquered Ireland, which consolidated its power at home. The War of Spanish Succession (1702–13) enhanced its status as a naval and military power and made inroads into Spanish spheres of influence in western Mediterranean and Spanish America, including a share of the slave trade. More independently the English opened up factories and plantations in North America, the Caribbean, Levant, India and China, as well as the control of fisheries over Newfoundland. (J. Darwin: 2012). This colonial supplantation and domination and its legitimacy began to be challenged in the later nineteenth century.

The European Empire and the Third World

The anti-colonial movements have had a long history and one of the earliest inspirations was the Haitian Revolution (1791–1804) and in 1928, the anti-colonial leaders gathered in Brussels for a meeting of the League Against Imperialism, and it was an early attempt to create a global platform to unite the visions of the anti-colonial movements from Africa, Asia and Latin America. Roger Casement who worked for the British Foreign Office related to European public the cruelties inflicted on the Congolese people by the Belgians. King Leopold II's successor Albert I and his Foreign Minister Emile Vandarvelde as the secretary of the Socialist International was pressured into holding the meeting of the League Against Imperialism at Palais d'Egremont in Brussels. 200 delegates representing 137 states or colonised regions attended and passed resolutions criticising the barbarism of the colonisers. This conference consisting of delegates from all the peripheralised areas of the world was considered to have been the bedrock of the anti-colonial movement.

The Soviet Communists had supported this movement and when they had taken control of the Soviet state they had abrogated all the treaties the Czar had made with other European powers to divide the territories of the peoples of Latin America, Africa and Asia. Albert Einstein was the patron of this organisation, alongside Madame Sun Yat-sen and Raymond Rolland the Swiss Nobel prize winner. (Prasad, p. 22) Prasad recounts the ways in which political movements in the three continents continued to meet at regional levels and established solidarities till the WWII; while the League of Nations played a paternalistic role in relation to the colonised people. Leaders like George Padmore and Henry Sylvester Williams from the Caribbean, Nnamdi Azikiwe from Nigeria and W.E.B DuBois from the U.S. made the case for Africa and when Ghana became independent in 1957 under Nkrumah it hosted the first Conference of African States and Nkrumah stated that the idea of 'Africa' was not a cultural one but of a 'political union.'

Following the ravages of the Arab world by the Europeans and the Ottomans, the Egyptians, Syrians, Lebanese and the Palestinians forged a united front in Brussels and by 1945 created the Arab League. The demands against American control over Latin America gathered force before WWII, but the regional organisations continued to be economically dominated by the Americans. The situation for the countries in Latin America was that they had gained independence from European states and hence they did not have a contemporary experience of being colonised.

The idea of Pan-Asianism was promoted by Nehru and Sun Yat-Sen and they argued for a continental unity against imperialism, including that of Japan. In March 1947, liberation movements in Asia met in New Delhi.

The regional formations had an appreciation for the universal struggle against imperialism and the embraced the United Nations as an organisation which would fight for justice of the colonised peoples.

However, there was little progress in this direction till after the Second World War. It was a decade after the War ended that newly independent countries from Asia and Africa met in Bandung in 1955. Prasad states: 'The Bandung dynamic inaugurated the Third World Project, a seemingly incoherent set of demands that were actually very carefully worked out through the institutions of the United Nations and what would become, in 1961, the Non-Aligned Movement.' (V. Prasad: Verso: 2012, p. 1). This phase of supplantation was not one based on the Third World as a place, but a Project which was galvanised by mass movements and the failures of the capitalism.

The anti-colonial movement sought greater democracy and was based on demands of greater peace during a period of bipolar Cold War; demand for greater economic equity through the UN Conference on Trade and Development (UNCTAD); and justice demanded by the Non-Aligned Movement (NAM) through the Group of 77 whose founders included Nehru (India), Nasser (Egypt), Sukarno (Indonesia) and Tito (Yugoslavia). The NAM recognised that there was a need for a greater international democratic structure through the UN systems which had been hijacked by the Security Council, as well as, the IMF and the World Bank, using GATT to undermine any new international economic order.

For the colonised peoples the liberation from the colonial powers itself presented a range of problems. Hence, the liberation following WWII was a period of grave political errors and setbacks for a large part of humanity. The colonial world was not directly exposed to the democratic values of the Enlightenment by the European colonial elite, including those of democratic political rights and secularism. Hence, it was the national liberation movements that had to confront the challenge of the values of universality of human rights of peoples. This was reinforced by the fact that socialists in Europe were not able to shift their thinking beyond its Eurocentric origins.

The national liberation movements opted for the unity of peoples in the struggle against imperialism and for the constructions of the nation-state beyond ethnic or religious horizons. Those who were on the right wing of the political spectrum invoked the myths of the ancient nations which were shrouded in the 'mists of time'.

However, these myths flew in the face of the complex histories of the past which embodied ethnic, religious, or linguistic diversity. They instead, harked back to the tributary river systems which were the founts of Hinduism, Islam, or the ideas of the biological and racial identity for instance, 'the Arab nation' rather than the modern constitutional bases. Many of these myths lie behind the many contemporary conflicts which have devastated many polities. They are in this sense not very different from European nations, which also believed in mythic beginnings. The Janus-faced nature of the nation with 'blood and soil' on the one hand and the modern civic nation based on democratic constitutions on the other hand have continued to pose problems to the present time.

There were also differences and divides within the national liberation struggles between the right and left, the centralists and the federalists, those who opted for multi-party political systems, and those who espoused unitary political party systems. Those nationalist leaders who subscribed to the progressive ideas were of the leftist tradition within the national liberation, and drew their inspiration from the philosophy of the Enlightenment.

These ideas and perspectives were not something that European elites and colonialists shared with progressive nationalists. For instance, the speech by Jawaharlal Nehru on the 14th August 1947 when India become independent included the following sentence: "And so we have to labour and to work, and work hard, to give reality to our dreams. Those dreams are India, but they are also for the world, for all the nations and peoples are too closely knit together today for anyone of them to imagine that it can live apart." (The Guardian, London 2007; Great Speeches of the 20th century No. 11 in series of 14) Nehru derived his ideas from Western, Indian and other sources from the colonised world and this syncretism of ideas do not have a purely European pedigree but result from struggles for freedom in different societies.

In addition to the recognition of diversity and difference at local and regional levels or in religious or linguistic terms, they have also stressed the notion of unity across these particularistic divides. The Non-Aligned Movement (NAM was founded in 1961) which grew out of the Bandung Conference in Indonesia, in 1955, made an important contribution towards the democratisation of the United Nations and developed into an instrument of justice. NAM brought together the progressive and democratically oriented nation-states and lasted till about 1975 in the form it was initially established.

The Bandung proposals for 'economic cooperation' and for an international system to diversify their economic base led, despite resistance of the Western powers to the formation of the UN Conference on Trade and Development (UNCTAD). The most powerful agreement at Bandung came over 'cultural cooperation' and condemned the cultural chauvinism of the imperialists and there was greater unity on this than on issues of political economy. The UNESCO based studies by Claude Levi-Strauss and Marie Jahoda on the biological fiction of race led to twenty nine new states condemning 'racialism as a means of cultural suppression' (V.Prasad: 2007. p. 45) and laid the foundations for what ultimately became the basis for intercultural exchange and cooperation and educational initiatives including the arts, culture, science and technology.

The movement was reactivated in Havana in the summer of 2006 and the gathering hoped that after Hugo Chavez's death, where the cry was 'We are all Chavez' (The Guardian, London, 9-March 2013). It was proposed that the movement would gather strength and become a force in progressive struggles of peoples around the world rather than being suppressed by the major imperialist powers.

If societies within the rubric of this system are analysed in horizontal terms, they reflect vast reverses experienced by the national liberation movements, peoples, and the negation of citizenship rights across many countries of eastern, central, and southern Europe and the Southern Hemisphere. These present a major challenge for reinstating the intercultural understandings, citizenship and human rights of the masses. However, for hundreds of millions of peoples in war-torn, corrupt, and collapsed states across the globe, this is a distant dream.

The challenge for inclusive polities and for the deepening of intercultural and civic education is not only to engage with the retreats of the ideologies and religions of the tributary epochs. These need to be deepened with the philosophy of the Enlightenment as well as the socialist movement and the progressive ideas of national liberation, as exemplified by the Bandung Movement.

The democratic practices organized around the notions of respect for difference need to be informed by the right to be similar. This is important to establish greater levels of mutualities and resemblances. These ought to bring about an erosion of the many injustices within and between societies and establish commonalities between and with struggles for equality and human rights globally. In order to help construct a new notion of 'us' and of shared belonging in European societies, progressive ideas from the Third World ought to become part of the ideas of inclusive citizenship in the body politic of Europe in the same way that Western ideas and ways of life have penetrated the Third World. Such initiatives are necessary at the present time to establish new bases of building solidarities which been fragmented by many negative political and economic forces.

The accumulation of the disengagements present major challenges to political systems and and the education systems. One of the issues which bears original thinking and which political systems need to consider is how can it enchant the disenchanted and disengaged younger generation. There is a need not only for establishing good intercultural political and citizenship education, but also how to ensure that this leads to active citizenship in impoverished and poor communities. Hence, how to socialise and educate young people who can live in socially diverse and massively unequal communities with a semblance of stability and intercultural amity is not a challenge which has been adequately been met. In this respect Mwalimu Nyerere, the former President of Tanzania practised statecraft which held the diverse Tanzanian polity together. He was therefore known as Mwalimu, a Teacher. (M. Mamdani: 2012) It is unusual that political leaders would consider themselves as teachers and think that this will enhance their political credibility. Therefore, Nyerere demonstrates an element of humility.

Contemporary Struggles and Solidarities

Do the past and common struggles for equality, human and citizenship rights provide any basis for progressive struggles to work together and learn from each other? William Katz has uncovered the hidden history of the shared and common struggles of the African and Amer-Indian peoples from New England to Brazil. This history of relationship and collaboration between the reds and blacks remains largely unwritten. (See W. L. Katz: Black Indians: A Hidden Heritage (New York: Simon Pulse: 2005)

Subsequently, the Civil Rights Movement in the United States in the 1960s inspired the feminist movement in its struggle to obtain greater degrees of gender equality. While in the bourgeois national and global contexts this has helped certain classes of women, there are many millions more who are still at the margins of society. In the next stage, can these contemporary struggles lead to some sharing of learning from the past?

The year 2008 commemorated the bicentenary of the abolition of the slave trade, especially the trading in peoples of African origin, who were transported by force to the Americas in large numbers and to the Arabian Peninsula in smaller numbers. One of the challenges posed at the present time is how these events can mark issues of better intercultural relations and equality of citizenship, not only for the descendents of slaves but for the many millions more who are currently denied citizenship and human rights.

How can educators functioning in modern state systems establish commonalities and mutualities with those who have experienced other kinds of oppressions? As an example, the liberation of slaves led to the recruitment of indentured labour, largely from India to work in the plantation economies in the Indian Ocean and Pacific Ocean and the Caribbean region.

First World Peoples and Interculturality

Discussions about interculturalism and multiculturalism do not normally take any cognisance of the most oppressed peoples in the world. The nomadic peoples like the Roma in Europe, the indigenous peoples of the Latin American continent; the Turag and Masai peoples in Africa or the Orang Asli people in Malaysia are examples of the First World Peoples. This paper cannot deal with major issue but would like to refer to two examples of the Samish people in the Nordic countries and the Inuit people in Canada.

In the Arctic Circle and the Nordic region the Samish people in the Scandinavian countries have been ignored by the governments which profess to be progressive and as upholders of human rights. The Nordic states are however, defined in monocultural and ignored the rights of indigenous peoples. As Sam Hall writes:

The Nordic governments, reputed to be the guardians of the world's conscience, have steadfastly refused to recognise Sami nationality. Legislators carefully avoid any reference to the Sami people, preferring to label them the Sami-speaking population. The Sami people are being assimilated into dominant Nordic cultures. (S. Hall: The Fourth World (1987) p. 138)

The Inuit peoples in Canada as historic minorities have acquired rights within Nunavet province present a different situation than most of the First World Peoples, including the Samish people. They have fared better by acquiring an autonomous region which they are able to exercise control over. The Constitution Act 1982 in sections 25 and 35 designated the Inuit as First Peoples and the province of Nunavut as their territory. While there are still major problems faced by them it is important that work in this field takes account of those people who are most marginalised in the world.

The Assembly of First Nations (AFN) represents the 1,400,685million people according to the 2011 Census and they constitute 4.3% of Canada's population. As an organisation of the Inuit, Metis and the First Nations was established by these communities to protect themselves against discrimination and demand their political rights. These communities also demand that there is the need to correct past injustices, protect their cultural survival and demand their human rights according to international, federal and provincial legislation.

Canada presents an important case study of the way in which issues of bilingualism and biculturalism between the French and English Canadians have been used to broaden the discussion to a much larger tapestry and range of issues of societal diversity. The use of 'interculturalism' in Quebec and 'multicultualism' in the other parts of Canada require a critical analysis which tends to get submerged by discussions and other literature in this field. The use of terminology which is not agreed upon tends to obfuscate rather than clarify issues in this field. Furthermore, research and literature emerges from the United States needs to be read more critically and circumspection. At an international level work in this field would intellectually benefit if new paradigms which takes account of all aspects of diversity, differences, divides as well as, unities and in most societies are based on original research evidence.

Such a perspective would have implications for policies, practices and the establishing of solidarities across the deep divides. So, for instance, are there possibilities of connecting the struggles of these disparate groups of peoples to attain equality, not only in the Americas, Australasia and Europe, but also feeding into the struggles of the first peoples in the countries where they were transported? Amerindian and Aboriginal peoples also suffered oppression and continue to wage isolated struggles without making connections with others who have fought similar battles. At the global level these struggles and solidarities are important forces to enhance intercultural understandings and unities.

There is also the massive movement of women who eke out a living in the globalized capitalist economies in the world. For every female executive there are multitudes of poorer women who migrate for work in factories and farms or as cleaners, caregivers, maids and sex workers. This feminization of poverty represents a fundamental denial of citizenship and human rights. How are these millions upon millions of people to be accorded their rights, and what can be learned from previous oppressions and struggles out of which new solidarities, similarities, and mutualities of interest can be established?

Concluding Section

This contribution has pointed out the dichotomies which exist in most societies at the present time and the need to deal with inequalities into greater levels of equality. Is it possible to turn the negative aspects of diversities into more productive and creative actions? Dominant groups and nationalities have construed many aspects of difference as deficits? It is important that these definitions of 'defectology' of the minorities in both the capitalist and socialist systems are eradicated. The notions of unities ought to include basic and fundamental rights of peoples and citizens and which vest them with rights and responsibilities. As stated earlier in this paper, this has been demonstrated in the recent months by the Scottish referendum by staying united within the British state and not separating from it.

This paper has raised challenges for intercultural education and for being active citizens in cohesive democratic contexts where people continue to struggle against hierarchies, inequalities and disenfranchisement. It also raises the issues of divides amongst peoples along gender, faith, social class and racial divides which the dominant groups and political institutions have failed to tackle in practical terms on the local, national and global levels. It is to be hoped that it also provides a basis through international exchanges to enhance intercultural understandings and provide depth of a more universal basis of knowledge. Education, knowledge and value creation require a social focus. A basis on 'huminatas' and the inculcation amongst citizenry ways and values of leading fuller lives have a long and ancient pedigree. The ancient Greek concept of 'paidea' and German notion of 'bildung' need to be cultivated in intercultural and humanistic terms

At the core of all these issues are ways in which the academe needs to universalise knowledge and shift away from dominant and 'centric' knowledge systems which have continued to provide singular and dominant versions of humanity and its histories. During this period of global transitions these separate realities and developments need to acquire multiple as well as universal legitimacies so that cohesive futures are based on more inclusive and realistic understandings of humanity.

Discussions about the intercultural curriculum within many countries including Britain cannot ignore these broader underpinnings of knowledge at the universal level. As mentioned earlier there are some attempts to make the history curriculum more inclusive of the knowledge of minority communities as well as the impact of slavery and colonialism. The issues raised in this paper have substantive implications for civic and citizenship education which do not appear to be currently taken on board by the national educational policy makers and educational institutions.

References

Amin, S. *Capitalism in the Age of Globalisation*. London: Zed Press, 1997.

Asante, M.K. *The Afrocentric Idea*. Philadelphia. Temple University Press, 1987.

Bernal, M. *Black Athena*. London: Free Association Press, 1987.

Chaudhuri, K.N. *Asia before Europe. Economy and Civilisation of the Indian Ocean from the Rise of Islam to 1750*. Cambridge: Cambridge University Press, 1990.

S. Desan, L. Hunt and W. Max Nelson. *The French Revolution in Global Perspective*. Ithaca: Cornell University Press: 2013. P. Serna; 'Every Revolution is a War of Independence' pp. 165–182.

Hamashita, T. "The Tribute Trade System and Modern Asia." *The Toyo Bunko*, no. 46; 7–24. Tokyo: Memoirs of the Research Department of Toyo Bunko, 1988

Huntington, Samuel. *The Clash of Civilizations and Remaking the World Order*. New York: Simon and Schuster, 1996.

Katz, William, *Black Indians: A Hidden Heritage*. New York: Simon Pulse: 2005

Küng, Hans. *Global Responsibility: In Search of A New Global Ethic*. London: SCM Press, 1991.

Mamdani, Mahmood Mamdani, *Define and Rule: Native as a Political Identity*. Cambridge: Harvard University Press: 2012

Prashad, Vijay. *A People's History of the Third World: The Darker Nations*, New York: The New Press, 2007.

Putnam, R. *Bowling Alone*. New York: Simon Shuster, 2000.

Putnam, R. D., Feldstein, L. M. and Cohen, D. (2003) *Better Together: Restoring the American Community*, New York.

Soyinka, Wole. *Of Africa*. New Haven and London, Yale University Press, 2012.

Voll, J. I. "Islam as a Special World-System." (1994) *Journal of World System History*, 5, 2: 213–26.

Wallerstein, Immanuel. *The Modern World-System, vol. I: Capitalist Agriculture and the Origins of the European World-Economy in the Sixteenth Century*. New York/London, 1974.

Wallerstain, Immanual. *European Universalism: The Rhetoric of Power*. New York: The New Press, p. 59, 2006.

Issues of Religious and Cultural Diversity

in Modern States

Introduction

The modern constitutional and democratic states have an important task in protecting the rights of all citizens as well as providing them the protection of the law. These rights and legal protections include the protection of religious institutions and the right of citizens to believe or not to believe in the sacred. This paper does not use the term 'secular' in its commonsense understandings of the separation of church and state. Jawaharlal Nehru the first Prime Minister of India, provided an Indian version of the European concept of the term secularism which meant that while religion was completely free, the state gave protection and opportunity to all (religions and cultures) to create conditions for tolerance and cooperation. The role of a secular constitutional state is therefore necessarily not in conflict with the sacred or the religious but to provide protection to those with no beliefs as well as those of different belief systems. The last election in India reinstated this version of secularism by securing a victory over the fundamentalist Hindu political parties and is perhaps a better political safeguard for the multi-faith Indian society.

This paper will analyze the Janus-faced nature of the sacred and the Janus-faced nature of the nation state and its implications for inter-faith understandings or of conflict. This is partly the case because Ferdinand Tönnies assumption of a historical movement from Gemeinschaft towards Gesellschaft has not taken place. Tönnies had formulated an understanding that in industrial societies, because of their association with modernity, the ethnic and kinship status of social differentiation would be replaced by social class as a driving force in social organization. Durkheim, Weber and Marx had argued this case and, while social class analyses are still valid, issues of ethnicity and the sacred have reasserted themselves.

Religions are both transnational and multicultural. This raises the complex issue of multicultural citizenship as articulated by Kymlica which is less associated with legal citizenship (Kymlica, 1995). Their strength also has the weaknesses of an Achilles' heel in achieving values in the 21st century. Hans Kung (1991), for example, outlines his major project for encouraging an ethical quest:

> No survival without a world ethic. No world peace without peace between the religions. No peace between the religions without dialogue between the religions (p.xv).

The conclusion of his book returns to this thought: "Therefore the programme which guides us and which comes together as one may be summed up once again in three basic statements:
- No human life together without a world ethic for the nations;
- No peace among the nations without peace among the religions;
- No peace among the religions without dialogue among the religions". (p.138).

Kung has come face to face with the absence of a value system as a modus for our present world. According to him, religious institutions (and by inference other self-selective bodies) need to learn a process of dialogue. Dialogue without an educational, public and social policy spin-off dies a natural death. One could also add that these spin-offs need to be institutionalized. Kung is moving toward one basic ethic. Although not wishing a unitary religion or ideology, he claims that we require some "norm, values, deals and goals to bring it together and to be binding on it" (p.xvi). A potential educational and public policy framework exists through the various international human rights instruments, all of which subscribe to a high common value. Such initiatives necessitate a policy mix between the universalistic definitions of citizenship and the 'politics of recognition' of the specificities of ethnicity and the sacred.

While a potential for such a process exists, trends and substantive realities in the current political situation does not lend itself to such lofty ideals; nor to inclusive constitutional citizenship nor to inclusive educational credibility. Rather, narrow identities and imaginations are also operative. Public and educational institutions may be failing to deal with the more complex and multiple identities amongst students. The recent past of humanity has been a major traumatic period in which politicians, administrators, teachers and educators on the whole have not understood the nature of the glue that has held different groups and communities together. The corruptions of values within the public domain, and the assertions of short-term private gains taking over from long-term public interest, have contributed to the corrosion of civil society and civic culture. This may have exacerbated civilisational incompatibilities, which may yet deepen civilisational conflict, as articulated by the late Samuel Huntington.

Instead of utilizing the potential contribution of public servants and teachers to enhance the best interests of society, education is seen as a handmaiden to strengthen the narrow interests of the liberalized market. In other words, broadly based issues of learning and knowledge are replaced by narrowly devised notions of schooling, and education is conflated with training. The ideas of a good broadly based liberal arts education seems to have evaporated over the last half of the twentieth century. Issues of education are conflated with training. Teachers, lecturers and their professions are neither cherished nor lauded, but instead chastised. The disenchantment and disenfranchisement of large numbers of groups, has debased the role of inclusive public policies and the educational process. In the final resort, this could also be potentially dangerous because it can lead to the destabilization of the polity where notions of multiple identities within an increasingly internationalising community are undermined. One of the ways in which the relationship between the sacred and the secular can be conceptualized is by building a repertoire of various phases of the religious and secular knowledge and action which can actually make a difference in the lives of ordinary peoples in many modern states.

Scholars in higher education institutions need to develop ideas of a non-centric basis of knowledge. This presents curriculum developers with the obvious dilemmas of the rootedness of cultures and civilisations as well as their inter-connectedness. Curriculum developers as well as academics, educators and other policy-makers need to examine these complex notions and to analyse the myths, feelings, understandings and concepts of the sacred surrounding them in order to develop rational ways of dealing with the resultant dilemmas. Education has normally been seen as a secular or religious phenomenon, but the division and divisiveness caused by this separation has been very damaging. However, if civilisational knowledge can be pooled differently to draw the best from each phase of human history, then a more syncretic understanding from across civilisations and periods of time could inform the educational process differently. This would help better inter-group and interfaith relations in the context of secular, democratic and the constitutional state.

Within the modern constitutional states vulnerable groups like the Aboriginal Australians and other fourth world peoples (including the mobile populations) ought to maintain their private rights to "Aboriginal Keeping Places" or the Maori "maraes" (ceremonial areas) which may choose of keep private or open to "outsiders" if they consider it appropriate. UNESCO and other international agencies should have mandatory powers to ensure that their cultures are not eradicated under the guise of modernization and superficial constitutionality or concepts of rights.

However, in arguing for the most marginalized groups in the world and the protection of their cultures, I do not want to argue for 'ethnic cultures' or cultural relativism which pertain to their groups in societies which reinforce notions of identity politics and at this level organizations need to reconsider the negative features of an unconditional acceptance traditional and local identities. (Wiktor Stockowski: 'UNESCO's doctrine of human diversity': A secular soterology. Anthropology Today, Vol. 25, No. 3, June 2009)

Civisational basis of sacred and secular knowledge

In the first phase between the fifth century BC and seventh century AD, Universalist concepts of humanity were established by great religions like Zoroastrianism, Buddhism, Christianity and Islam and the Confucian and Hellenistic philosophers. However, as Amin states:

> The declaration of a universalist vocation did not establish a real unification of humanity. The conditions of tributary society did not permit it, and humanity reformed itself into major tributary areas held together by their own particular universalist religious-philosophy (Christendom, Dar Es Islam, the Hindu world, the Confucian world). It is still the case however; that tributary revolution, like all the great revolutionary movements in history, projected itself forwards and produced ahead of its time. (Amin, 1997, p.80)

This focus on the particular faith by each of the tributary religions is indicative of the necessity of the secular state to attempt to develop better inter-faith relations, understandings especially within the public domain and societal contexts. This is however, not any easy task for educators because inter-faith as well as intra-faith legacies are not only about cooperation to develop a common legacy about common and shared culture. It is a legacy of crusades and jihads which are sometimes too complex for educators to teach about. This becomes even more of a problem when political leaders get involved in exacerbating religious conflict. A retired Indian judge Mr. Liberhan has produced a report on the destruction in 1992 of the Babri Mosque in India and named the previous Indian Prime Minister Vajpayee and his deputy Advani of being complicit. The judge recommends that the use of religion in furthering a political agenda be outlawed. (The Guardian, London 25-11-2009) Within such religiously biased regimes educators have little chance of promoting inter-faith understandings.

The second phase of the development of knowledge especially in the Mediterranean region was the Renaissance. During the 11th and 12th centuries it was the collaboration of progressive Catholic, Muslim and Jewish faiths working on Greek scientific and other texts which led to translation of these Greek works from Arabic to Latin and contributed to the Renaissance. Hence, what underpins interfaith dialogue is not the rhetoric of dialogue but an actual project which involves faith communities. This process of interfaith intellectual work is just one example of action and active participation to give life to dialogue. It has a long pedigree in human history and needs revisiting.

Religions have also left a legacy of conflict and much of the current religious strife is based on the memories of wars, terror and persecution derived from religious particularism and specificities of their belief systems. In socially diverse public and educational institutions it is very difficult different versions of these stories, because religious stories and imaginations are deeply engraved into the psyches of believers and therefore not amenable to rational discussions and argument within public and secular institutions. Here it is perhaps important to stress that religion is only one aspect of the multiple identities of many people.

The third phase during the modern period has made a contribution to universalism through the philosophy of the Enlightenment. This social vision of society was based on the notions of a social context and the French Revolution sought a nation based not on ideas of blood and ancestors but of free citizens. The abolition of slavery and ideas of secularism went beyond mere religious toleration. However, despite the fact that the nation was not an affirmation of the particular, but of the universal, such Universalist objectives have not been achieved. During the American Revolution, in a nation largely based on immigration, the right to be 'different' was recognized. Nevertheless, there has been little defense of the right to be 'similar' within a constitutional state, especially of the descendants of slaves and indigenous Americans. Hence, inclusive social and political frameworks for all peoples in diverse states across the world have not been optimally developed.

Fourthly, the rise of socialism in the nineteenth century further contributed to notions of radical transformation especially through Soviet Bolshevism. The price paid by socialism in respecting difference and not building inclusive rights to be 'similar' has been very evident in the dissolution of Yugoslavia and the Soviet Union. These states did not develop inclusive citizenships with common and shared values and the colonized nations did not have substantive options to develop the public policies to liberate the colonized from class inequalities, minoritised status, gender inequalities or narrow nationalisms or racism.

Fifthly, the post-colonial states likewise faced great challenges of maintaining unity, with divisiveness being foisted upon them by the colonizers and their own national elites. Most of them have tried to maintain notions of nominal national unity despite tendencies towards fragmentation. The Bandung Principles (1955) of non-alignment that avoid polarities need to be revisited to develop the notions of secular, inclusive, equal and democratic polities in the Commonwealth. The post-colonial nations were largely based on constitutions, which embody powerful features of the modern state. However, the reversals of these very important principles need to be challenged to strengthen more equal, inclusive and socially cohesive societal frameworks.

The super powers undermined many of the initiatives of the Non-aligned Movement (NAM), especially in relation to the creation of international institutions for greater levels of economic equalities. The most powerful agreement within NAM at Bandung was on issues of 'cultural cooperation' and this was an attempt to curb the cultural chauvinism of imperialist powers. UNESCO had sponsored a critical study of racism and racial attitudes in different cultures. This work included monographs by Claude Levi-Strauss and Marie Jahoda and it reinforced the ideas of race as a 'biological fiction.' The 29 Bandung states condemned 'racialism as a means of cultural suppression' and stressed the need for the study of national cultural history as well as developing measures of cultural cooperation. It is important to remember that the NAM countries helped to strengthen the basis of UNESCO's work on culture, education and scientific cooperation in the post-WWII period.

The educational and political challenge for democratic ideas is to hold notions of respecting difference but at the same time ensuring the right to be similar. Such an approach could begin to break the polarizations between particularism and universalism. The establishment of a common set of resemblances amongst citizens of many states can largely be activated in the political and education systems.

The Sacred and Racism in the Middle Ages

Europe is not immune from the need to reconceptualise the validity of Indian and Nehru's ideas of protective secularism. The history of religions and racism in the middle Ages provides a sanguine backdrop for this reconsideration.

These early interactions between different groups cannot be ignored in discussing issues of the sacred and diverse identities in Europe. The Greeks and the Romans distinguished between the civilized and the barbarous but these categories were not regarded as hereditary. While there was colonization and there were slaves, there was no concept of race and racism although ethnic prejudice did exist in antiquity.

Anti-Judaism was endemic to Christianity from the beginning. Writers like George Fredrickson state that anti-semitism became racism when the belief took hold that Jews were intrinsically and organically evil rather merely having wrong beliefs and wrong dispositions.

This stereotype lasted through the Crusades, the Black Death in the mid-fourteenth century and Jews were massacred when racism adopted the garb of Christianity. However, Robert Bartlett argues that this racism or proto-racism of the late middle Ages extended beyond the Jews. As the core of Catholic Europe expanded, the attitudes towards the conquered and colonized peripheries of Europe were based on notions of superiority including the subordination of the Slavic people on one side and the Irish on the other side of Europe. This anticipated the feelings of dominance and entitlement that would characterize the later expansion of Europeans to Asia, Africa and the Americas. "Ghettoisation and racial discrimination marked the later centuries of the Middle Ages" (Bartlett, 1993). Bartlett states that this was ethnocentric because German descent was a requirement for holding office, as was belonging to a guild and marriages between Slavs and Germans were forbidden. Hence, this drive for uniformity and homogeneity provided a backdrop for lack of cultural pluralism in Europe.

In the fourteenth and early fifteenth centuries the Iberian peninsula saw the rise of anti-black racism; the beginning of identifying blacks with servitude, since sub-Saharan Africans were seen as descendants of Ham (James, 1997).

However, Islam itself and especially the Moriscos and the Jewish Conversos suffered a terrible fate in Spain especially after the Reconquista of 1492. In the period 1609–1614 the entire Morisco population of one third of a million was driven out of Spain by the powerful religious champions of the True Church.

The situation is more complex because during the Renaissance the rise of Christian Humanism points towards a totally different direction and further change in the relationship of the sacred with the society.

The Role of Imperialism and Colonialism

The rise of imperialism and colonialism in the nineteenth century British Empire provides a further complication to the issues of the sacred and the secular.

The Concordat of 1801 between the church and the French imperial state led to the revival and the strengthening of the papacy across the Roman Catholic world. John Stuart Mill wanted to relegate religion from the realm of politics to the domestic domain. Saint Simon and Mazzini envisioned a rational deity, which was for secular "progress" and instead of belief in grace focused on a belief in justice for humanity and its humanization. The Marxists and socialists after 1848 had their own scientific doctrines and thought of religion as a result of "false consciousness".

The major problem, which the 21st century seems to have inherited from the nineteenth century, is that while some intellectuals remained progressive others have turned to religious belief and most of the masses remain devout. This is true not just in Europe and the Americas but in Asia, Middle East and Africa as well. Hence, there is no simple equation between low levels of education and high levels of devoutness because many people at the present time from the educated elites have become devout.

As imperialism and colonialism spread in the nineteenth century empires of Europe, intellectuals from the European dominated coastal cities in Asia and Middle East also challenged the older forms of religious institutions and philosophic elements in their religious inheritance. Hence the strengthening of the nation state, and its spread through colonization, led to the religions also strengthening and modernizing themselves. This dialectical inter-relationship between the sacred and the state cannot be ignored in enhancing our contemporary understanding of this intricate and problematic relationship between the sacred, the secular and the state. Part of this complication is that the secular is not seen in the protective Nehruvian sense but in oppositional terms to the sacred, although the recent Indian election has vindicated the strengths of a socially inclusive multicultural Indian state. Is there an object lesson here for the other member states of the UN system and are there new ways of thinking which can placed into action now in the international conventions which related to cultural and belief systems?

The recent economic crises have thrown up the issue of ethical ways of dealing in the financial sector. Here the role of the Islamic version of working in the financial and banking sectors has provided many states with another model of working in the financial markets. The neoliberal and light touch regulation in most of the worlds markets have failed to be transparent and have an ethical basis. Hence, Sharia compliant financial arrangements have become popular. In Britain HSBC offers a home ownership scheme with the name Amanah. This means trust, in the moral and legal sense and has been successful in Britain. Obviously, here the important issue is how faiths can help to bring greater levels of transparency in the financial world.

Religion, Culture and World Heritage

In this section a few issues will be referred to briefly: (i) the destruction of heritage sites by other faiths; (ii) the attempts to renovate which lead to negating the heritage site status: and (iii) the claim of heritage artifacts by the countries of origin currently stored in the so-called encyclopedic museums.

At the present time when religions and other belief systems, speak of heritage, frequently they can only make utterances from behind the barriers of privileged positions, protected under domestic law. In most cases they are protected by secular states and by secular constitutions, which many of these groups try to denounce. For example, believers largely think of heritage sites which pertain to their own faiths and not to those of others and the destruction of the Ajodhya Mosque in India by Hindu fundamentalists is one recent example of this issue. More recently, the Taliban destroyed the Bamiyan Buddhist monuments in Afghanistan, which UNESCO is currently trying to reconstruct.

States can also try to makeover monuments to cash-in on tourism as has happened with the Tiwanku civilization in the village of Tiwanaku where the Bolivian archeologists gave a facelift to the Akapanka pyramid. This civilsation reached Bolivia, and parts of Peru, Argentina and Chile, existed from 1500BC to AD1200. The Pyramid was supposed to have been built between AD300 and 700 and was supposedly built in stone and has now been plastered during renovation UNESCO is considering whether to withdraw its listing as a world archeological treasure. (*The Guardian*, London, 21-10-2009)

There are also current debates about the way in which European and American museums which now refer to themselves as 'encyclopedic' institutions are facing demands for return of artistic heritage by countries of origin. These include the demands for the Parthenon and Benin sculptures by Greece and Nigeria from the British Museum; the Pergamon alters now in Berlin and moved from Turkey as well as the Louvre which Egyptian artifacts. What are the best ways of resolving these fairly serious inter-state and intercultural conflicts for artifacts of human heritage?

From one perspective, major religious bodies are seen to be caught up in reactionary movements that do not respect the heritage artifacts and sites which pertain to those of other faith groups. In multi-faith and secular societies this necessitates the intensification of interfaith and intercultural activities and there are examples of social action projects where the smoothest religious discourse on citizenship issues can and has taken place, and where leadership in nongovernmental organizations' has been both positive and dynamic. For instance, cooperation between Christians and Buddhists takes place through the coordination of different non-governmental organizations engaged in citizenship and development activities in urban and rural areas. In 1980, the Thai Interreligious Commission for Development was founded by leading Buddhists and Christians in the field of development. This is a forum where religious leaders and lay people, mostly from Buddhism and Christianity, came together in order to share experiences in social action and in the life of the community (Phongpit, 1986). Nevertheless, unless such ecumenical dialogues are accompanied by institutional measures and social action to strengthen inter-faith links, they do not serve functions of better intercultural relations in secular constitutional and democratic states.

There are numerous examples of organizations within civil society which are not just making superficial nods to inter-faith dialogue but use faiths to work towards achieving certain social goals. Hence, faith groups are working together to achieve Millennium Development Goals. In this respect the Tony Blair Foundation and its project Malaria No More to eradicate malaria and preventable deaths through health education and practical health measures. Churches, mosques and temples are ideally placed to deliver integrated health care and community-based health care education initiatives. Hence, faith communities can be mobilized to work across faith groups to deal with various common and shared levels of problems, exclusions and inequalities. Likewise, in Sri Lanka the Buddhist Sarvodaya Movement has set up a centre using health education programmes to foster conflict resolution across religious divides. Islamic and Christian organizations like Islamic Relief, Muslim Aid, Christian Aid, CAFOD and the Aga Khan Foundation have worked in countries like Pakistan. These initiatives help not only those within the faith but outside them as well. It is possible that such action based projects can then become a basis for establishing respect for religious and cultural heritage sites of other groups in socially and culturally diverse societies.

Inclusionary Initiatives and Measures

Exclusion of groups on religious or social groups' ethnic or racial grounds poses major challenges for all involved in teaching and pedagogical planning. Similarly, fundamentalist beliefs about such elements as the economy or the market can have similar exclusive effects, and can give rise to other fundamentalisms. For example, Islamic law reform, which will reinforce and emphasize those verses of the Qur'an which counsel freedom of religion and equality principles (regardless of gender or religious faith), is a major issue. In a very real sense, the direction of reform of modern Islamic Shari'a, with concern for matters such as the principle of reciprocity, will have a substantive impact on global citizenship rights and religious freedom in a contextually different world. Abdullahi Ahmed An-Naim (1990) argued for instance:

> I have distinguished between Islam and Shari'a in the sense that the latter is a particular interpretation of the former in a given historical context. Although I believe that a modern interpretation of Islam will produce a version of Shari'a which is capable of sustaining the whole range of human right.... The fault is that of contemporary Muslims who insist on implementing archaic concepts in radically transformed circumstances. (1990: 68; see also Art, 1990).

One of the strengths of Islamic knowledge is that it has drawn on a wealth of cultures, which include Semitic, Hellenistic, Iranian and Indian. The Hellenistic role of Aristotelian philosophy has been profound. This syncretic influence needs to be maintained by dialogue not only with the faithful but those who are not of the faith. The power of the concept of knowledge is recognised by the Islamic notion that "kings are rulers of people but scholars are rulers of kings". In the contemporary context however, kings, scholars and people increasingly need to ascribe to democratic engagements and values.

The rise of strong belief systems in modern secular states may be a reflection of how secular states have failed to provide a safe inclusive and secure framework for different faith communities. It also may be partly attributed to strong assertions of the rights of citizens, which are not accompanied by effective measures to ensure their implementation, at both the political and social levels. While notions of universalism are cited they do not seem to have any substantive or dynamic meanings in tackling, for instance, narrow nationalisms in many European contexts. The division that took place at the international human rights conference in Vienna between the Western and Asian countries on individual and group rights is another case in point. This distinction was not shared by the Asian non-governmental organizations or by the Dalai Lama. Speaking to that conference on 15 June 1993, he stated that:

> Recently some Asian governments have contended that the standards of human rights laid down in the Universal Declaration of Human Rights are those advocated by the West and cannot be applied to Asia and other parts of the Third World because of differences in culture and differences in social and economic development. I do not share this view and I am convinced that the majority of Asian people do not support this view either, for it is the inherent nature of all human beings to yearn for freedom, equality and dignity, and they have a right to achieve that. I do not see any contradiction between the need for economic development and the need for respect of human rights. The rich diversity of cultures and religions should help to strengthen the fundamental human rights in all communities.

Yet, we do need to examine carefully the recognition of group rights and their implications for an embracing polity especially as it focuses once again on the distinction between universality and particularity.

The application of principles for constitutional citizenship within the major world religions will go a long way towards the enhancing of human dignity—in concert with inter-faith and intercultural education in nation states. These concentric interests have forced the religious factor to be cognizant of secular value standards. Except at the margins, the creative edge of growth in humanistic/secular values has had a positive effect on the scholastic and popular presentation of religious formulations and identities.

Research and Curricular Issues in Higher Education Systems

In dealing with such complexities teachers, learners and institutions would need an enormous amount of support to acquire relevant skills, knowledge and understandings. These virtues can be developed through enabling participation of learners and lecturers in situations which embody greater levels of equality.

The ways to good life at community and educational levels do not depend on singular conceptions but on a mutual realization. The evolution of cosmopolitan unity lies in recognizing the values of civilisational and cultural diversity as mentioned earlier, which as Alain Locke suggests can draw on the principles of cultural reciprocity. Hence, both within the informal lifelong learning and formal university education as well as the cultural aspects of the arts, music, and drama have been used to enhance interfaith understandings as well as giving specific faith groups an opportunity to speak for themselves at an educational level, without being misrepresented.

In this sense the role of those in education is to engender an interest in students to become active citizens, based on public policies which are inclusive. Here, it is important to examine the kind of history is taught within education systems. Is it a history of conflict, of militarism, triumphalism or is it a history of building friendships? Is it a history, which leads to ethnic cleansing, or is it history which is disarmed and helps intercultural understandings? The real challenge is how the democratic processes in society and experiential democratic education can guarantee social integration in highly differentiated contexts. Yet there are already positive examples amongst many young British folk. The following are examples from the British context and people of immigrant origin. Das, of the Asian Dub Foundation, describes himself as a '*Hindi British Asian, English, Bengali European*'. Pandit G, describes himself as a *half-Irish, Asian, Scot*' (*The Times*, London, 2nd July 1999). These modern multiple identities are of great significance in modern democratic states because there no 'hidden hatreds'. Paradoxically, at the level of historical diversities, another set of issues come into play with devolution of power. For instance, it may be easier in UK, to enhance cordial relations especially between England, Wales and Scotland. However, in devolved Northern Ireland, it may be more difficult to make links and solidarities across religious and nationality divides. Here the notion of the *Kulturnation* on basis of the ethnic and the sacred is more powerful than the *Staatnation* based on constitutions and citizenship.

There are also difficult lessons to be learnt from ethnic cleansing in the old Yugoslavia. Can the same Kosovo fields be understood by both the Albanians and the Serbians to build shared meanings and not triumphalism and imagined histories and imagined pasts, which exacerbate intercultural conflicts? Can the symbols of the battles in Kosovo fields or the Battle of the Boyne in Northern Ireland be used to develop shared heritage sites?

The importance of history is also shown by the Tbilisi Initiative of the Council of Europe in the Caucasus region to develop a non-militaristic and non-conflictual intercultural history in countries like Georgia, Armenia and Azerbaijan. This has however; failed because of the political interventions and in its aftermath there was the invasion of Georgian expansion into the smaller republics leading to Russian intervention in 2008. This is an object lesson to the members of the Council of Europe where these issues are also of a major political, educational, historical research and curricular significance.

Hence the role of history in secular, multicultural and multifaith societies is to build shared and common values and resemblances among individuals and groups and to be used to develop active democratic citizens who can work for greater levels of equalities. Greater levels of equalities can also help reduce binary oppositions such as the winners/losers; religious/atheist; us/them; and belongers/non-belongers.

Since constitutional citizenship legally bestows equality, which is both gradable nor divisible, then racial justice and equity can be actualized only if institutional racism is absent. These issues become more critical as the rise of xenophobia, chauvinism, and racism can have consequences for even the dominant nationalities, within many countries. However, for those who are not citizens, indigenous peoples or even immigrants, their rights are more tenuous, especially groups like refugees and asylum-seekers.

The simmering of religious discrimination also takes on exclusionary significance at public institutional levels and Islamophobia has resonance for other faiths. In other words if in many states which discriminate against Muslims and the other faith do not take any action, then they can be next. Hence, inter-faith dialogues and initiatives need to include measures against the pillorying or victimization of any one faith group.

Intercultural education within higher education systems ought to recognize the possibility of the rise of reactive identities in many European countries. Amongst minority communities a 'siege mentality', largely sustained by language or religion, can develop. Amongst the dominant groups this may be based on racism, xenophobia and territorial ownership to the exclusion of those seen as 'the other'. Intercultural conflicts based on a combination of these differences have already taken place. For instance, 'ethnic cleansing' returned to south east Europe fifty years after the defeat of fascism. The challenge for political and modern constitutional systems is to turn singular notions of identities to notions of identities which are multiple.

Changing nature of Human Rights

In historical terms not only societies but also the nature and types of human rights change. For instance within modern constitutional systems, rights changed over time from the eighteenth century, when the first generation of rights were largely civil in nature, to the nineteenth century when political rights became a reality, to the third generation of social rights in the twentieth century, which also include human rights. Given the various levels of inequalities, the state also tries, as Marshall indicates, to initiate a 'tendency towards equality' by creating basic conditions that lead towards social equality. This is a dynamic and active concept, not a passive one. However, political devolution, regionalism and centralization within many countries introduce a new set of issues. They create a new political logic, because not only are there issues of inter-relationships between the devolved and regionalized polities, but also between the contemporary and historically diverse groups within them. These devolutions in turn need to be reconciled to the harmonization and centralization processes especially at the level of the nation states and an international organization like UNESCO.

The challenge is to build social and cultural cohesion and inclusive polities, which can accommodate notions of difference but also create conditions for the belongingness and equity of diverse groups. From a higher education and research perspective this presents a 'creative moment', since notions of intercultural and inter-faith education as well as, secular values can be utilized to develop integrative mentalities based on notions of differences and multiple identities. Such academic work cannot just be based on well meaning rhetoric but on sound social science and humanities research. In this respect for those who work in higher education systems some aspects of cultural diversity may need to be challenged.

There is already a legacy of the exclusive and negative phenomena of racism, xenophobia, chauvinism and sexism. However, constitutional citizenship and human rights is a recent concept as part of the modern nation state because in ancient and medieval societies, (where monarchies, empires, and chiefdoms existed) people's rights were more circumscribed.

Toleration

Ethnic and religious toleration continues to be a delicate issue in our times. At the international level, there is a growing sensitivity to changing patterns of acceptable behaviors and continued escalation of threats about the 'clash of civilizations'. The topic is central in any contemporary considerations of societal conflict—and its prevention and resolution. Religious toleration is among the most basic universal rights, but does not extend to practices that conflict with other basic democratic rights. Frequently, lack of respect for each others' human dignity and the cause of conflict occur when cultural distinctions are exacerbated by and through religious differences and identifications. In other contexts political and economic exclusions and marginalization can also exacerbate conflicts.

A programme "Face to Faith" was launched last summer to enable exchange between young people from different faiths. The programme has the function of improving religious literacy and to nurture amongst new generation to become champions of religious tolerance and peace. It will work in 15 countries in the first year and try to reach 20,000 children. (I. Linden, Tony Blair Foundation, launch by Tony Blair, 9th June 2009)

Religion can contribute to human liberation as well as to human oppression:

> Certainly religions can be authoritarian, tyrannical and reactionary and all too often were so in the past: they can produce anxiety, narrow-mindedness, intolerance, injustice, frustration and social isolation; they can legitimate and inspire immorality, social abuses and wars in a people or between peoples. But religions can also have liberating effects, oriented on the future and beneficial to human beings, and indeed often have had. They can disseminate trust in life, generosity, tolerance, solidarity, creativity and social commitment, and can encourage spiritual renewal, social reforms and world peace. (Kung, 1991, p. 46)

There is a commonsense understanding that it is the duty of a constitutional secular state to protect diverse sacred and faith systems. It therefore follows that the faith and belief systems have reciprocal obligations to protect the state and its institutions, which guarantee their safety, security and freedom.

A contemporary addressing of the increased problem of intolerance and lack of respect penetrates the heart of citizenship and fundamental freedoms. There cannot be a full appreciation of values until there is an understanding of the religious factor.

Theoretically, respect and toleration constitute a major values taught by and through religions. The role of religions in human values can be paramount through identification with values of citizenship. More precisely, most societies or sovereign states have become linked to international instruments through their Constitutions and as signatories to treaties. Are there ways the religions and religious communities can subject themselves to the same scrutiny, which they often demand of "the other"?

Are religious bodies prepared to face the intensity of their obligations as citizens thinking in an even more radical manner? The remarkably rapid international and national expansion of citizenship rights could be the subject for analysis in it, but one thing is clear, citizenship can be the interfacing edge of religion and culture in any society, in the search for an articulation of social values.

Religions are not strangers to the field of citizenship rights, and continue to occupy a significant position in the struggle to ensure implementation of citizenship rights and the 'conscientisation' internationally and domestically—most lively at the international and broader national levels, but locally as well. Religion is a significant factor in global analysis—as long as it participates and does not pontificate. The dilemma is clear, that if the major religions projected their innate ecumenical sense of universality, that is, if they could communicate a spirit of solidarity, toleration and unity, then distinctiveness would become a creative moment in present-day culture. Hence, distinctive identities may not be exclusive of the notions of multiple citizenship and identities.

Issues of Acceptance, Inclusion and Human Rights

Following the havoc of the Second World War, the nations of the world accepted a set of standards or goals, which have penetrated every society from that day to this. The opening phrase of the Universal Declaration of Human Rights recognizes the inherent dignity of all members of the human family. The now widespread use of the elastically defined concept human dignity serves as the cornerstone for the most broadly accepted document in human history. The other parts of the complete document, the Covenant on Economic, Social and Cultural Rights and the Covenant on Civil and Political Rights, flesh out and add to the principles of the Declaration. Being Conventions they do have the status of law since entering into force in 1976. The Universal Declaration and the two Conventions (with an Optional Protocol) constitute the finest achievement of standard setting for and by the human community to date; the International Bill of Human Rights. More than 60 additional human rights instruments adopted by the United Nations cover most aspects of behavior in order to protect, enhance, and develop human dignity. One of the instruments commanding attention is the 1981 Declaration on the Elimination of all Forms of Intolerance and Discrimination based on Religion or Belief (see Walkate, 1989, for the Declaration's history).

Modern value dilemmas (in what Saul Bellow describes as the "moronic inferno") do contain exceedingly dangerous manifestations, the rise of narrow nationalism, chauvinism, fanaticism, neo-fascism, racism and sexism. The rise of these phenomena is not restricted to the USA and Europe, but poses even graver threats outside those regions of the world. There is an elastic linkage between ethnicity, multiculturalism and religion, but in our own mind and experience it is these arenas which have most to do with each other. In the European context, close ties exist between religion and national identity. Similarly, the August 1991 revolution gave the Russian Orthodox Church a unique opportunity to be identified with the people after years of subordination to communism. One can almost be certain that if the religious factor is not cognizant of citizenship rights standards, the relationship will sour. One senses the tension in huge democracies such as India where communal violence flashes. The situation in Poland changes rapidly as the Roman Catholic Church loses the luster of Father Popieluszko's martyr complex, and becomes another centrist power. Indications are that anti-Semitism has not lessened its grip. On the Russian borders, we are all aware of the Armenian-Azerbaidzhani ethnic/religious disputes with mosques and churches as pawns in a complex war. The interplay of Catholic, Orthodox and Muslim cultural forces haunts us daily from the Balkans, where citizenship rights seemed to have drowned in the European pond. The Irish/English tribal dispute is so subtle; we sometimes forget its antecedents.

The younger generation is also orientated towards vandalism, violence and crime, and some of it may be the result of experiencing injustice, marginalization or the lack of a voice. Such behavior may result from an attempt to resist the denial of citizenship values and the continued stereotyping of victims as the cause of social problems. The lack of a voice for certain groups of university students may be one practical manifestation of this, and lecturers and higher education institutions can deal with this issue by developing inclusive institutional policies, practices and curricula.

Higher ducation systems may need to consider whether interculturalising Greek ideas of paidea and German notions of Bildung to build a broadly based framework of values amongst university students.

Conclusion

Potential conflicts which have implications for heritage sites have recently been arising between social diverse groups. This is especially true of societies in the process of democratization which need to lead towards specific recognitions on the one hand, but also grounded in generally accepted constitutional principles. Thus, dialogue based research and teaching within higher education institutions within democratic frameworks can lead to the discovery of shared values or, at the least, to an appreciation of differences and diversities out of a shared societal base.

As educators and others attempt to overcome potential conflict through sustaining a democratic union of diversities, this paper has suggested that education for constitutional citizenship and human rights offers an approach to values in which communities can have a dialogue about that which is sacred. Since common basic values centre on relationships which in many societies are influenced by the religious factor, it is worth inquiring whether or not world religions can contribute to enhancing inter-faith values education within intercultural encounters by sharing a commitment to citizenship and human rights precepts and standards. Can they also accept the legitimacy of modern democratic and secular constitutional principles and help to protect the sacred pillars of the independent judiciary, legislature and democratically functioning governments?

References

Amin, S. (1997) *Capitalism in the Age of Globalisation* (London: Zed Press)

An-Naim, A. (1990) *Toward an Islamic Reformation* (Syracuse: Syracuse University Press)

Art, D. (1990) *The application of international human rights law in Islamic states. Human Rights Quarterly*, 12, pp.202–230.

Bartlett, R. (1993) *The Making of Europe: Conquest, Colonisation and Cultural Change* 95–130, (Princeton: Princeton University Press)

Fredrickson, G. (2002) *Racism: A Short History* (Princeton: Princeton University Press)

James, H. (1997) The Iberian Roots of American Racist Thought, *William and Mary, Quarterly* Vol. 54, pp. 143–166

Kung, H. (1991) *Global Responsibility: in search of a new world ethic* (London: SCM Press)

Kymlica, W. (1995) *A Multicultural Citizenship* (Oxford: Clarandon Press)

Phongphit, S. (1986) The cooperation between Christians and Buddhists. In: G Kung & J. Moltmann (eds.) *Christianity Among World Religions* (Edinburgh: T. & T. Clark)

Walkate, J. (1989) *Conscience and liberty. International Journal of Religious Freedom*, Winter, pp. 21–35

The Times, London: 2nd July 1999

Inequality, Diversity and Life-long Learning:

Intercultural Perspectives

Introduction

The last year has evidenced dramatic changes at both political and economic levels in many parts of the world but especially in Europe and the Islamic countries in the Mediterranean Sea and Arabian Peninsula regions. In the European Union the globalised neoliberal market has led to a collapse of the economies of Greece, the Irish Republic and Portugal. This is not just a serious moment for these three countries but the European Union and Europe as a whole since these economic cataclysms have significant political consequences. In the case of Portugal three countries which were former colonies want to help their European friend by buying five and ten year bonds. The President Ramos Horta of Timor stated that three members (including Brazil) of the Community of Portuguese Language Countries from the "third world" would show unprecedented solidarity to fight market speculators. (*The Portugal News*, 23-4-2010). There are probably friends of the Irish Republic who would demonstrate similar solidarity and support for the peoples of this island.

As the Stock Exchanges improve their ratings it is the citizens who experience the pain. As the neoliberal ideology allows the state to better its competitive position the population suffers more. This is what my friend at University of Athens, Professor George Markou calls: 'an era of global dictatorship of financial markets.' With the disappearance of social solidarities distress has now been created at planetary levels and cultural nationalism is not the answer to the state we find ourselves in. The question now is how to organise mass movements at national, regional and international levels which can ensure the public and institutional basis for the fast eroding social democracies, public institutions and the social and public policy safety nets.

In the southern Mediterranean and the Arabian region the collapse of the political systems brings possibilities of a new perhaps less authoritarian and more democratic forms of governance. But in this region with a youth bulge of the 18–25 year population forming part of the massive unemployed group what are these groups up against? These young and poor people confront a long legacy of religious and cultural nationalism, as do people in Europe and the Americas. We therefore, need to rethink of what drives hierarchal, authoritarian and religious regimes. This recent collapse of authoritarian regimes have challenged the culturalism which has opposed the secularism and has been politically based on atavistic tribalism and religionism, The ordinary citizens in this region are trying to reconfigure the nature of the social democratic forces they want to establish but this progressive change is not a foregone conclusion because for instance, in Palestine the nationalism of the fundamentalist Hamas is opposed by an even more radical Fundamentalist Salafi Islam which aims to build a single Islamic commonwealth in place of nation states. Tawheed and Jihad means 'oneness of God and holy war or struggle.' In Cairo most recently, this was demonstrated by the burning of two Coptic Churches and killing of 12 Copts, an act of the very same Salafis, who have links with Saudi Arabia. (*The Guardian*, London. 9-5-2011)

Benedict Anderson argues that for nationalism three basic cultural conceptions have to lose their 'axiomatic grip' on human consciousness: these are the endowment of sacredness to languages (be it Sanskrit, Latin or Arabic); the acceptance of divine monarch and an idea of time that does not distinguish between history and cosmology. The World Muslim League and Wahhabism for instance, replace quam (nation of equals) with the idea of ummah (a community of believers). This reversal of history does not distinguish between history and cosmology. It instead argues for a community based on sacred languages, divine concept of the Caliphs and time as being eternal. Hence, the crooked line that history travels is banished and divine religiosity becomes the heart of statecraft and the ordinary citizens in the Islamic states face a daunting challenge to reverse these powerful forces. Lest we think that these issues only pertain to Islamic state, we should try to remember the power of similar forces on the European continent or of Fundamentalist Christianity in the U.S. arguing for Creationism and the necessity of establishing secular democratic values within our own societies. This is especially needed at a time when it might seem more comfortable to retreat into the safe havens of glorious, secure and mono-cultural pasts. In fact, the real challenges we and the young people in countries like Tunisia and Egypt need to think about should move us beyond nationalism of Benedict Anderson into thinking about secular, cosmopolitan, multicultural and more economically equal global polities—not just neoliberal economies.

Let me illustrate this by referring to the case of the Irish Republic. On the 16th June 1995 I spoke at a very memorable Conference in Dublin. The then President Mary Robinson addressed the Conference on Intercultural Issues at Drumcondra

College. The President did something very simple—she went through her diary from 1st January 1995 to the day she attended our conference. She started out by stating that the Republic of Ireland was not generally perceived to be a multicultural society. However, recounting her diary engagements between 1st January & 16th June she painted a picture of a very complex intercultural set of experiences. The President outlined her involvement in policies and other engagements of an intercultural nature. This is being stated here as an indication of the fact that there are hardly any states in the EU region or Europe generally which are not historically and contemporaneously multicultural and do not have issues of intercultural understandings, cooperation or conflict to address. Later on I offer some detailed thoughts about the different meanings of the terms 'multicultural' and 'intercultural'. For now I just want to highlight the essence of 'multicultural' is that it is a descriptive term of a society inhabited by different socio-cultural groups. These include those based on linguistic, social class, religious, ethnic, territorial or non-territorial nationalities (like the Roma or the Irish Traveller community.) The essence of intercultural is the basis of social interaction; developmental dialogues as well policies and practices which enable these interactions. Hence, the term 'multicultural' is a descriptive term and the other is about activities. The Life Course Institute could be in the forefront of developing these intercultural policies and practices which have the advantage acting as glue between generations as well as establishing connectivity in inter-generational terms and try to reduce inequalities especially with the inclusions of the disabled and older groups.

It is over 100 years since the publication of James Joyce's book *Ulysses*. As in the past there will be celebrations of his work on the 16th June next month. In this literary book Joyce portrays Dublin through the characters in *Ulysses* as a cosmopolitan city with echoes from all over Europe, yet, they all are genuine Dubliners. Stephen Dedalus has elements of being Greek, Molly, Leopold Bloom's wife was born in Gibraltar and Bloom (her husband) is Middle European, Austro Hungarian. Bloom's fantasises on the New Jerusalem as a New Bloomusalem which he Bloom would rule: "New worlds for old, Union of all Jew, Moslem and Gentile ... General Amnesty, weekly carnival with masked licence, bonuses for all, Esperanto the universal language with universal brotherhood. Mixed races and mixed marriages" (U. 15, 1683–99).

One could also say that Joyce's perceptions of Dublin as a cosmopolitan and multicultural city in a complex and plural Irish polity virtually interprets the Ireland of today with its firstly economic success and then its downfall. The economic success was reflected through through pharmaceuticals, IT and technology; financial one through the Dublin of luxury cars and property boom; and cultural success was evidenced by U2, West life and the Corrs; or designers like Kennedy and Rocha.

This boom had banished the sense of doom in the Republic and as in James Joyce's formulation 'a nightmare from which I am trying to awake.' The Irish university community now might wish to reflect on how to capture the positive creative and imaginative energies of this period and genuinely recreate an economic infrastructure which benefits the whole of the Irish polity.

A colonial Ireland of Joycean day in which emigration was common is changed in the 1990's to one which there is immigration from both rich and poorer countries took place. Now, three decades after the last emigration of young Irish people there is another emigration of the highly qualified and motivated professionals. Hence, while the earlier migrations might have been referred to as 'brawn drain' the current one is more of a 'brain drain'—the very people who are needed to rejuvenate the Irish polity and economy. The meanings of these diasporic realities for individuals and their families are of critical importance. The question for the Lifecourse is how these macro-levels changes can be mapped at micro-levels and what are the implications for families and children.

These peaks and troughs of the last half century have also given Roddy Doyle in his latest collection to paint a picture of Ireland after the death of the Celtic tiger, and the Barrytown trilogy documents the recession of the 80's and the early 90's, and the short story collection on economic immigrants and *The Deportees* of the of the flavour of them and the boom-time in between.

It portrays the contradictions and complexities which exist in all member states of the Europe and other regions of the world as mentioned earlier. More recently, Doyle picks up after the broadcast of the *Family* and *Bullfighting* the complexities of family life and the changed times.

Fintan O'Toole's controversial book *Ship of Fools* explained why the Celtic Tiger died such a spectacular death and now in *Enough is Enough* he offers a way forward for this small and creative country. This is a map to the future of the Republic where there is shelter and security; a viable health system; which provides good education, equality and citizenship.

Political and Social Contexts

Discussions about the need for inclusion, interculturalism and citizenship in the Ireland, Britain and the European Union are taking place at a time when powers have been devolved to Scotland, Wales and Northern Ireland. The ten newer member states in the EU also present new challenges for positive integration. Both these developments in the EU provide an opportunity to develop ideas about interculturalism and inclusion especially to capture the imagination of all citizens, who are frequently reported to be disaffected with the political process. Within this broader process of intercultural relations, consideration of human rights and inclusive citizenship initiatives are issues of great importance.

Harmonisation and centralisation at the level of the European Union are leading to calls for eliminating racism, under Article 13 of the Amsterdam Treaty (European Community, 1999, Article 13, XEX Art. 6a). The Racial Equality Directive adds a force to establish minimum standards for legal protection and these issues after the boom years are not new to the Republic.

This contribution will discuss the idea of developing a framework based on historical and contemporary aspects of diversity beyond the minimum standards and their relevance to an inclusive society, which integrates issues of historical and contemporary diversities. In particular terms, issues of identity in singular or multiple forms—are relevant for intercultural relations and citizenship. Within complex democratic societies where economic globalisation, collapse of financial institutions and technological changes may be leading to high levels of unemployment, democracies and democratic institutions are subject to great stress. The need to deepen democracy entails a critical appraisal of societal diversity and the development of collaborative community participation to strengthen active citizenship. Strategies of cooperation and collaboration open up discussions about the 'belongingness' of diverse groups to a society and its institutions. This needs to be strengthened for all groups in society from the preschool education to lifelong formal and informal education. This is necessary not just to provide skills to get jobs but to ensure that in multicultural and diverse communities the good intercultural education that a school provides is not reversed by parents and adults in xenophobic and racist communities. Hence, the Lifecourse Institute can explore the need for parental, family and adult learning to facilitate intercultural understandings.

Secularism and Religion

Modern constitutional and democratic states in the EU have an important task in protecting the rights of all citizens through the law. These include the protection of religious institutions and the right of citizens to believe or not to believe in the sacred. This paper does not use the term secular in its commonsense understandings of the separation of church and state. Jawaharlal Nehru the first Prime Minister of India, provided an Indian version of the European notion of the term secularism which means "that while religion is completely free, the state gives protection and opportunity to all (religions and cultures) and thus brings about an atmosphere of tolerance and cooperation." (Santihder, p.3). The role of a secular constitutional state is therefore necessarily not in conflict with the sacred or the religious but merely to provide protection to those with no beliefs as well as those of different belief systems. The Janus-faced nature of the sacred as well as the Janus faced nature of the nation state has implications for inter-faith understandings or of conflict which merit detailed consideration. Can this help the Irish polity to develop powerful secular ethic in the public domain and allow for genuine inter-faith understanding in the private domain.

Religions are both transnational and multicultural. Their strength also has the weaknesses of an Achilles' heel in achieving inclusive public values in the 21st century. It is not only the Dalai Lama but also Hans Küng (1991), for one, who outlines his major project for encouraging an ethical quest as such: "No survival without a world ethic. No world peace without peace between the religions. No peace between the religions without dialogue between the religions" (p.xv).

In Britain and Ireland, the numbers who are religious and regularly attend the Church has declined dramatically (although still about 46% in Ireland) but for the younger generation is below 10%. Nevertheless, religious institutions and especially schools play a very powerful role in maintaining separate institutions. In Northern Ireland Peter Robinson of the DUP called for a 'roadmap' to a single education system. He called the current system a 'benign form of apartheid' and the need to 'breakdown divisions and build for a better future...given our divided history'. The express purpose according to him was to overcome difficulties of building a shared and united community. (*Irish Times*, 8-4-2011) After the killing of Constable Ronan Kerr, Robinson attended his funeral and this was the first time he had been to a Catholic mass. A few days later Martin McGuiness attended the funeral of Mr. Robinson's mother-in-law, the first time he had been inside a fundamentalist Free Presbyterian Church. (*The Economist*, 30-4-2011, pp. 31–32) Should these acts of chivalry and friendship not have positive resonances in the educational discourse and public political life of the Republic?

While a potential for such a process exists, the current political situation lends itself neither to such lofty ideals nor to educational credibility. In practice however, narrow identities and imaginations are also operative and national public institutions may be failing to deal with the more complex and multiple identities amongst European cities. The recent past of humanity has been a major traumatic period in which politicians, administrators, and educators on the whole have not understood the nature of the glue that has held different groups and communities together. The corruption within and of the public domain, the assertions of short-term and private gains taking precedent over long-term public interest, has corroded civil society and public and civic culture and citizenship values. Now, is the time for the citizens to hold the political class accountable and to call for public ethic, morality and probity which is beyond reproach? This is necessary so that they utilize the potential contribution of public institutions to enhance the best interests of society, and not remain handmaidens to strengthen the narrow interests of the liberalised market.

Interculturalism and citizenship

Issues of interculturalism, inclusion and human rights should be an integral part of an entitlement to being a citizen.

Democratic engagements of adults and young people in a democratic context partly get formed within the education system. So, a democratic ethos in education is important, and this needs to be experienced in the context of the wider community (International Centre for Intercultural Studies, 1996). Youth work, further and other formal and non-formal lifelong learning are all important. There is an African adage that 'it takes a whole village to educate a child'. There is obviously a lot to this adage, but nowadays it is possible that the village itself needs reeducating. This is especially true because both young people and adults may not sufficiently understand the historical and contemporary underpinnings of society and the issues of its complexity and 'belongingness' within it. The changing nature of identities, in particular, may lead either to conflict or to peace and stability.

The terms 'social diversity' and 'multiculturalism' are used descriptively, and therefore raise issues about which there is no agreement. Firstly, there is the commonsense notion that European societies have become multicultural. It is assumed that it is the post-World War II immigrants to Western Europe who have caused diversity, leading to a loss of national identity. The comparative educationalist, Nicholas Hans (1949), referred to factors such as language, religion, social class and territory as forming the historically diverse basis of nations.

Multicululturalism

Social diversities which are evident in the European context are also evident in most other societies. In some of the ex-colonial European countries the experience of decline of the imperial power and external colonialism and the distance from it, allows the members of the polity(ies) an opportunity to reflect on the dominant nature of historical 'internal colonialism'. This reflexive distance can provide an opportunity to 'see themselves from the perspective of the defeated in the questionable role of victors who were called to account for the violence of an imposed and disruptive process of modernisation.' (Habermas 2007)

In this paper the term 'multiculturalism' is used as a descriptive term and refers to aspects of social and cultural differences in institutions, communities and societies. However, in many English speaking countries the term 'multicultural' is used as a policy term and has led to interminable debates about 'political correctness'. In many European countries and other societies these multicultural policies are also perceived to have consequences for 'Western' and 'Enlightenment values', which are perceived by these critics as being undermined by 'the others' and especially Muslims in Europe. These tensions between the religious and the secular have been highlighted by Ian Buruma and other contemporary writers. (Buruma 2010) Another writer Gilles Kepel argues that multiculturalism used by British and Dutch has echoes of the old colonial practices of indirect rule through organised religious and ethnic communities and that this 'communal' approach, prevents successful integration of Muslims and other immigrants in Europe. (Kepel: 1997). These issues of immigration, integration and the role of Islam are also raised by other authors as, are the dilemmas which have resulted from them for the policy makers in most European societies. (Caldwell 2009); Anderson 2009)

Another fairly strong critique of the use of multiculturalism as a policy term is that this tends to obfuscate the much bigger questions of inequalities in society. It tends to legitimise economic inequality and diverts attention away from the deeper issue of class politics in societies like the United States. (Michaels 2007). Worse still is the way in which conservatives in many societies try to underplay the importance of equalities for all groups in society. Richard Wilkinson and Kate Pickett's research and book on 'evidence based politics' received praise from British Conservatives but soon after assuming power, they have used their right-wing think tanks to rubbish the evidence used by the authors. (Wilkinson and Pickett 2009); and *The Guardian*, London 14-8-2010: 3.) However, Wilkinson and Pickett, claim that where inequality exists in socially diverse communities 'ethnic divisions may increase social exclusion and discrimination, but ill health and social problems become more common the greater the relative deprivation people experience—whatever their ethnicity'. (Wilkinson and Pickett: 178) Where there are class differences, people nearer the bottom of society almost always face downward discrimination and prejudice. Where there is also racial discrimination there is a greater social division and greater levels of discrimination which may impede the processes of intercultural understandings through educational and other social and public policy measures. They contend that more equal societies are safer and better places to live for both the wealthier and poorer groups.

There is also another argument about the need to break from the national container of history and to develop a 'transnational memory'. This would enable societies to reflexively modernise by institutionalising a cosmopolitan civil society having learnt lessons from the Holocaust, imperialism and colonial history. These events have barbarised both the brutalisers as well as the brutalised.

The normative cosmopolitanism would need to correct the democratic deficit of the public institutions and the negative historical legacies and create levels of institutional equality and inter-dependence. These measures would lead to cosmopolitan integration both internally and externally, by reinterpreting the creative tension between unity and diversity. Beck and Grande state that this is 'a paradigm shift resting on the principle that diversity is not a problem but a solution'. (Beck and Grande 2007: 242). They however, recognise that living together can be explosive and therefore necessitates enhanced capacities for intercultural interaction. (Beck and Grande: 249). The reduction of social inequalities and within the school a non-centric curriculum and the learning process have an important role to play in giving substance to enhancing intercultural understandings.

This difficulty of living together is most pronounced for groups who are viewed as being very different by those who are settled and consider the norm as being the national sovereign territories which have boundaries. They view those groups which are nomadic as not having the same rights and there are huge tensions between settled and nomadic communities, like the Roma and Traveller communities in Europe. The French government has recently deported 1,000 members of this community to Romania and Bulgaria and has been forced into a defensive stance by the European Union's Justice Commissioner, Viviane Reding, who cited this as a violation and a denial of fundamental right of the freedom of movement. The Sarkozy government may land in the European Court in Luxemburg for this violation. (*The Guardian*, London, 15-9-2010: 17) The constitutional, human and social rights of these groups are ignored and the education of their children is generally of a very low standard. This issue presents one of the greatest challenges for intercultural education in democratic societies and schools within them.

Within the British context, the devolution of Scotland, Wales and Northern Ireland is an indication of the political acknowledgement of the historical multinational nature of British society. This historical legacy presents ongoing challenges. Wales has a functioning Assembly and the Scottish Parliament has greater powers than the Assembly. The Northern Ireland the Assembly has functioned sporadically and the solutions may ultimately lie with the governments in Dublin and London.

The complex processes of devolution, centralisation and integration are simultaneously taking place within many socially diverse societies. It is important to reflect on the features of democracy, citizenship and public and social policy issues within most societies generally. There is also a need to educate young people about the multicultural nature of societies and the importance of democratic features and cosmopolitan citizenship issues within such complex societies and region. The multicultural contexts in historical and contemporary terms are dynamic and not static. (Bakhtin) There are also trans-cultural crossings, shifts and leaps which can result in dissensus since the dominant group may attempt to undermine consensus to remain dominant. There is an ethical imperative to engage in a dialogue with issues of difference in society. While the need for grounding by many groups can be understood, it can be temporary and changing, and based on critical reflection. Grounding and uncertainty can go together and open possibilities which are not necessarily relativist in nature. It can open up in pedagogical terms where dissensus and consensus can be seen to be contingent on changing circumstances. In Raymond Williams's terms this would require the unlearning of the 'inherent dominative mode.' (Williams 1958: 376). This sort of perspective can form the basis for intercultural dialogue and intercultural education.

The liberal market economies have deepened the divides between winners and losers, but the elites continue to use the political rhetoric and conventions of compromise. They try not to allow the basis of discontent and opposition to 'respond energetically or imaginatively to new challenges.' (Judt 2010: 157). While democratic societies provide constitutional protection for dissent, there is a general swing towards conformity and the minority dissenters may find themselves as outcasts. Neither at the level of citizens or of contemporary intellectuals are there informed discussions about public policy issues, which are undertaken by policy specialists and 'think tanks.' In the U.S. the mantra of holding taxes to the minimum and 'keeping the government out of our affairs' is further strengthened by the demagogy of keeping 'socialism' out of government. In Switzerland a referendum banned the building of minarets by Muslims; in Britain citizens have accepted high levels of closed circuit television and intrusive policing and in most European countries citizens find it difficult to challenge economic policies. The education systems bear part of the responsibility for not educating young people to be well informed critical citizens, and allow them to remain apolitical. Young people are more likely to join single issue interest groups but do not engage in 'the management of public affairs,' and the development of strategies to dissent within the law. This can happen if young people develop a new language of politics which recasts public conversation. (Judt: 156–173). This is partly the result of young people not being taught history properly and the absence of understanding of who 'we' are and who the 'others' are. A critical reading and understanding of the past can help young people to refine their analytical skills to understand the complexity of contemporary societies. At the underlying level the absence of the study of history may add to the failure of citizenship education to deal with issues of dissensus.

A consideration of such a pedagogic practice is necessary because most states face similar issues which have led to pressures on the political, economic and social systems. At this level contrasting valuations can be placed on politics and the market and reinforce 'confidence in the civilising power of a state that they expect to compensate for "market failures." (Habermas (2007): 47) There are pathological consequences of capitalist modernisation which requires an ongoing political evaluation to promote citizen's 'awareness of the paradoxes of progress'. (Ibid,: 47) This can possibly form the basis for the bringing together of differentiated regions in most continents to develop cosmopolitan strategies beyond the national boundaries.

Education has a powerful role to play in the strengthening of democracies and to make them more inclusive. It can also enable young people to understand their rights, obligations and responsibilities as active citizens, within most complex democratic societies. This presents educational institutions with a challenge of bridging divides by providing access to diverse groups to social goods in society. They can also assist in nurturing conversations which can lead to the creation of shared values within the public domain and public institutions. However, educational processes should not only be considered to be taking place in the formal school system but they should include the use of visual media and a critical reading of media messages.

There are also some elements of diversity which can be counterproductive if they conflict with citizenship and liberal democratic principles. Given that there are deep divisions caused by historically derived 'hidden hatreds' and uneven development, what can be done to develop new friendships and creative imaginations? There is already a legacy of exclusive and negative imaginations of racism, xenophobia, chauvinism and sexism. These issues pose complex challenges to teachers of citizenship to try to bridge these divides which cannot easily be dealt through rational discussions. While at the classroom level these issues present pedagogical challenges they also present institutional challenges. In democratic educational institutions, intercultural and anti-racist policies which disallow negative behaviours. These policies can also be used to provide greater levels of access to knowledge, skills and shared values through institutional initiatives. Hence, while there have been genocides and Holocausts of particular groups and peoples the role that educators along with other public and social policy makers have to undertake is how to build solidarities and commonalities between and within these different groups at transnational levels. The issue at this level is: without losing sight of the particularities of a loss of different groups: what can be done to bridge the divides between different groups?

To ensure that young people do not accept binary divides but adhere to their rights, obligations and responsibilities, the political culture has to have a broad basis. It cannot be based on the narrow national, dominant group or on the acceptance of simplistic ethnic divides. Young people need to develop notions of inclusivity which symbolically and substantively are based on inclusive good values from all groups and which capture the imagination and enchant the disenchanted young people, especially those from subordinated and marginalised communities. The cosmopolitan constitutional and human rights principles and other progressive and democratic struggles can also form part of this teaching and learning process.

Amongst many young people the notion of being part of, and belonging to complex localities is important. Hence, the acceptance of territorial belongingness which is not exclusive but shared is worth exploring within schools and youth clubs. There is a need to develop non-exclusivist neighbourhoods which are not no-go areas for others but are as Bookchin has called them "confederal communities". It entails turning the biological affinities into social affinities. (Bookchin: 1992). Such communities would be based on shared resemblances which are neither racist nor patriarchal. This necessitates the revamping of the old Greek concept of "paidea" or the German notion of "bildung" to develop their interactive and intercultural aspects within complex and socially diverse schools and communities. These purposes of education ought to ensure that they are enablers of citizens in contributing to the life of the communities and societal institutions. These confederal values ought perhaps to give a new meaning to an intercultural paidea or an intercultural bildung. Chinese and Indian civilizations also embody similar notions which can lend strength to developing intercultural shared value systems which strengthen the social affinities within multicultural polities in Europe. The UNESCO Chair at Galway University and other colleagues can initiate pioneering work in the important field.

The importance of the work of the Life Course Institute is that it can work on issues of the formal education and developing issues of a non-centric school curriculum. In terms of the informal education it can with other agencies try to tackle the issues of negative imaginations whether they are racist, sexist or xenophobic which are enacted in the playgrounds when unsupervised by adults. Organised games can provide discipline and rules which can help ensure fair play and rules of play and assist in the development of intercultural understandings. In the case of Ireland the role of hurling especially at Croke Park are intricately related with nationalism.

Earlier this year the Irish Cricket team playing in the World Cup in India defeated the English team in a spectacular match. This might have made Arthur Young, the English economist turn in his grave. When he witnessed a game of hurling in the 1770's he called it 'the cricket of savages.' How the wheel of history have turned as the colonised win the colonisers at their own game!

In the case of hurling at Croke Park the Gaelic Athletic Association has slowly moved the game of hurling from the violent republicanism which stressed its anti-British identity to a non-reactive Irish identity. This is illustrated by the impending visit of the Queen to Croke Park and as hurling par excellence represents a sport from the classic Victorian times with codified sports with written rules and centralised organisations. As a sport it is not damaged by the professionalism of football and rugby with their snob appeal. O'Toole suggests that Queen will find here 'the old Corinthian spirit—character, community, playing for the sake of it—alive and well and living in Croke Park.' (Fintan O'Toole, *The Observer*, 8-6-2011)

How can these processes at the broader level are replicated with young people, families and local democratic community levels so that they contribute to intercultural understandings.

Citizenship and Diversity

The challenge for inclusive citizenship within many European Union societies is the moulding of one out of the many and the construction of appropriate public and social policy responses to difference and diversity, especially in the light of the new and emerging constitutional and institutional arrangements for harmonisation and the new proposed EU Constitution.

There is a need to avoid racialising intercultural and citizenship policies by focusing on immigrants and national minorities, which ignore the fundamental historically diverse groups within European Union member states. Public and social policy initiatives of antiracism or multiculturalism, directed at 'immigrants' or national minorities, which exclude the dominant groups, are not useful. Within the new member states this issue becomes even more complex, and previous assumptions about dominant and subordinate groups require reexamination. Inclusive citizenship policies become an important issue within devolved nations because otherwise the immigrant, Irish Traveller and Gypsy and national minorities within them may be treated as second-class citizens.

The essentialist rhetoric of some public bodies and civil society organisations has led to the designation of some communities as 'other' groups and the creation of binary oppositions (for example, majority/minority, black/white, dominant/subordinate, 'belongers'/'non-belongers'). This has negated the possibilities of creating an inclusive polity based on inclusive policies, with long-term institutional and everyday implications. After September 11, in the US, July 7th in London and March 11 in Madrid, the 'us-them' divide in Europe has become sharper, and it needs to be narrowed. As I briefly mentioned religious issues this necessitates public policies and institutional mechanisms to deal with religious bigotry and promote interfaith and intercultural understandings.

The issue becomes more critical as the rise of xenophobia, chauvinism and racism can have consequences for even the dominant nationalities and devolved societies. However, the rights of those who are not citizens, for instance refugees and asylum seekers, are more tenuous. The simmering issue of religious discrimination takes on increasing institutional importance in the secular European context, and therefore necessitates consideration within citizenship and human rights initiatives and integrative public policies.

These initiatives ought to recognise the possibilities of the rise of reactive identities on religious and racial grounds in Europe, which can become stronger in the aftermath of the above events. Amongst the minority communities a 'siege mentality', largely sustained by religion, can be developed. Amongst the dominant groups, this may be based on xenophobic notions of territorial ownership and racism, which can lead to the exclusion of the 'other'.

In historical terms, societies and the nature and types of citizenship and human rights change. For instance, rights have changed over time, from the first generation of rights, which were largely civil in nature (18th century) to include political rights (19th century) and, the third generation, social rights (20th century). Given the varying levels of inequalities, states try, as Marshall (1977) writes, to initiate a 'tendency towards equality' by creating basic conditions for social equality. This concept is dynamic and active, not passive.

The challenge is to build inclusive polities, which can accommodate notions of difference, and also create conditions for 'belongingness' of diverse groups. From an EU perspective, this presents a 'creative moment' since notions of citizenship and human rights can be utilised to develop integrative mentalities, based on differences and multiple identities. Diversities can be intrinsically counterproductive if they conflict with citizenship and liberal democratic principles. Given that deep divisions and uneven development, exist not only within states in Western Europe but between Eastern and Western members of the EU, what can be done to develop new friendships and constructive and creative imaginations? There is already a legacy of exclusive and negative phenomena of racism, xenophobia, chauvinism and sexism. However, citizenship and human rights as part of the rule of law in modern nation state are recent concepts; because in the monarchies, empires and chiefdoms of ancient and medieval societies, people's rights were more circumscribed and people were not considered to be citizens.

In the public domain in the UK and especially the Republic there is a need to reappraise the public values, and the institute the power of republication ethic and citizenship values. These need to move beyond the theocratic private values which citizens might hold. Hence, the role of citizenship education in the curriculum and the classroom, to be supplemented by the experience of democratic school culture, which in turn encourages active citizenship in the communities are something which can inform the development of collective and public democratic values, based on freedoms and responsibilities but also rules and regulations which strengthen public accountabilities of all societal institutions.

Communities: Intercultural and Inclusive Society

One of the ways in which history has been disarmed (that is, not used for triumphalist and narrow nationalistic purposes) in democratic states is the settlement of disputes not by war, but through the courts, tribunals and, of course, through democratic elections.

In terms of everyday problems, the roles of communities, identities and customs are important. Access to institutions which sustain citizenship and human rights is particularly important in relation to gender in a socially diverse society, where a group or community (but not the state) wants to deny girls or women access to education especially, higher education or employment. The conferring of citizenship and human rights entails opposing particularistic practices that deny girls equality in all institutions of the state. Hence, here barriers to equality may not come from the state, but from the customs and practices of specific communities. The question for us is how to unpick those aspects of an identity which are legitimate and which are not. There is not likely to be a consensus on this issue.

Justice as a supreme asset in society is a social asset and Aristotle refers to it as a "social virtue." Aristotle distinguishes between "corrective justice" which related to relationship between groups and "distributive justice" which related to the whole of society and its parts. (G. Economou (2007) *Direct Democraccy and the Critique of Aristotle.* (Athens: Papazisi)). For us at this point in history if some groups are excluded from, or marginalised within, the education system, should the state remain neutral or should it intervene? In other words, is the state 'fair' or is it impartial? Rawls (1997, p.60), using the different principle, argues that the better off should not do better than the 'worst off'. So, to accord equity, the state must be 'fair' but not impartial. In a democratic state, citizens are entitled access to all public institutions to equalise their life chances. If the state remains impartial, it cannot create level playing fields in public and social policy terms; it can only do so by intervention. Other major concerns are raised by the liberalisation of economies, partly by many European governments, but also by the major changes brought about by economic and technological globalisation. Not only do these changes negate notions of inclusiveness, but they can also fragment stable economies, industries and communities. How can the enlarged EU use the new EU Constitution at a time of deep economic crises help to protect its economies, industries and communities?

We currently face an additional dilemma, because old solidarities based on class have been destroyed, especially as the younger generation confronts greater levels of polarisation by being divided into 'winners' and 'losers'. Such polarisation, where the 'losers' feel that they owe nothing to the 'winners' and vice versa, poses a new challenge to inclusive citizenship and human rights. How can the EU help build a set of mutualities and resemblances, or a stake amongst divided groups in society? These ought to have the object of developing new solidarities and resemblances Citizenship and human rights initiatives, therefore, has the complex role of addressing the sense of exclusion and loss amongst both dominant or subordinate or majority and minority groups. In this context, genderised exclusion presents added level of complexity and needs to be dealt with firmly, but delicately. Former policies, which privileged one or other group, may prove to be counterproductive by exacerbating differences and reducing features of commonality between different groups. The issues here are how to develop 'positive action' or 'affirmative action' which addresses inequality not just amongst disadvantaged minorities but also the poor in the majority communities. Hence, the state is not impartial but intervenes through its institutions to create greater levels of equality in all the EU member states. Here it is important to examine institutional exclusions through customs practices and processes. Effective policies and practices which are monitored to demonstrate effective outcome of equality are needed.

Furthermore, intercultural initiatives to develop inclusion ought to bridge the gaps between those who are considered a 'permanent minority' and the majority and nurture notions of citizenship and human rights of both. Such policies and processes can instil the enduring notion of fraternity or new solidarities and develop 'communities of development and hope', as Judith Green (1998) describes it. Yet, this is easier said than done, because Britain, like many other states, confronts complicated issues. Habermas writes:

> Today, as the nation-state finds itself challenged from within by the explosive potential of multiculturalism and from without by the pressure of globalisation, the question arises of whether there exists a functional equivalent for the fusion of the nation of citizens with the ethnic nation. (Habermas, 1998, p.117).

Multiple Intelligences and Identities

In the UK, U.S. and the Republic there are still deeply held notions of the singularity of intelligences. However, as Howard Gardner of Harvard University has suggested people have multiple intelligences, at least seven. Hence, the debate about I.Q. and genetics which strengthens educational and subsequently societal inequalities and it is the opposite of what the schools should be doing: which is to accept the ideas of equalising educational potentials of all pupils and reducing inequalities of educational attainment.

So, the real challenge is how the democratic processes in society and experiential democratic education can guarantee social integration in highly differentiated contexts. Yet there are already positive examples amongst many of the young folk all over Europe. In Britain for instance, Das, of the Asian Dub Foundation, describes himself as a '*Hindi British Asian, English, Bengali European*'. Pandit G, who operates the decks, describes himself as '*a half-Irish, Asian, Scot*' (Williamson, 1999, p.40).

This example from amongst recent immigrant groups in one member state needs to be examined to develop similar broadly based identities in other member states in which there may be historically entrenched notions of singularised identities or nationality.

Many citizens currently demand their rights, but do not necessarily accept that they have obligations. The public culture and domain therefore include values derived from both the minority and the dominant groups in society. Intercultural and citizenship initiatives need to have an inclusive notion that symbolically and substantively captures the imagination and enchants disenchanted people. To engage citizens who are disaffected by the political process, it is appropriate to use constitutional, citizenship and human rights principles and other progressive and democratic struggles as part of becoming active citizens.

Amongst young people, the notion of being part of, and belonging to, complex localities is important. Hence, the notion of territorial 'belongingness', which is not exclusive but inclusive and shared, is worth exploring within schools and youth clubs. There is a need to develop non-exclusivist-neighbourhoods that are not 'no-go' areas for others, but are confederal communities. Such communities would be based on shared resemblances and values, which are neither racist nor patriarchal. If this process is not undertaken through academic and formal political or citizenship and human rights education, and through active citizenship engagement, underclass or pauperised groups of whatever nationality or religion will activate their own separatist 'politics of recognition'. Such dynamics could heighten fragmentation and division, with political consequences. Even if these groups are statistically small, they cannot be written off as having no political consequences. The corrosive potential of urban ghettos and rural blight has a way of permeating the body politic, which prisons and internal security cannot contain (Habermas, 1998).

Active Citizenship and Unemployment

Following the very deep current crises in the Republic there is a great need to expand educational attainment in Ireland so as to be part of the world class knowledge economy. As in the UK the situation in Ireland demands addressing the needs of groups which are not plugged into the system. As O'Toole states 'Ireland can't close its skills gap unless it closes it social justice gap.' There is a large proportion of the workforce that has only primary or lower secondary schooling. In the 55–64 age groups, 42 per cent have only primary education. In the 45–54 age groups, 44 per cent have only a lower secondary education. Even in the 25–34 age groups 18 per cent have been educated only as far as Junior Certificate. This is partly due to the fact the free secondary education started later in Ireland than other European countries. This therefore points to the great need for adult and lifelong learning which is systematically implemented to ensure that the current adult population as other European countries like those in Scandinavia.

A focus on the economic inclusion and technological aspects of globalisation, which ignores the political, social and cultural aspects, does not help citizens to become active participants. This becomes critical in socially diverse societies because of the massive unemployment this can create, especially amongst young people. Inclusive citizenship policies, that nurtures political knowledge, understanding and skills is crucial to strengthen engagement in public life and the public domain. Active citizenship that solely relies on weak and impoverished civil society institutions is not sufficient, because it does not currently possess leverage to interest disaffected people, although in many parts of Europe, where civil society institutions are strong, dynamic people who are involved in programmes of active citizenship are making a difference in their communities and localities.

Inclusive employment, social and economic policies are needed. Policies that separate out different groups with stereotypical identities can be counter-productive. Issues of unemployment and lack of jobs are important if they create brick walls which thwart ambitions. Since there will be no jobs in the virtual and privatised technological factory, and governmental institutions are shrinking, how will social cohesiveness in the context of social diversity be strengthened? Unless the public domain and the public sector are brought together with the civic and community sector, the only viable civil society of strength and glamour is the criminal fraternity, whose growth will increase levels of imprisonment and raise social and inter-group tensions? It is here that economic measures from micro community level to the EU level are needed to stabilise neoliberal globalised economies.

Such a political initiative needs to establish the basis for social policies, measures, strategies, actions and institutional changes. These initiatives need to be monitored to ensure that EU and international standards are met. Without these strategies, combined with the analysis of the negative aspects of exclusion, there would be further proliferation of racial and ethnic conflict.

There is an urgent need for the formation of a network of institutions and structures to initiate further work: the collation of good public and social policy practices at national, EU and Council of Europe levels; the development of electronic and other information networks; the dissemination of findings; the establishment of civil society, economic, educational and political strategies for different contexts. All the member states and the EU ought not just to focus on anti-discrimatory measures. These are a good and necessary starting point in legal terms. These need to be strengthened with active measures at governmental and across the EU particularly as the National Consultative Committee of Racism and Interculturalism, Human Rights Commissions and the Equality Authority in Ireland and in other countries are wither being weakened or abolished. The effective implementations of these positive measures to develop intercultural, inclusive policies, and practices right across Europe are needed. This is not only desirable but necessary because of all the regional bodies in Europe, the OSCE, The Council of Europe, and NATO—the EU is the most cohesive and integrated in political, economic and social terms.

Other Works

Books

Intercultural Europe: Diversity and Social Policy (ed.) J. Gundara and S. Jacobs, (Aldershot: Ashgate/Arena: 2000) Translated into Greek by N. Palaiolgou, (Athens: Atrapos: 2006)

Intercultural Europe: Diversity and Social Policy. Jagdish Gundara and Sidney Jacob (Eds.) (Athens, Greece: Nebio: 2012) 2nd Translation into Greek. (Translator: Nekatria Palaiogou)

Interculturalism, Inclusion and Education (London: Paul Chapman Publishing Ltd: 2000)

Racism. J. Gundara and R. Hewitt, Lifew File Series, (London: Evans Brothers Ltd: 1999)

Intercultural Education (ed) D. Coulby, J. Gundara and C. Jones: World Yearbook on Education (London: Routledge: 1997)

The History of Blacks in Britain: (ed.) J. Gundara and I. Duffield (Aldershot: Avebury: 1992)

Racism, Diversity and Education: (ed.) J. Gundara, K. Kimberley and C. Jones (London: Hodder and Stoughton: 1986)

Chapters

Intercultural Education: Conceptual and Empirical Challenges in a New Age (ed.) Nektaria Palaiogou (LondonRoutledge: 2014) Chapter: Jagdish S. Gundara: 'Ancient democratic knowledge and citizenship: connectivity and intercultural implications'

Education Across Borders: Comparative Studies, (ed.) E. Buk-Berge, S. Holmes Larsen, Wiborg (Oslo: Didkata Norsk Forlag AS: 2004) Chapter: 'Issues, Potential and Problems for Intercultural Education In Higher Education' pp. 99–113

Encyclopedia of Diversity in Education (ed.) James A. Banks: Chapter: Jagdish S. Gundara and Barry van Driel: 'History and Development of International Association for Intercultural Education.'

Ministerio da Educacao, Departamento da Educacao Basica, *Flexibility in Curriculum: Citizenship and Communication* (Lisboa: Colibri – Artes Graficas: Marco 2004) Section II – 'Citizenship Education' Jagdish Gundara and Paddy Walsh, pp. 123–233

World Yearbook of Education 2005, *Globalization and Nationalism in Education* (ed.) D. Coulby and E. Zambeta (Oxford and New York: 2005) Chapter: 'The global and the national: inclusive knowledge and linguistic diversity', pp.237–251

Gestione dei Conflitti e Mediazione Intercultural (ed.) Agostino Potera and P. Dusi (Milan:Franco Agenelli: 2005) Chapter: 'Globalizzione, Intercultural e Gran Bretagne' pp. 78–91

Racism in Metropolitan Areas, (ed.) R. Pinxten and E. Preckler, (New York: Bergham Books : 2006) Chapter: 'Racism and Intercultural Issues in Urban Europe

The Standing Conference on Teacher Education (SCOTENS), *Teacher Education for Citizenship in Diverse Societies* (Dublin and Belfast: Cross Border Studies: 2006) Chapter: 'Intercultural Teacher Education in Multicultural Societies', pp. 15–26 Expert Meeting on Intercultural Education, UNESCO HQ, Paris, 20th to 22nd March 2006, Section of Education for Peace and Human Rights Report of the Expert Meeting, (Paris: UNESCO: 2006)

Pereyra, Miguel A. (ed.) Changing Knowledge and Education Chapter: 'Educating the Police for a Multicultural and Globalised Britain.' (Frankfurt am Main: Peter Lang: 2008) pp

Georgi, Viola B. (ed.) The Making of Citizens in Europe: New Perspectives on Citizenship on Citizenship Education. Chapter 'Civilizational Knowledge: Complex Issues for Intercultural Citizenship Education.' (Bonn: Bundeszentrale fur politische Bildung: 2008) pp. 191–203.

Mahatma Gandhi Institute, Moka, Mauritius. Gandhi Memorial Lecture, Paper: 'Mahatma Gandhi: Political Creativity and Intercultural Understandings.' (published by MGI, Moka: 2008) R. Cowen and A. M. Kazamias (eds) International Handbook of Comparative Education, Vol. 2. Chapter: 'The Future of InterculturalStudies in Multicultural Societies.' (Berlin: Springer: 2008) pp. 995–1012.

Education and Social Policy in Europe (ed). J. S. Gundara and S. Jacobs (Ashgate) Greek translation (by N. Palaiologou, published in Athens: 2009)

Mapping the Broad Field of Multicultural and Intercultural Education Worldwide: Towards Development of a New Citizen. Nektaria Palaiologou and Gunther Dietz (Eds) (Newcastle Upon Tyne: Cambridge Scholars Publishing: 2012) Foreword, Jagdish Gundara pp. xii–xiv. Chapter Two: 'Intercultural Education, Citizenship and Civicism in a Multicultural Europe.' Jagdish Gundara, pp. 45–62, Chapter Nineteen: 'School Language Curricula in Dynamic Linguistic Contexts' Jagdish Gundara and John Broadbent, pp. 334–347

Intercultural and Multicultural Education: Enhancing Global Interconnectedness. Carl Grant and Agostino Portera (Eds). (New York: Routledge: 2011), Chapter 19. 'Citizenship and Intercultural Education in an International and Comparative Context'. pp. 294–314

Encyclopedia Diversity in Education. James Banks (Ed). (New York: Sage: 2012) Chapter: Barry van Driel and Jagdish Gundara: 'IAIE and the Development of Intercultural Education in Europe' Chapter: Jagdish Gundara: 'Globalisation and Intercultural Education' pp. 1015–1021

Intercultura, Rome. Publication. Chapter: Jagdish Gundara: 'Cultural Diversity and Interculturalism' based on: UNESCO World Report; Investing in Cultural Diversity' (Paris: UNESCO: 2009)

Conference Publication: World Heritage Centre, Brandenburg Technical University, Cottbus, Germany and UNESCO, Deutschland. A. M. Albert (Ed.) (2010). Paper: 'Issues of Religious and Cultural Diversity in Modern Constitutional States.'

Journal Articles

'Intercultural Studies: Diversity and Adult Continuing Education' , *LLinE, Lifelong Learning in Europe*, Vol.XI, Issue 3, 2006, pp.142–148

Intercultural Education, (Routledge, Oxford) Guest Editors: J.S. Gundara and Agostino Portera. Joint Editorial: Theoretical reflections on intercultural education.' pp.463–468. Article: 'Civilisational knowledge, interculturalism and citizenship education'. Pp. 469–479. Volume 19, Number 6, December 2008.

Article: 'Complex Societies, Common Schools and Curriculum: Separate is not Equal', *International Review of Education* (2008) 54: 337–352.

Intercultural Education Journal of IAIE. (Abingdon, Oxon: Routledge) Volume: 23, Number 5, October 2012. Special Issue: Comparative and Intercultural Education: Possibilities and Problems. Guest Editors: Robert Cowen, Jagdish Gundara and Thyge Winther Jensen. Editorial: Robert Cowen, Jagdish Gundara and Thyge Winther Jensen. Pp.381–2. Article: Leslie Bash and Jagdish Gundara: 'Contesting borders; a challenge to some paradigmatic assumptions of intercultural and comparative education.' pp. 383–395.

Intercultural Education, Journal of IAIE, Volume 22, Number 4, August 2011, pp. 231–241, Article: 'Ancient Athenian Knowledge Democratic Knowledge and Citizenship: Connectivity and Intercultural Implications.'

UNESCO APCEIU, Seoul, Korea. *Sang Saeng*, No. 28 (2011) Article: Jagdish Gundara: 'Intercultural Education and APCIEU'

Journal: *Engage*, Steve Sinnott Foundation, London (2011) Article: Jagdish Gundara: 'Girls, Conflict, Violence, War and Education.

Finnish Journal of Ethnicity and Migration. (March 2011). Jagdish Gundara: Article: 'Citizenship Education in a Socially Diverse and Cosmopolitan Europe'

Intercultural Education. (August 2011) Vol. 22, No. 4, Article: Jagdish Gundara: 'Ancient Athenian democratic knowledge and citizenship: connectivity and intercultural implications.' Pp. 231–241.

Intercultural Education (October 2012) Vol. 23. No. 5. Special Issue: 'Comparative and Intercultural Education Possibilities and Problems'. Guest Editors: Robert Cowen, Jagdish Gundara and Thyge Winther Jensen. Joint Editorial, pp. 381–382. Article: Leslie Bash and Jagdish Gundara: 'Contesting Borders: a challenge to some paradigmatic assumptions of intercultural and comparative education' pp. 383–395.

Intercultural Education (June 2013) Vol. 24 No. 3. Jagdish S. Gundara and Namrata Sharma: 'Some issues for cooperative learning and intercultural education.'

Published Conference Papers

Korean Association for Multicultural Education, (May 9–11 2013). Hanyang University, Seoul, Korea. Conference Title: Reconstructing Education, Culture and Identity in a Global Age'. Keynote Address: 'Intercultural and International Understanding: Non-Centric Knowledge and Curriculum in Asia.' Pp. 25–47.